JEDBURGH ABBEY

JOHN H LEWIS & GORDON J EWART

Cover illustration shows Jedburgh Abbey from the S with insets (left) the walrus ivory comb showing a knight fighting with a dragon and (right) detail of the N side of the choir of the Abbey church.

JEDBURGH ABBEY

THE ARCHAEOLOGY AND ARCHITECTURE
OF A BORDER ABBEY

JOHN H LEWIS & GORDON J EWART

with

RICHARD FAWCETT & DENNIS GALLAGHER

A FOREWORD BY CHRIS TABRAHAM

and contributions by

DAVID H CALDWELL, THEA GABRA-SANDERS, C PAMELA GRAVES,
RICHARD GROVE, GEORGE HAGGARTY, JOHN HIGGITT,
NICHOLAS McQ HOLMES, ROBIN MURDOCH, CLARE THOMAS
& ROBERT WILL

ILLUSTRATION

DENNIS GALLAGHER, PAMELA GRAVES, ANGELA TOWNSEND
& MARION O'NEIL

SOCIETY OF ANTIQUARIES OF SCOTLAND
EDINBURGH 1995

MONOGRAPH SERIES NUMBER 10

SOCIETY OF ANTIQUARIES
OF SCOTLAND

MONOGRAPH SERIES

EDITOR ♦ ALEXANDRA SHEPHERD

This volume is published with the aid of a generous grant from

British Library Cataloguing-in-Publication Data.

A catalogue record for this book is available
from the British Library.

ISBN 0 903903 10 5

Produced by Alan Sutton Publishing Limited, Stroud, Glos

CONTENTS

ACKNOWLEDGEMENTS

The authors would like to express their thanks to the numerous people whose contributions, both in terms of fieldwork and for specialist input, have led to the compilation of this volume. The excavation staff were: John Cannell, Eoin Cox, Richard Grove, Alison Haggarty, David Pollock, David Reed and David Stewart. We would also like to thank the following for their assistance during the excavations: John Godbert, Garrett O'Brien, Alan Radley, David Stalker, Jane Todd, Jonathon Triscott and Jonathon Wordsworth. Those who contributed to the final report as specialists were: Dr David Caldwell, Dr Richard Fawcett, Thea Gabra-Sanders, Dennis Gallagher, Pamela Graves, Richard Grove, George Haggarty, Nicholas Holmes, Robin Murdoch, Clare Thomas and Robert Will. Information concerning the animal bone assemblage, environmental samples and soils was supplied by Lin Barnetson, Dr Brian Moffatt and Dr Robert Shiel respectively. We are also grateful for the advice given to us during the post-excavation process from the following: Dr Michael Baillie, the late Geoffrey Collins, John Higgitt, Roderick McCullagh, Nigel Ruckley and Richard Welander.

The line drawings are the work of Dennis Gallagher. The pottery was drawn by Angela Townsend, the window glass by Pamela Graves and the bone and metal artefacts by Marion O'Neil. All photographs reproduced are Crown copyright.

Finally, the authors wish to express their gratitude to Chris Tabraham for reading several drafts of this paper, for guiding the project from its inception and for his enthusiastic support throughout.

The responsibility for any factual or interpretative errors that remain within this volume rest on the authors' shoulders.

DISPOSAL OF FINDS AND DOCUMENTS

The site records and the full specialist reports are deposited with the National Monuments Record of Scotland. The full finds assemblage is in the care of the National Museums of Scotland; the ditch assemblage is on long term loan to Historic Scotland from the Trustees of the National Museums and is on display at Jedburgh Abbey.

John H Lewis & Gordon J Ewart

ILLUSTRATIONS

LIST OF TABLES

FOREWORD

In 1913 the ruined abbey church of Jedburgh was placed in the guardianship of HM Office of Works, the first of the great Border abbeys to pass into state care.

1913 did not mark the beginning of the abbey's new role as a visitor attraction. That effectively had begun in 1875, largely on the initiative and at the expense of the ninth Marquis of Lothian. In that year the old parish kirk that had stood in the nave since 1671 was replaced by a new building on the other side of the Jed Water, enabling work to begin in earnest on repairing the old abbey church.

Such was the scale of that task that thoughts did not turn to excavating and laying out the cloister buildings until the 1930s. Scarcely anything of the conventual buildings survived above ground, but between 1936 and 1937 most of the available ground on the south side of the church was 'excavated' and the exposed wall foundations laid out. No written account was made of those investigations but the drawings and photographs made by the Office of Works formed the basis of the interpretation of the claustral ranges, published by the Royal Commission on the Ancient and Historical Monuments of Scotland in 1956.

The programme of excavation, begun in 1936, had been intended to include all the land between the abbey church and the Jed Water to the south, but war intervened and the scheme was abandoned. In 1983 the plan was resurrected and exploratory excavations were carried out in the area of The Bow. The main excavation followed in 1984. In 1986 the completed scheme, including a new visitor centre, was formally opened by Michael Ancram, the Scottish Office minister responsible for Ancient Monuments and, coincidentally, a descendant of the ninth Marquis of Lothian.

This volume is a record of the archaeological discoveries made by John Lewis and Gordon Ewart and their team in 1984 and financed by the successor to the old Office of Works, the Scottish Development Department (Ancient Monuments). Its own successor, Historic Scotland, has financed a grant towards the publication of this volume. In addition to the record of the excavations, the volume includes some thoughts on the lay-out of the abbey complex by Dennis Gallagher and a re-assessment by Richard Fawcett, Principal Inspector of Ancient Monuments, of the architecture of the great abbey church.

Chris Tabraham
Principal Inspector of Ancient Monuments

INTRODUCTION

1.1 HISTORICAL BACKGROUND

The ruined church of Jedburgh Abbey (illus 1; 2) has long been acknowledged as one of the finest examples of Romanesque architecture in Scotland – an inspiration for generations of poets, writers and artists. However, it was only when the opportunity arose to thoroughly excavate the claustral ranges to the south of the church that direct evidence of the abbey's eventful history emerged. In unravelling the complex sequence of building, clearance and conversion, new information was released regarding the everyday life of the community, from its colonisation to abandonment, as well as showing the abbey in a wider perspective. For the first time, the range and detail of the data retrieved during the excavation revealed the abbey in context – historically, socially and topographically. Evidence retrieved over a large area, and covering an extended period of history, was then synthesised within the broad phases of the abbey's construction, occupation and decline.

Illus 1
Jedburgh Abbey, from the S, after the construction of the new visitor centre. The Jed Water is in the foreground.

Illus 2
The West front of the abbey
church.

Despite the paucity of primary documentation concerning the abbey, it is apparent that most of the site's history has been coloured by the frequent warring between Scotland and England. Lying so close to the Border and near an important N–S route for armies of both sides, the abbey's development, and from the late 13th century its decline, became inextricably linked with the effects of war.

The effects were physical, in terms of destruction, repair and fortification, but were felt on a social level, too. The brethren were frequently obliged to be either manifestly partisan or to tread a fine, diplomatic line between the two warring nations. Through necessity, political expediency became a constant aspect at Jedburgh (as at all the Border abbeys), apparently a far cry from the ideals and aspirations of those who first colonised the abbey in the 12th century.

David I, King of Scots, with the assistance of John, Bishop of Glasgow, founded a priory at Jedburgh in *c* 1138 and invited Augustinian canons from Beauvais in northern France to settle there (Cowan & Easson, 1976). The fertile land of the area offered the colonists both prosperity and the potential for expansion. By 1154, its status had been raised to that of an abbey and it eventually came to have dependent priories at Blantyre, Canonbie and Restenneth (*ibid*).

The political climate for such a major investment by the Crown was very favourable. The Border was stable and '. . . it divided communities with the same language. . . the same social structure and agrarian practices.' (Duncan 1975, 538). Up to the late 13th century a stability prevailed which enabled western European monasticism to establish itself securely in the Borders.

Moreover, the foundation of a great house at Jedburgh demonstrated to the English the individual power of King David and the independence of the Scottish church. Bishop John of Glasgow had long been at odds with the Archbishop of York, to the extent of his self-imposed exile in Tiron in 1136–7, and it is likely that John's return to Scotland and the foundation of Jedburgh in 1138 were part of a policy by King David to emphasise his power on the eastern Border.

By 1138 the popularity of the Augustinian order in Scotland owed something to the influence of Bishop Turgot of Durham and two successive Archbishops of York, Thomas and Oswald, on the predecessors of King David, resulting in foundations at Scone, Inchcolm, Loch Tay and St Andrews. King David was, in turn, greatly influenced by his intimate followers: three of his ex-chaplains, Alwin, Osbert and John, were all instrumental in the establishment and running of Augustinian houses at Holyrood and Jedburgh. There were, however, other factors which recommended the regular canons to David.

The order encompassed a wide variety of spiritual ideals embracing almost every aspect of religious life. '. . . No other order offered the founder of a religious house such a choice of spiritual prospects.' (Dickinson 1950, 137). To a very marked extent, this doctrinal adaptability enabled the Augustinians to liaise closely with the *caput baroniae* and to involve themselves with the secular world on a variety of levels. The 'association between the regular canons and the administrative or curial classes . . . became one of the more outstanding characteristics of the first phase of the Augustinian settlement' (Platt 1984, 31) – an association even more significant in Scotland because it involved the royal house itself. The foundation of Jedburgh Abbey close by the royal castle should be viewed alongside those at Holyrood and Cambuskenneth which served the royal castles of Edinburgh and Stirling.

The reoccupation of early Christian sites, both Celtic and Anglian, by the Augustinians was very marked during the 12th and 13th centuries, thus presenting the canons as the most effective vehicle for the promotion of reformed monasticism and the preservation of a tradition of Christian observance. This sense of continuity, combined with sound economic strategies and expertise, proved a successful formula in the peaceful transition towards new attitudes and doctrines, both spiritual and secular.

Thus it was that with the introduction of the Augustinians to Jedburgh, political prestige and effective administration were assured by the combination of royal castle and great abbey. This association had proved highly significant in the Norman conquest and settlement of England – and so could be seen as the key to the effective control of older territorial units in Scotland, whether secular or ecclesiastical.

Having established the need and desirability of such an arrangement, the '. . . principal concern must have been for the physical establishment in the most literal sense. Only as an abbey's future became more secure would the mandated range of first structures become realistic . . .' (Ferguson, 1983, 82). In one sense, this process is colonisation (because of the time taken to construct the great stone ranges) and demonstrates the priorities of the community in establishing key structures to enable the house to start running properly.

At Jedburgh, building in stone was concentrated on the great church, commencing from the E to establish altar and crossing. The community itself was accommodated in various temporary timber structures which were only superseded as the stone building progressed (initially completing the nave of the abbey church and the East range before converging on the S and W of the complex), a process which lasted some 120 years.

When Edward of England's army, under Sir Richard Hastings, became the first on record to damage the abbey in 1305, the great building and the strategy behind it were altered forever. In 1410, 1416, 1464 and 1523 the abbey buildings were variously damaged and subsequently repaired, only to be burned again during the campaign of 1544–5.

The damage caused by the Wars of Independence probably gave rise to the extension of the cloister and consequent development of the South and West ranges. The castle of Jedburgh was destroyed in 1409 and the abbey's defences were extended as a result – including the construction of a series of towers forming a line along Canongate. Damage incurred later in the 15th century is likely to have prompted the rebuilding of the Chapter house. Into the 16th century, the subdivision of larger rooms to form cells towards the SW of the abbey and the presence of a series of crude buttresses outside the S wall of the nave demonstrates the re-use of rubble from demolished buildings and the general decline in numbers of individuals actually living in the abbey.

Whereas the abbey may not have been as well burnt as the Earl of Hertford claimed in 1545, the crude repairs completed by a tiny complement of canons certainly suggest that it was fairly dilapidated. As the community gradually diminished during the early 16th century, the role of the abbey as part of the town defences became increasingly important in the face of English invasion. The most graphic of these changes as a result of war was the partial fortification of the abbey in the mid-16th century by the addition of an earthwork to the E of the East range and the conversion of abbey structures at the SW of the claustral circuit to mount artillery. This conversion probably gave rise to the development of The Bow and marked a period of extensive stone robbing and gradual encroachment by the town. Nevertheless, much of the abbey church survived and, with some modifications, was used by the new, reformed kirk until a completely new church and manse were built on the opposite bank of the river in 1875.

1.2 LOCATION

The town of Jedburgh, in Roxburgh District, lies 80km (50 miles) SE of Edinburgh and just 18km (12 miles) N of the Anglo-Scottish border (illus 3). The medieval burgh developed on the left bank of the Jed Water, a fast-rising river which runs from Carter Hill to the River Teviot, 4km (2.5 miles) to the N of the abbey. At Kelso the Teviot joins the River Tweed which reaches the North Sea at Berwick, an important Scottish burgh and seaport until 1488.

On the S edge of the town the river deviates from its S–N course and flows E for about 200m. Here, on the N bank, the abbey complex (NGR: NT 651 205) was laid out on a series of terraces cut into the sloping ground (illus 4), with the great abbey church at the summit of the slope, some 80m from the present course of the Jed Water. The river's alignment allowed for the standard monastic layout, with the reredorter (latrine-block) positioned at the bottom (S) end of the East range.

A post-Reformation graveyard to the N of the church and tarmac roads (Abbey Place, The Bow and Abbey Close) on its remaining sides gave the abbey a rather cramped appearance prior to excavation in 1984. The effect was misleading, however, for the monastic precinct had once extended well beyond these limits, particularly to the E and SE. Unfortunately, much of the archaeological record was probably destroyed during the construction of a textile mill in Victorian times. The works were demolished in 1967 and the area (known as Murray's Green) subsequently landscaped as part of the town by-pass development.

1.3 PHYSIOGRAPHY

THE GEOLOGY OF THE SITE

The bedrock at Jedburgh is of Upper Old Red Sandstone age. Its soft, dark red, horizontally-bedded strata have been cut by the Jed Water, forming vertical cliffs to the S and E of the town and, in places, exposing the underlying Silurian rock. The solid geology is overlain by a thin layer of glacial till belonging to the Hobkirk Association (Muir 1956, sheet 17) which, on the abbey site, is represented mainly by coarse sands and gravels. The typical soil profile on Old Red Sandstone is a dark brown topsoil (A horizon) over light brown subsoil (B horizon) with a dark red-brown parent material (C horizon). Outside the East range at Jedburgh, the B horizon and some of the A horizon survived, whereas in the W part of the site, the soil had been removed down to the C horizon in antiquity.

Most of the abbey's stonework is derived from the higher levels of the Upper Old Red Sandstone (MacGregor & Eckford 1952, 244) and was quarried from one or more sites close to Jedburgh (illus 5): Ulston Moor (three quarries), Ferniehirst (four quarries), Tudhope and Hundalee (RCAHMS 1956, 239–40). Initially, the very friable sandstone from the abbey's immediate environs was used only for wall-core, but its softness and ease of cleavage prompted its exploitation in later times, particularly during the remodelling of the refectory and the construction of the so-called 'infirmary' to its S (*ibid*, 205). However, although easily worked, this stone laminates readily and consequently the masonry of these two buildings has eroded badly. A major component of wall cores and foundations was dolerite, a dark grey, intrusive igneous rock of Carboniferous age that occurs locally at Lanton Hill, Dunion Hill and Black Law. Although glaciation

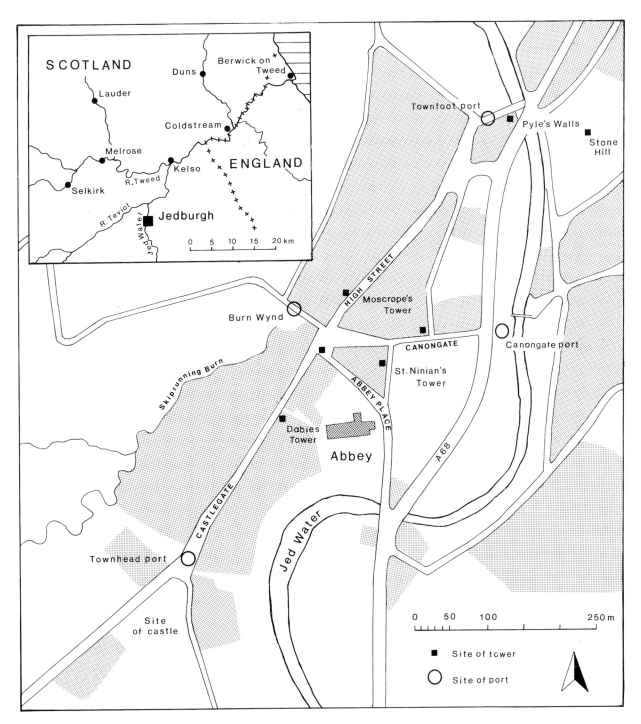

Illus 3
Location of the abbey and town of Jedburgh.

Illus 4
Aerial view of the abbey before the 1984 excavation with The Bow extending around the S side of the abbey. The flower beds within the cloister garth were intended to show the two phases of the South and West ranges.

has littered the soils near these outcrops with boulders of this rock, it is unlikely that many of those on the abbey site had been deposited in this way (Dr R Shiels pers comm). Enormous quantities of sandstone were carried more than 2km from the quarries and it is likely that the abbey builders were just as willing to transport dolerite similar distances from its more accessible hilltop sources.

THE TOPOGRAPHY OF THE SITE

There were considerable problems building a large monastery on such a steep slope. Excavation showed that terraces had been cut into the river bank so that the claustral buildings could stand on level ground and that the crumbling cliff face had been consolidated to protect the buildings close to the river. Furthermore, the Jed Water itself had had to be diverted to allow the S end of the East range to be built.

Terracing the river bank was an enormous task although the excavated material was probably put to good use: topsoil in gardens and orchards; the underlying sand and gravel for making mortar and concrete; bedrock for building stone; and other debris for levelling the ground, particularly at the river's edge. Indeed, there were some positive advantages to the abbey's location. Waste could easily be carried away from the cloister, downhill into the Jed Water, and an elevated situation protected most of the complex from the sudden and severe flooding that still afflicts parts of the town.

The river, however, was probably not the source of the abbey's domestic water supply for its transportation uphill to the claustral ranges would have been a laborious and impractical task. Streams running off hills to the W and NW of the town seem more likely sources. The nearest of these streams is the fast-flowing Skiprunning Burn which courses along a narrow, steep-sided ravine through the W part of the town but which is now culverted from a point 100m NW of the abbey as far as its confluence with the Jed Water. The

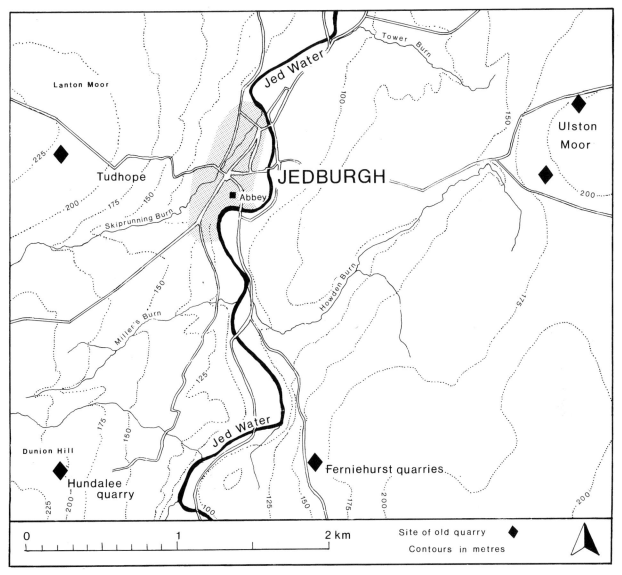

Illus 5
Jedburgh in its topographical context, showing the probable quarry sites for the abbey building stone.

route by which water might have been conveyed from the burn to the abbey is open to speculation although piping the water from some distance upstream would have obviated the need to pump it uphill from the ravine. Monastic plumbing was frequently very elaborate. This is apparent at Melrose Abbey and even more so at the Cathedral Priory of Canterbury where lead piping passed along a complicated route through the city walls, workmen being employed to ensure the pipe's regular maintenance (Urry 1967, 205).

Other possible water sources at Jedburgh were rainwater cisterns, of which no evidence has come to light, and wells. However, the two wells so far located within the claustral area were both cut through demolished medieval walls and are therefore assumed to be post-monastic structures.

1.4 THE ABBEY WITHIN THE TOWN

The great antiquity of Jedburgh as a settlement site long before the arrival of the Augustinian canons in the 12th century is attested by numerous finds covering a wide historical spectrum. The advantages of this sheltered valley site, with its strategic significance in terms of natural routeways and river crossings, were exploited from at least the Celtic Iron Age.

The decision to build the abbey on such a steep river bank may have been influenced by existing patterns of land ownership, habitation, river crossings and, perhaps, by the tendency for many Augustinian houses, in contrast to those of other orders, to be founded on earlier religious sites (Robinson 1980, 35). Furthermore, an elevated situation close to a major route through border country could have served as a statement by King David I as to the wealth and power he could exert on even the far corners of his realm.

The following appraisal of the town's early development is based on an analysis of a series of 18th- and 19th-century maps of Jedburgh, the earliest being a survey by John Ainslie which, although undated, was probably the predecessor of his town plan of *c* 1775 (illus 73).

THE EARLY SETTLEMENT

According to Symeon of Durham, in his *Historia de Sancto Cuthberto* (Arnold 1885), *Gedwearthe* and *alterum Gedwearthe* were among the lands given by Ecgred of Northumberland to the church of Lindisfarne in AD 830–45. The nature of these settlements is unknown although an ecclesiastical presence near the site of the Augustinian abbey is indicated by several pieces of Anglian sculpture, found before and during the 1984 excavation. These include a fragment of late 8th-century date (Cramp 1983, 280) which suggests that there was a church there prior to Ecgred's donation. However, the earliest documentary reference to an actual church dates to the early 12th century when *Geddewerde* is cited as the burial place of Eadwulf Rus, the murderer of Bishop Walcher (Arnold 1885, 198).

The pre-Augustinian church was probably a minster, a status suggested by a grant to a pre-existing '*Monasterium Jeddew*' in a charter of William I which confirmed the privileges of the Augustinian abbey (Barrow 1971, 163–4). This *monasterium* is likely to have been close to, or even on the site of, the extant abbey church although a position slightly to the N, within the present kirkyard, would have enabled the new building to be constructed whilst the old church continued in use. It may be assumed that some form of secular settlement existed along the line of Canongate, before Castlegate and High Street were laid out.

THE BURGH

The new burgh of Jedburgh was founded by the king before 1170. It was arranged in a line extending NE from the castle. The integral relationship between the castle and the abbey was hinted at in a charter of 1165 x 1170 which refers to Jedburgh '. . . *ubi castellum est* . . .' (Lawrie 1905, 151–52). Its precise extent, however, is uncertain. Originally, the S limit may have been to the W of the castle, on the line of the present drive of Glenburn Hall which appears on Ainslie's plan as Chatows Wynd. Evidence of regular, planned burgage plots survives as far N as the line of Jewellers Wynd and Smith's Wynd. Beyond, in an area later to include the Franciscan Friary, the properties were generally wider and more irregular.

Pronounced angles in the property boundaries suggest that the burgage plots were laid out over the open fields of an earlier settlement. In the S half of the burgh (the present Castlegate), the limits of the plots were restricted by the Jed Water and the Skiprunning Burn. To the N, there were back lanes. Queen Street, known earlier as Walkers Wynd or Back Gate, lies to the E of High Street; Friarsgate, or Back of Friars, lies to the W. In this part of the burgh the burgage plots appear to have been laid across the line of the Skiprunning Burn.

THE MONASTIC PRECINCT

The monastic precinct lay within the area bounded by the Canongate to the N, Castlegate to the W and the Jed Water to the S and E. Its precise limits are unknown although it encompassed an area later occupied by Abbey Close, the High Kirkyard and the properties on the S side of Canongate; all of which remained outside the jurisdiction of the burgh until they were purchased in 1669.

To the W of the abbey was Abbey Close which provided access to the ceremonial West door of the church and the West claustral range. Augustinian canons normally undertook full pastoral duties and the nave of the abbey church would also have served the parish throughout the medieval period. There is a reference, dated 1220, to an altar in the nave which was appropriated for parochial use during a dispute between the Bishop of Glasgow and the canons of Jedburgh (Glasgow Registrum, 97); and a document of 1502 states that a mortgage repayment must be made 'on the altar of the parish church of Jedburgh'

MONARCHS ENGLISH	SCOTTISH		KEY EVENTS IN THE HISTORY OF THE ABBEY	SUPERIORS OF THE HOUSE	
WILLIAM I	MALCOLM III		1080 *Murder of Bishop Walcher of Durham* 1087 *Body of Eadwulf Rus cast out by Turgot*		PERIOD I
WILLIAM II	DONALD BANE EDGAR	1100			
HENRY I	ALEXANDER I				
STEPHEN	DAVID I		1138 *House of Augustinian canons founded* 1148 *Burial of Bishop John of Glasgow* 1152 *Priory raised to abbey status*	PRIOR DANIEL	
	MALCOLM IV			ABBOT OSBERT	
HENRY II				RICHARD	PERIOD II
RICHARD I JOHN	WILLIAM I	1200		RALPH HUGH PETER	
	ALEXANDER II			HENRY PHILIP	
HENRY III				ROBERT DE GYSBORNE	
	ALEXANDER III			NICHOLAS DE PRENDERLATHE	
EDWARD I	JOHN BALIOL		1285 *King Alexander III married at Jedburgh* 1297 *English army damages abbey*	JOHN MOREL	
	ROBERT I	1300	1315 *Canons flee to Thornton on Humber*	WILLIAM DE JARUM	
EDWARD II				ROBERT	
	DAVID II		1346 *English forces hold Jedburgh Castle*	JOHN	
EDWARD III					PERIOD III
	ROBERT II			ROBERT	
RICHARD II					
HENRY IV	ROBERT III	1400	1410 *Castle and abbey damaged by Scots* 1416 *Town and abbey damaged by English*	JOHN	
HENRY V	JAMES I				
HENRY VI	JAMES II				
	JAMES III		1464 *Town and abbey damaged by English*	WALTER	
EDWARD IV RICHARD III				ANDREW ROBERT JOHN HALL	
HENRY VII	JAMES IV	1500		THOMAS CRANSTON ROBERT ROBERT BLACKADDER HENRY	PERIOD IV
HENRY VIII	JAMES V		1523 *Town and abbey damaged by English*		
			1544/5 *Town and abbey burnt by English* 1548 *French troops occupy Jedburgh*	JOHN HOME	
EDWARD VI MARY I	MARY				
ELIZABETH I	JAMES VI			ANDREW HOME	
		1600			
JAMES I and VI			1606 *Abbey lands combined with those of Coldingham Priory and erected into a temporal lordship*		PERIOD V
CHARLES I					
CHARLES II			1668 *New church built in abbey nave and first manse* 71 *built on abbey West range*		
VICTORIA			1875 *New parish church built*		

Table 1 Historical table showing the main events in the life of the abbey.

(Anderson 1899, no 267). Access to the church from the main area of the town was probably through the kirkyard – along the 'Kirkstilegait', according to a charter of 1539 (*ibid*, no 267) – to a door on the N side of the nave.

The graveyard to the N of the abbey church is bounded on the NE by The Rampart. If a 16th-century date is accepted for this earthwork (**6** below), then it is likely that Abbey Place developed as a thoroughfare after its construction and that the medieval graveyard was defined on the E by Deans Close. Ainslie's survey shows the properties to the N of Abbey Close and to the W of Deans Close as having no back properties, suggesting that they were an infill along the N boundary of the graveyard. This was probably the medieval lay cemetery, the monastic burial ground being to the E and SE of the abbey church in the area of Murray's Green (Simpson & Stevenson 1981, 19).

Deans Close may have provided public access to the abbey's industrial buildings, including mills and a building identified as a malt barn, the remains of which lie beneath the public hall in Deans Close (*ibid*, 31). The properties to the S of Canongate and to the E of Deans Close are shown on Ainslie's plan as a very regular block, in contrast to the sinuating property lines of the Castlegate. These may reflect a separate medieval development laid out by the abbey although its chronological relationship to the planned burgh is unknown.

With the exception of the Canongate properties, the area to the E of Deans Close was known during the 18th century as Convent Gardens, or Ladies Yards (illus 6), and was used for orchards and other horticultural purposes until the late 19th century. These properties are described as part of the abbey lands in a charter of 1588 (SRO.CH6/1 f86v), confirming similar usage during the medieval period, and some of the land divisions shown by Ainslie may date from that time.

PORTS AND TOWERS

There is no record of the abbey's precinct walls although there was probably some form of physical boundary between the monastic lands and those of the burgh. There were towers at several points along the abbey boundary (illus 6), three of them defending gates into the precinct. Dabie's Tower, demolished in the mid-17th century, stood at the junction of Abbey Close and Castlegate. Another was sited on the W side of Kirk Wynd, near the junction of Canongate and the Lawnmarket (later to be part of Castlegate) and now within the area of the Market Place. St Ninian's Tower stood at an unlocated point in Dean's Close and, being on abbey land, it probably defended a gate (Simpson & Stevenson 1981, 26). A charter of 1551 (SRO.CH6/1 f32v) describes St. Ninian's Tower as the residence of the chaplain of the altar of St. Ninian's which was in the nave of the abbey – thus confirming that the tower was part of the pre-Reformation abbey properties.

Entry into the burgh was controlled by four ports, situated at the ends of the town's main lines of axis and serving the dual purpose of defence and the regulation of trade by the collection of tolls. A watercolour, painted from a pencil sketch by Thomas Girton in 1800, shows an apparently medieval crenellated wall with a string course extending from the N side of Castlegate. This wall and a corresponding one on the opposite side of the street are indicated on Wilson's 1762 'Plan of the Castle Wood Field of Jedburgh and Castle Hill' (Simpson & Stevenson 1981, 26). Their late survival was probably linked to their use as the Townhead Toll, the building to the S of the gate being the tollkeeper's cottage. This and another two ports are depicted by Ainslie as restrictions of the streets. Other known ports were at the E end of Canongate and at a point where Burn Wynd (now Exchange Street) crossed the Skiprunning Burn. There was evidently another at an unknown location towards the N end of the town (*ibid*, 25).

The ports were complemented by a number of towers (illus 6) whose situations suggest that they defended the burgh rather than the residences of private individuals. One, at 30 Canongate, supervised entry into the town from a back lane (now Queen Street); another, known as Moscrope's Tower, may have controlled the entrance into the market area to the N of the market cross; while from Pyle's Walls watch was kept on the ford that led to Bongate (Simpson & Stevenson 1981, 27).

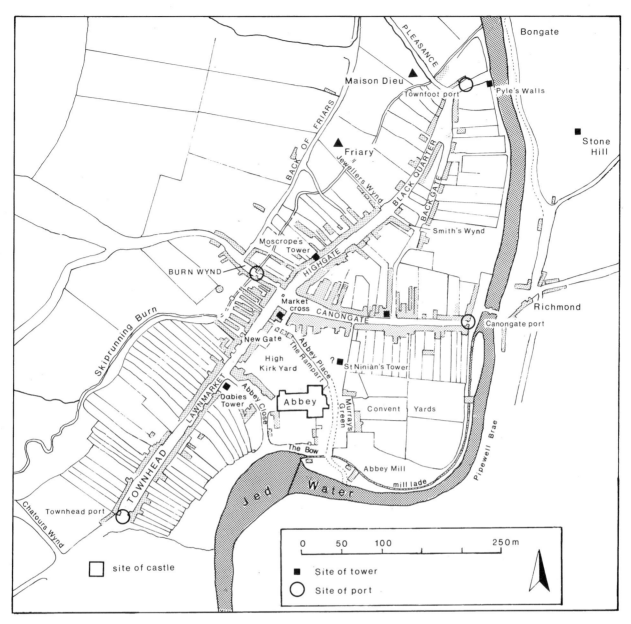

Illus 6
The abbey and its environs in the late 18th century.

CONCLUSION

The abbey complex was defined by Castlegate, Canongate and the sweep of the Jed Water and protected by a series of defensive towers. The cruciform plan of the burgh, based on Castlegate/High Street and Burn Wynd/Canongate, represents the integration of a primary route between a probable early ford at modern Bongate and the castle hill with the boundary of an abbey precinct defined by the river and Canongate. The monastic area covers some 35,000m², with the church and cloister occupying less than 25% of the available ground.

Given the presence of both an 'ancient' church on the site, probably monastic in style, together with a major royal castle close by, the chosen site of the abbey fulfilled two of the main criteria for colonisation by the Order. The Jed Water and its tributaries ensured a good water supply as well as providing defence and power, while the rising ground to the N of the river was well suited to accommodate the full range and mass of the abbey buildings.

1.5 REPAIRS AND EXCAVATIONS PRIOR TO 1984

THE POST-REFORMATION CHURCH (1560–1875)

After the suppression of 1559, the abbey church continued in use as a parish kirk until a new kirk was built on the S side of the river in 1875. Immediately after the Reformation the congregation worshipped in make-shift premises below the central crossing tower, but in 1671 they transferred to the W end of the nave. The fabric of the building was repaired many times and on several occasions the Town Council had to prevent the theft of masonry from the decaying edifice. The ordeals of this period are chronicled in some detail by Watson (1894).

REPAIRS TO THE CHURCH (1875–1913)

Apart from some consolidation work on the crossing tower between 1824 and 1826 (SRO 1833), little thought was given to preserving the abbey as an historical monument until 1875, when the ninth Marquis of

llus 7
The S side of the abbey church.
Note the doorway on the left,
reconstructed in 1875.

Illus 8
The 1936–37 excavations: a) the view S from the abbey during the excavations; (note the parish kirk of 1875 on the far side of the Jed Water);
b) (below left) the West range from the N; the well in the middle of the picture dates to the occupation of the manse which covered this part of the site;
c) (below right) the SW corner of the refectory; the depth of soil covering demolition debris indicates the extent of landscaping over the abbey ruins within the claustral area; from the W.

Illus 9
Trial trenching across the W end of
The Bow in 1983.

Lothian undertook to repair and reconstruct some of the church's medieval masonry (illus 7). Lothian wanted to remove all trace of recent work and consequently had to stand the entire costs of the exercise himself (Watson 1894, 102).

Following the demolition of a belfry tower above the N wall, concrete was laid around the bases of the NE and NW piers of the crossing tower and the piers themselves were buttressed. Piers and arches were stripped of 18th-century plaster and paint although no attempt was made to renew any of the arch mouldings or capitals. Some of the pillars and most of the corbelled eaves course on the N side of the clerestorey were replaced and, for reasons of safety, a series of tie beams inserted. The wall heads above the clerestorey were capped with Caithness flags; elsewhere they were sealed with cement. The N wall of the church was partially repaired, the ruined W end of the S wall (demolished in the 1670s for the kirk) was almost completely rebuilt and a reconstructed Romanesque-style doorway inserted into it. However, the alignment of the West cloister walk indicates that the position of the doorway differs somewhat from that of the 12th-century original.

According to Watson (1894, 133): 'No cost was spared to improve the amenity of the Abbey . . .' and consequently the 18th-century manse and several other houses near the church were demolished during this programme of work.

THE ABBEY IN STATE CARE (1913–)

In 1913 the abbey was entrusted into state care, being maintained by HM Office of Works (now Historic Scotland). The first task was to repair the NE and NW piers of the crossing tower, by consolidating the masonry and replacing the cores of soft, crumbly, 12th-century concrete with modern cement concrete. Exposure of the pier foundations revealed numerous human bones, but details of these findings were not recorded (SO 1959). Between 1919 and 1921 several artefacts (mostly post-Reformation coins) were recovered from the 'south end of the cloister' (SRO 1938) (perhaps within or adjacent to the refectory) but whether they were stray finds or unearthed during excavation work is not clear.

In 1936–37 most of the area bounded by the church, Abbey Close, The Bow and Abbey Place was 'excavated' and the foundations, and occasionally upstanding walls, of most of the claustral ranges exposed. No written account of these investigations has been found although the excavation drawings and numerous photographs (illus 8a, b, c) formed the basis of the Royal Commission's interpretation of the claustral ranges (RCAHMS 1956, 194–209). The finds from the excavation were listed on file (SRO MW/1/1088). They comprised mainly post-Reformation coins although a few medieval coins, pottery sherds and other artefacts were also recorded.

Early in World War II the Home Guard commissioned a blacker bombard to be trained upon the road bridge to the SE of the abbey. The mortar was placed within the abbey precinct, '. . . practically under the trees, in the flower bed on the Western range . . .' (SRO 1942) – presumably in the NW corner of the cloister, high enough to command a view of the bridge. The mortar's bedding trench comprised a circular hole, 2.44m (8') in diameter and 1.07m (3' 6") deep, within which was found a 'foundation stone', assumed to be part of the 18th-century manse and evidently considered unworthy of detailed recording before it was removed. The foundation trench for the gun was not located in 1984.

In 1957 a partial re-examination of The Royal Commission's so-called infirmary (RCAHMS 1956, 205) was carried out, probably as part of an investigation into the building's drainage, which continued to be inadequate until the 1984 excavation.

The programme of excavation, begun in 1936, had been intended also to include the area between the 'infirmary' and the Jed Water, thereby removing the road known as The Bow, but work was halted by the outbreak of World War II. There were several proposals to resume the scheme once hostilities ceased but the ground in question did not become available for excavation until 1983, when several exploratory trenches were opened in order to assess the archaeological potential of the abbey's S limits (illus 9) (Lewis 1984, 259). The main excavation work then followed in 1984.

THE 1984 EXCAVATIONS

The principal objectives in 1984 were: to excavate below The Bow; to re-excavate elements of the claustral buildings uncovered, consolidated and laid out for display in 1936–37; and to investigate the available area beyond the East claustral range, thus allowing structures partially uncovered, but evidently not understood by the earlier excavators, to be fully exposed and interpreted. Illustration 10 shows the extent of the excavated areas and the structures exposed and colour illustrations I–IV show work in progress.

The excavation findings have enabled the site's development to be divided into five main periods:

PERIOD I   Pre-Augustinian activity (before *c* 1138)

PERIOD II   The building of the abbey (*c* 1138–*c* 1300)

PERIOD III Remodelling and rebuilding (*c* 1300–*c* 1480)

PERIOD IV Late repairs and alterations (*c* 1480–1559)

PERIOD V   Post-Reformation activity (1560–1875)

Phasing an excavation can be a subjective exercise (Rahtz 1979, 45) and it is realised that the boundaries between the periods listed above may not always reflect precise moments in time. For example, both the evidence of excavation and a consideration of the abbey's architecture (**8** below) suggest that the initial building campaign had largely been completed by the middle of the 13th century but, because the first major rebuilding work began after the English attack of 1305, the preceding half-century is included within Period II. In addition, the widespread redeposition of materials, associated with numerous repairs and alterations, calls for extreme caution when attempting to date many of the excavated features. This was vividly demonstrated by the discovery of a coin of Aethelred II (978–1016), found in the backfill of a robber trench associated with the final phase of the Chapter house, and by a 1st-/2nd-century AD Roman *dupondius* recovered from a monastic drain in the East cloister alley.

2.1 PERIOD I – PRE-AUGUSTINIAN ACTIVITY (BEFORE *c* 1138)

Pre-12th-century artefacts recovered from the abbey and its environs prior to 1984 have suggested that this was an important centre, with a monastic presence, in the late first millennium (Duncan 1975, 464) although the physical evidence of contemporary occupation has been lacking. Nevertheless, several features discovered in the area of the East cloister range (illus 11) most likely represent a pre-Augustinian presence although none of these features could be ascribed an absolute date.

OUTSIDE THE EAST RANGE

Outside Room 4 was a reasonably level surface of water-washed pebbles (916) which was cut by a ditch (928) of probable 12th-century date, implying that the metalling was a pre-Augustinian feature. Nearby were the remains of two parallel, rubble walls (914, 915) (illus 12a), apparently contemporary with the metalling although the width, 1.1m, of wall 915 and its location suggested that it might be the S wall of an 18th-century building (John Preston's House) (illus 67). Unfortunately it was not possible to expose more than 5.5m of these walls and hence the problem remains unresolved.

Both walls were cut by an irregular trench (probably the work of stone-robbers), the backfill of which comprised rubble and mixed soils containing a 15th-century Nuremberg jetton (**4.7**, no 47 below). The S limit of the metalling (916) had been truncated although a drop in level of 0.42m along its surviving length of 6.5m suggests it had been an external surface – perhaps a path or courtyard – rather than an internal floor.

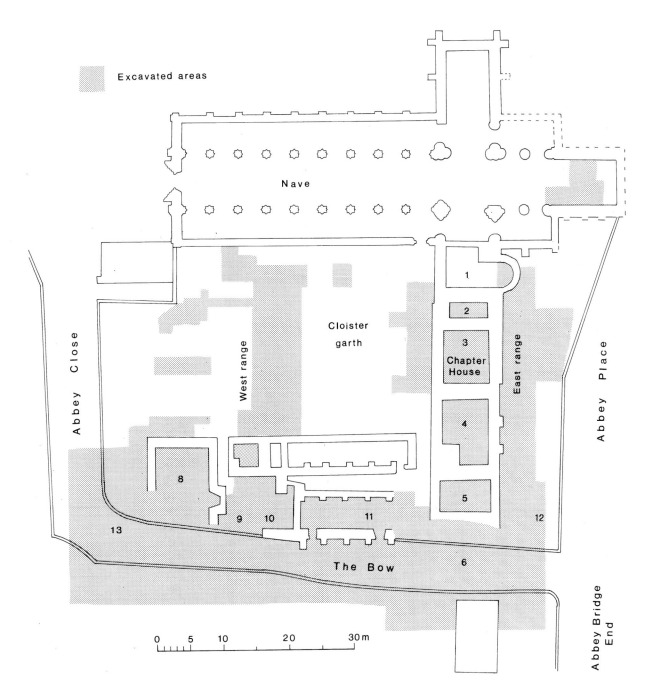

Illus 10
Plan of the area of excavation in 1984 and 1990.

ROOM 4

Pressed into the sandy subsoil within Room 4 were two areas of compacted gravels. The gravels predated levels known to be associated with the building's construction and were, perhaps, contemporary with the area of metalling (916) although here the stones were unsorted. In the NW corner of the room was a quernstone and, elsewhere among the gravel, many dolerite boulders with worn surfaces that suggested a footpath or yard pre-dating the Augustinian East range.

THE CHAPTER HOUSE AREA

Early occupation of this area was suggested by charcoal-rich soils, disturbed during the construction of the first Chapter house, and by numerous disarticulated human bones, many of them juvenile, within the room's floor-levelling deposits. This concentration of human remains clearly indicates an early graveyard; the juvenile bones within it implies that it served a secular community.

Illus 11
View from the S of the excavation of the East range and adjacent area. Ditch 928 is in the centre.

2.2 PERIOD II – THE BUILDING OF THE ABBEY (*c* 1138–*c* 1300)

PRIMARY OCCUPATION

From the onset of construction, temporary housing for the canons and builders, as well as the latter's workshops, must have covered a wide area for a considerable period of time. Little evidence of such transient accommodation might be expected to survive the construction of the main stone complex; although traces of a ditch adjacent to the East range and two timber structures in the West range can be ascribed to the primary occupation by the Augustinians.

FEATURES ADJACENT TO THE EAST RANGE

DITCH 928 (illus 12a, b, c)

The ditch, approximately 1.0m deep, cut through the metalling (916) and the fluvio-glacial soils below. It had been truncated at a point 7.46m from its rounded N terminal, probably during the construction of the East range. Over that distance the ditch narrowed from 1.8m to 1.1m at the top whereas the narrow channel at its base widened from 0.37m to 0.64m. Within the channel was a grey-green silt containing fragments of bran, ova of whipworm (an helminthic gut parasite) and high levels of *Potentilla*-type pollen (*Potentilla* spp were frequently used as astringents); these together with high levels of organic and organic-rich phosphates, indicate that the ditch was used as a sewer.

Minimal accumulation of the organic-rich deposit suggests either that the ditch was in use for only a short period or that it was emptied regularly – but not immediately prior to backfilling. The pollen was generally undeteriorated and hence typically water-borne, its assemblage representing a catchment area that included forest and scrub, woodland, tussock, turf and open ground. The hills to the W and NW of Jedburgh would provide such an assemblage and in all probability these hills were the source of the abbey's water supply. High values of metallic lead within the ditch suggest that the water was piped at an early stage, the pipes presumably running below or through the foundations of buildings.

DRAIN 1173

The only other evidence of plumbing to survive in this part of the site was a stone-sided drain (1173) (illus 15a) in the East cloister alley. The drain appears to have accommodated a (?lead) pipe and may have served the lavatorium in the South cloister alley or perhaps an infirmary beyond the East range.

GRAVE 38

Near the truncated end of the ditch, against its W side, were the partial remains of a human torso (Grave 38) (5 below) whose position and lack of orientation were indicative of a non-Christian burial. Although the skull and limb bones were missing (perhaps removed during later landscaping), the articulation of the surviving rib-cage indicated that, had the corpse been moved, this must have taken place within several months of death (Dr RAA Macaulay pers comm). Near the skeleton were several very interesting artefacts : a small walrus ivory comb; a seal/pendant, also of walrus ivory; a horn buckle; and a whetstone (**4.1**; illus 78; colour V; VI below). All four objects were of high quality and, assuming single ownership, belonged to someone of wealth and importance. Whether that person was the same whose skeleton lay nearby is unproven but the circumstantial evidence is strong. The objects were evidently made between the late 11th and the late 12th century and perhaps disposed of in the third quarter of the 12th century.

Following these depositions the ditch was backfilled, apparently in a single phase with no obvious pattern or consistent direction of tipping. Within the infill were an almost intact ceramic cresset lamp (**4.6**; illus 83, no 51 below), sherds from a straight-sided cooking pot of local white gritty ware (*ibid*, no 29), three worked flints, pieces of tracery and fragments of two more whetstones. Near the top of the ditch infill was a barely worn Henry II 'Tealby' penny identified as Type C (1161–5), Type D (1165–68) or most likely Type E (1168–70) (**4.5**, no 4), indicating that the ditch was infilled no earlier than 1161 and probably at least a decade later.

THE TIMBER STRUCTURES AT THE W OF THE SITE

The fragmentary remains of two timber structures were discovered towards the SW corner of the site (illus 13). They were built on terraces cut into the natural N bank of the Jed Water (illus 27) and appear to represent a fairly lengthy period of occupation within this area of the monastic complex: this is suggested by the successive phasing of the two structures and by the apparent sub-division of Timber Structure 2. They were precursors to the Period II structure, 8, with its undercroft and pend (below), but their precise functions are not clear. They were apparently domestic in character (despite the absence of hearths) and are most readily interpreted as part of the extensive temporary accommodation required on site during the construction of the church and other major stone buildings. In addition to the slight structural evidence from the buildings themselves, further evidence of the occupation of the site during the later 12th and early 13th centuries was reflected by deep, tipped deposits of domestic midden associated with the timber buildings (see below).

TIMBER STRUCTURE 1

Evidence of the earliest building phase identified on the W of the site was limited to a narrow rectangular area immediately N of the

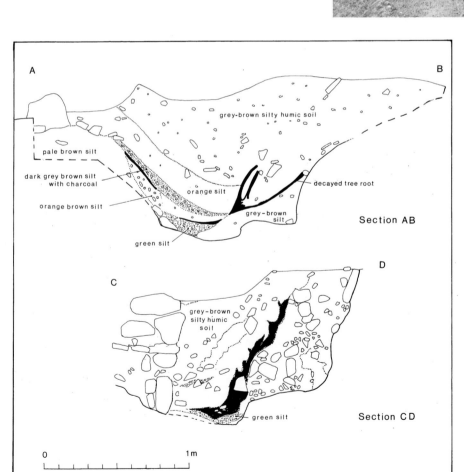

Room 4

914

915

916

928

Section AB

Section CD

general location

0   1   5   10 m

Illus 12
Ditch 928 and adjacent
features: a) plan;

b) the N terminal of ditch
928; from the E; note the
proximity of the East range
foundations to the ditch
edge;

A   B

grey-brown silty humic soil

pale brown silt

dark grey brown silt
with charcoal   decayed tree root

orange silt

orange brown silt

grey-brown
silt

green silt   Section AB

D

C

grey-brown
silty humic
soil

green silt   Section CD

0   1m

c) sections across the ditch.

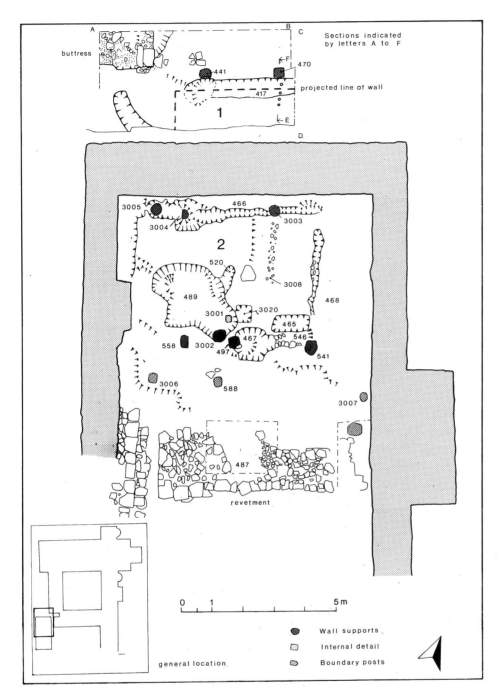

Illus 13
Plan of Timber
Structures 1 and 2. Part
of Structure 8 is shown in
outline.

N wall of the later Structure 8 (illus 13). After the removal of 1.8m of deposits associated with the construction of the 18th-century manse and garden, an artificially-levelled terrace surface was uncovered. This surface comprised three composite lenses of compacted mortar (411, 476, 432) (illus 14a), with an overall depth of 0.2m, which sealed a localised group of features and associated levels lying towards the extreme S of the area.

SLEEPER BEAM AND POST PITS

The structural elements comprised a sleeper beam slot (417) and two small squared post pits (441, 470) (illus 13; Table 2). A series of midden deposits (473) ran up to the S side of 417, suggesting that their deposition occurred when the wall over the beam was standing. Context 473 was, in fact, a composite midden deposit with lenses of ash, charcoal, animal bone and pottery, all suggesting domestic debris accumulating over an extended period.

Quantities of charcoal in the lower fills of all three timber features indicate that they were burnt *in situ* rather than dismantled and the holes backfilled. Although such fragmentary remains make the reconstruction of the building difficult, the characteristics of this group of features are sufficiently distinctive as to represent a single structure, reconstructed as Timber Structure 1 (illus 27).

The two post pits (441, 470) were basically square in plan with no packers. Both, however, had flat stones at their bases to receive the weight of a timber upright, the dimensions of which were not traced. The fill of both – charcoal and redeposited midden (473) – suggests that Timber Structure 1 was first burnt and the debris cleared and flattened thereafter.

The overall regularity and fill of the associated beam slot (417) reflect the same sequence of destruction as in the two post pits. Its shallow depth implies the use of a sill-beam, a constructional device intended to avoid rotting (a common problem in earthfast

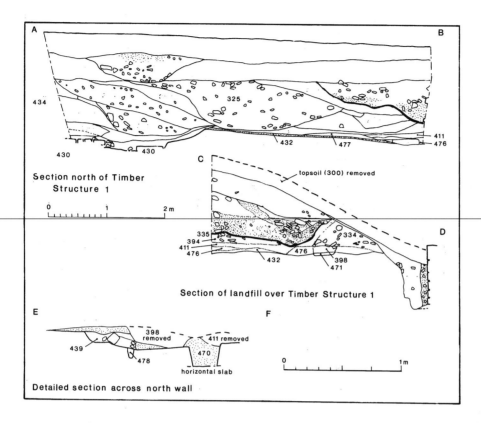

A   B

434   325

                                                              411
                                                              476
430   430
                              432   477

**Section north of Timber
Structure 1**

0   1   2 m

C
                            topsoil (300) removed

335   334
394
411   476
476   432   398
                                      471

Section of landfill over Timber Structure 1

E   F
                    398
                  removed   411 removed
439   470
    478
                  horizontal slab

0   1 m

Detailed section across north wall

Illus 14
a) Sections through deposits
overlying Timber Structure 1,
mainly reflecting extensive
post-monastic landscaping in
the claustral area;

b) section across midden
deposits to the S of revetted
bank 487.

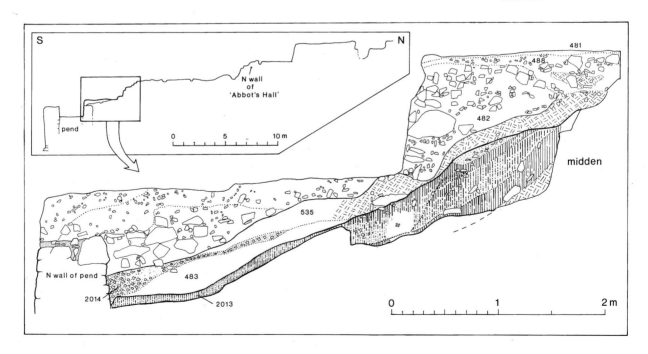

S   N   481
                                                                        488
                  N wall
                    of
                  'Abbot's Hall'   482
  pend   midden

0   5   10 m

                                              535

N wall of pend   483
2014
            2013

0   1   2 m

timbers). Such a beam would have been laid directly onto the cleared ground surface, thus providing a firm footing for the main infill of the wall – possibly wattle, planking or small stave uprights set into the sill-beam itself.

STAKEHOLES

A small cluster of stakeholes, again sealed by the flattened midden (473), was found to the S of post pit 470: these were contemporary with Timber Structure 1 but their function was impossible to determine.

TERRACE

The deposits against which Timber Structure 1 was cut comprised not only the upper levels of the natural hill but also the underlying clays and sands located at least 0.6m below the top of the natural soil profile (Ian Mate pers comm). This terrace, moreover, was truncated by the construction of Timber Structure 2 which lay immediately to the S. Its further progress N was not pursued because of limited time but, using the evidence of the uppermost terrace level upon which the cloister was built, it could not have extended more than 1m or so. This suggests that the terrace for Timber Structure 1 was a precursor of that prepared for Timber Structure 2 and had been abandoned when the latter was built.

TIMBER STRUCTURE 2 (illus 13)

TERRACE AND MIDDEN DEPOSITS

A wide, level terrace, uncovered within the N half of the later Structure 8 but probably extending further W than that structure, would have covered originally an area some 16m E–W by 10m N–S, its limits determined by the steep river bank to the S. The steepness of the original N bank of the river was determined by the pitch of a series of tipped midden deposits associated with Period II occupation and which lay against the face of the natural bank. This midden, along with two covered drains (573, 490) (illus 28), were part of the terrace for Timber Structure 2's occupation phase: the structural remains are, however, limited probably to the NE corner of a rectangular building on an E–W alignment.

STRUCTURAL REMAINS • PITS AND OTHER FEATURES

Timber Structure 2 can be described as the E end of a rectangular building. The main uprights of the walls rested in shallow and irregular slots which defined the N, S and W sides of the building. The walls appeared to have been constructed with wattle and daub, fragments of which were retrieved. These earthfast posts occurred in two groups: the N wall, pits 3005, 3004, 3003, and the S wall, pits 558, 497, 546, 541 and possibly 3002. The pits were fairly regularly spaced at an average of 1.3m apart. There is some evidence to suggest that the wall posts were paired and, as such, could have supported tie beams spanning the building to form three roof supports. Table 2 lists the dimensions of the main structural elements.

The wall slots were of such irregularity that sill-beams do not appear to have been used; instead, the wattle infill was sunk straight into shallow trenches which ran between the main earthfast posts.

A large and complex pit (489) was contemporary with pits 3002, 3001, 497 and 465. All had very similar fills characterised by the presence of daub and other burnt debris which included animal bone, pottery and the leg of a bronze cauldron (**4.2** no 69, below). The function of pit 489 is, however, obscure. It consisted of a large, shallow, rounded depression backfilled with burnt material around a central core of random stonework (probably backfill). It

may have been the robbed-out setting for a simple hearth or oven or some demolished industrial feature associated with the main building programme of Period II. Moreover, the role of the pit is linked with a pair of regular, shallow, rectangular depressions lying to the E of it. These features (520, 3020) proved to be only 30–40mm deep and, because of this lack of depth and yet regular plan, they were probably settings for robbed stone pads or low plinths.

The other main internal feature was the rectangular pit 465 – a well-defined, large, earthfast post setting which may have been a repair or structural refinement to the building. The feature retained its packers (although displaced), suggesting a post of some 0.35m or more in diameter. Its position, offset from the wall lines, suggested an association with a possible entrance to the building – itself a secondary feature. The wattle infill between posts 541 and 497 in the S wall was removed to create a cobbled threshold (546) within a primary wall slot. This feature comprised two rows of neatly set pebbles in a roughly rectangular area overlying the narrower wall slot. The reason for the creation of a doorway at the SE corner of the building may be linked with the construction of a probable light, internal wall running S from post 3003 in the N wall. The shallow foundations of this wall (3008) were marked by a line of pebble packers within a gully, resulting in a narrow passage 1.4m wide at the extreme W of the building. Therefore, pit 465 may have acted as some form of door support or wall reinforcement necessitated by this secondary work.

TERRACE BOUNDARY POSTS (illus 13)

The remaining timber features contemporary with the occupation of Timber Structure 2 were not, however, part of the building. At this stage, as they appear to define the S limits of the contemporary terrace activity, they are described as boundary posts.

This small group of post pits was of very similar character to the wall posts (Table 2), being roughly 0.2m in diameter with packers still *in situ*. Significantly, 3007 was found below the masonry of the upper course of the main E–W revetting wall (487). It may also be associated with a series of similar post pits (452, 453, 454) (illus 27) cut against the riverside terrace immediately E of Timber Structure 2.

THE COVERED DRAINS 573 AND 490 (illus 28)

Running N–S for a distance of 3.8m between walls 487 and 384, was a stone-lined drain (573), sealed by tipping in advance of the construction of Structure 8. The drain was readily identified as a primary Period II feature as it lay below later Period II build-up and was truncated by the later Period II revetting wall 487 which, in turn, post-dated primary Period II timber settings.

Another similar drain (490) also dated from primary Period II. Both served the early terrace occupation and flowed down to the original N bank of the Jed Water: both were adapted as sub-basement drains, taking away any natural accumulation of water from the hill which might have undermined the standing masonry.

The fills of both drains were similar in that the presence of burnt material was particularly marked. In the case of 490, this proved to be mainly burnt heather, apparently used as fuel. All traces of the W extremity of Timber Structure 1 were obscured by later building but it is likely that the W riverside terrace, against which 490 is cut, was linked in some way to the terrace of Timber Structure 1.

DRAIN 573

The drain was built predominantly of flat slabs of sandstone, both to define the edges of the channel and to cap it. There was no

Timber Structure 1

Context	Depth (mm)	Upper Dimensions (mm)	Length (m)	Width (mm)	Description
441	310	400 x 393	-	-	squared post hole
470	396	390 x 383	-	-	squared post hole
417	120	-	3.3	500 - 630	beam slot

Timber Structure 2

Context	Depth (mm)	Original Diameter (mm)	Overall Diameter (mm)	Description
3005	190	195	210	rounded post hole
3004	206	75	180	rounded post hole
3003	208	100	123	rounded post hole
541	263	200	256	rounded post hole
497	198	298	310	rounded post hole
3002	288	216	288	rounded post hole
558	306	300	308	rounded post hole

Context	Length (m)	Upper Width (m)	Lower Width (mm)	Description
466	5.7	1.0	75	wall slot
468	3.1	0.3	65	wall slot
467	3.5	1.0	600	wall slot
546	1.0	0.4	275	wall slot

Context	Depth (mm)	Upper Dimensions (m)	Lower Dimensions (m)	Description
3001	30	0.1	0.03	internal support
489	307	2.5 x 2.4	1.5	internal support
465	498	0.58 x 1.08	0.56 x 1.0	internal support

Boundary Posts

Context	Depth (mm)	Upper Dimensions (mm)	Lower Dimensions (mm)
3006	275	180 x 220	90 x 75
588	304	300 x 246	100 x 64
3007	260	290 x 250	165 x 75
452	250	260 x 220	70 x 64
455	30	-	250 x 216
454	50	–	100 x 88

Table 2 (left and above):
the dimensions of the timber structures.

stone bottom to the drain: the sides were simply pressed into the accumulated midden deposits adhering to the river bank immediately S of the primary Period II terrace. The drain had partly collapsed under the weight of successive building although, for most of its length, it retained its capstones *in situ*. The channel was an average of 250mm wide and 157mm deep.

The drain disappeared under the N face of wall 384 (the N wall of the Period II pend) and was realigned to flow out through the E end of the pend. Its original outflow was probably straight down the slope to the river – a straightforward attempt to remove effluent from primary Period II terrace activity. Indeed, it probably helped to prevent the kind of noisome accumulation into which the drain was cut.

It was sealed by three major tipped deposits – 488, 482 and, most significantly, 2014. The first two were basically redeposited clays and rubble whereas 2014 proved to be a key indicator of

secondary Period II work, being a distinctive deposit of crushed yellow sandstone, stonemason's debris in all probability.

DRAIN 490

In the main, this drain was constructed from unbonded sandstone slabs defining a narrow channel, 150mm wide and 120mm deep. A flattened 'S' shape, it ran for a distance of 5.5m across an artificial terrace (115) cut into the natural bedrock immediately N of the river to form a riverside platform.

Like 573, it was retained for use under later buildings – in this case, the basement of Structure 13 where it was refined by the addition of a sump (see below, Period III). The drain was also truncated by the cutting-back of the river bank to accommodate the angled outflow of the original Period II garderobe and drain (see below).

OCCUPATION DEPOSITS FROM THE TIMBER STRUCTURES

The limited area between late Period II walls 487 and 384 contained an intact, stratified sequence of deposits (illus 14b) which clearly predated the construction of the main stone claustral buildings. The material was sectioned to a depth of 1.2m from its upper profile as defined by the drain 573.

The material was deposited in thin lenses. The uppermost of these (535) was characterised by large amounts of animal bone, shell and pottery sherds. This gave way to increasingly organic deposits with much charcoal, some of which was up to 0.2m deep, culminating in deposit 2013. This soggy, black layer was not fully excavated but sherds of pottery, animal bone and other domestic debris were found alongside large pieces of bark and wood. The overall depth of the lower, organic rich sequence of deposits was a maximum of 0.4m at the N end of the section (a combination of layer 2013 and a deep tip of charcoal). The gradual nature of the depositional sequence and the depth of material on the upper reaches of the natural slope imply that the midden was the product of a lengthy period of occupation on the primary Period II terraces.

THE MAIN BUILDING PHASE

THE CLOISTER

The reconstruction of the cloister lay-out by the Office of Works after 1937 reflected two supposed phases in its development (RCAHMS 1956, 204). The second-phase cloister alleys were retained, the garth was planted with roses and, on dubious evidence, wall-lines were re-established. Partial excavation of the cloister in 1984 attempted to substantiate (or refute) this two-phase theory.

THE EAST CLOISTER ALLEY (illus 15a, b)

Placing contexts in specific periods of the abbey's development proved impossible here and consequently all of the excavated features in the East alley are described in Period II.

The trench consisted of a 16.0m-long section of the alley, itself 3.0m wide, with a short extension at each end. Below the topsoil and other recently deposited materials was a hard-packed layer of red sand and clay, cut by 1930s excavation trenches and other modern features as well as by a few medieval features which included five graves (5 below). Two of the graves (24 and 25) were stone-lined although their skeletons had been removed. One (Grave 28) had held a wooden coffin and two (Graves 26 and 27) were simple pit burials. The surviving skeletons were in a similar state of preservation to most of those within the Chapter house and, although the evidence is inconclusive, it suggests that they too were monastic.

One or two courses of the W wall of the alley (1131) had been rebuilt after the 1936–37 excavation. Its removal exposed the wall's clay-bonded, rubble foundations, the width (1.0–1.3m) of which indicated that the wall was unlikely to have carried much weight.

Running below the S end of the wall was a badly damaged drain (1173), its base of pale yellow clay still bearing the impression of a (?lead) pipe. A 1st-/2nd-century Roman *dupondius* (**4.5**, No 1 below), recovered from the drain fill, is assumed to be residual for the cloister wall respected the drain's course and the two structures were probably contemporary.

THE W SIDE OF THE CLOISTER

Excavation at the W side of the cloister (illus 16) was intended to shed some light on the two-phased cloister and the character of the West range. The excavation was not comprehensive and the excavation of the West range was limited to three trenches. The evidence, therefore, is fragmentary.

As much of the area in question had already been excavated earlier this century, the standing remains and their associated stratigraphic contexts were often found to be isolated from each other by the linear trenches of the previous excavations. However, sufficient evidence survived to confirm that the cloister had, indeed, been extended.

Of the cloister walls, both sides of the East alley survived whereas only the inner or E wall of the West alley remained, its W wall having been almost entirely robbed out.

THE EAST ALLEY

The East alley averaged 3m in width. Its upper surface (which showed no sign of cobbling or paving) was cut by intrusive features: five proved to be monastic burials (5 below) and another a clay-lined drain.

Both inner cloister walls (1212, 3011) were built on cobbled footings – mainly large river stones, apparently bonded in clay. Nothing of the upper masonry of 1212 survived; but 3011 showed that the main fabric of the walls was mortared sandstone.

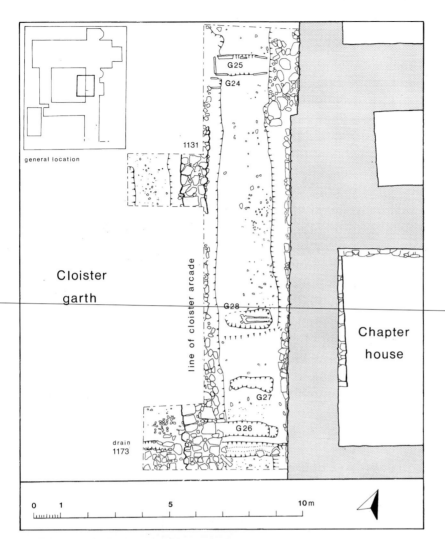

Illus 15
The East cloister alley: a) plan;
b) (below) view of the alley showing
some of the graves partly exposed;
from the N.

THE WEST ALLEY

The West alley was also approximately 3m wide, although its putative W wall was almost completely missing. Photographs of the 1936 excavation seem to show extensive masonry but all that remained in 1984 was the E side of its shallow foundation trench (1205). This feature echoed the line of 1212, ultimately being cut by a modern drainage trench. To the E of this shallow cut were four shallow rounded pits (1219, 1237, 3013, 1221), much eroded by later garden activities (indicating some sort of claustral feature). On average, they were only 0.1m deep but were spaced reasonably regularly at intervals of about 1.5m.

THE NORTH AND SOUTH ALLEYS

A short section of primary W wall did survive beneath the South alley. The wall (1307) was badly damaged by modern pipe trenches to such an extent that only the W face remained. The wall had the characteristic footings noted in 1212: a few stones from the core of the upper masonry survived, giving an overall width of 1.1m and a maximum height of 0.41m. The wall which had once run for over 20m was reduced to a 3m length.

The N wall associated with 1212 (the S wall of the North alley) was of identical build and dimensions. However, due to the almost complete masking of the contemporary S wall (N wall of South alley) by later restoration, there was no opportunity for a detailed examination of the relationship of this wall which was ultimately abandoned in Period III along with other elements of the first cloister.

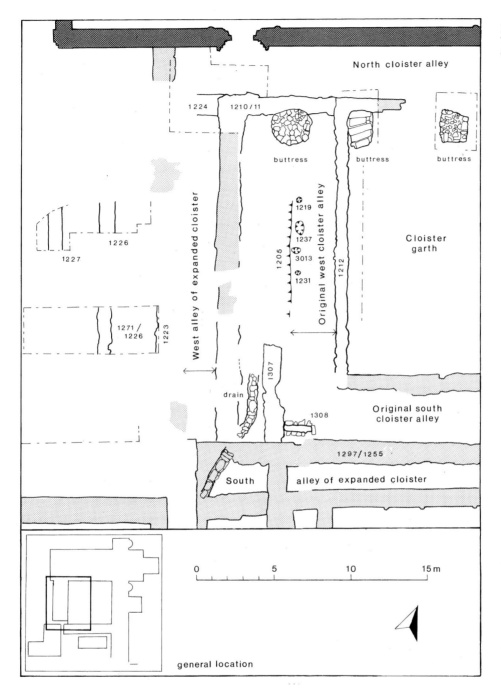

Illus 16
The W side of the cloister.

The wholesale remodelling of the two-phased refectory N wall (1297) and the secondary South alley S wall (1352) also obscured the complete sequence of re-alignment of the South alley of the cloister in Period III (as described in RCAHMS 1956, 205).

In a re-examination of the chronology of the claustral circuit development, the original refectory formed the S limit of the cloister although all that survived was the undercroft, terraced some 2m below the surviving alley surfaces. This would have necessitated a stepped entrance if there had been direct access between cloister and refectory undercroft, although the only surviving door, located at the end of the S wall of the refectory, suggests that access, at least during Period III, was only from the S.

The original South alley (illus 17) was 3.4m wide: only one damaged feature from this period, Grave 1308, survived within it. The contents of the grave had been removed before 1984, leaving

a boulder-lined trench located towards the W end of the South alley. Although fairly small (2.0 x 0.3m), its position under a cloister alley and its E–W alignment all tend to suggest a grave cut against the E face of 1307 and partially disturbed by modern pipe trenches. The grave, of well-laid boulder construction, was unlike any of the other five cloister inhumations.

Photographs taken in 1936 show that the S wall (1297) of the South alley was an extremely well-built section of masonry superior to and more massive than its successor, the Period III N wall of the enlarged cloister. It was apparent, however, that the earlier masonry was not demolished to a uniform height and that the succeeding cloister walls were not built directly onto the cleared earlier stonework but rather a substantial depth of soil. This evidence suggests that there was a delay between the first refectory being demolished and the new cloister being laid out.

Illus 17
Drain and the foundations of the
walkway in the South cloister
alley; from the W.

THE MAIN BUILDING PHASE

THE WEST CLAUSTRAL RANGE

The evidence for the original West range is inconclusive due mainly to the extensive disturbance to the surviving walls. It was detected in the 1936 excavation (illus 8b) as photographs and plans from that survey clearly show that the S end of wall 1307 was linked to a wall lying further to the W. This wall, apparently only surviving for 2–3m in length, was not revealed in 1984 but, on the evidence of similarity of build and dimensions as well as the overall symmetry of the site, it most likely joined with wall 1223 (illus 16), creating a major building 19m × 6m.

STRUCTURAL EVIDENCE

The N limits of the building were suggested by 1224 which appeared to be of Period II build (later re-used as cobbling in the Period III West alley) over which Period II blocking wall 1210 was built and which was redefined by the N end of the Period III West range.

Other than the broad outlines of the structure, there was little else found from this period of the West range, mainly due to the disturbance caused by the subsequent construction of the Period III range. It is likely that the mortared surface (1230),

against which all the Period III walls were cut, dates from Period II and, as this surface, which resembled a floor surface, lay to the W of 1223, there may have been another structure in this area.

The likelihood that wall 1223 was a Period II wall line was further suggested by the fact that it was exactly aligned with the Period II W wall of Structure 8 (see below). Wall 1307 was removed during Period III; 1213 formed the E wall of the West alley and 1223 became the W wall of the West alley.

THE MAIN BUILDING PHASE

THE EAST CLAUSTRAL RANGE

During the excavation all rooms within and adjacent to the East range were given identifying numbers (illus 10; colour III). This system functioned satisfactorily except in the Chapter house, where the relatively small Room 3 proved to be the third and final manifestation of a chamber which had formerly extended well beyond the E wall of the range. In addition to the rooms partially uncovered in 1936–37, the S end of the range (buried beneath The Bow) and an adjacent area to the E were also investigated.

The East range had been greatly disturbed during the 1936–37 excavation. Narrow, frequently deep, trenches had been dug alongside walls, resulting in the loss of evidence associated with the walls' construction and their relationships with adjacent levels. Thereafter, one or more courses of the exposed walls had been rebuilt and pointed with a very hard gritty mortar, thus further masking contextual relationships and making the interpretation of structures difficult, if not impossible.

The several phases of construction, together with stone-robbing and other detrimental activities, left little evidence of the environment that faced the builders in the 12th century and it can only be assumed that turf had been removed and the ground levelled before the East range was begun. The length of the building was such that localized problems, and the techniques employed to counter them, must have varied considerably. Near the church the ground was flat and the subsoil a stable, sandy clay, minimising difficulties whereas, further down the range, both the gravel slope and the river bank were always liable to erode.

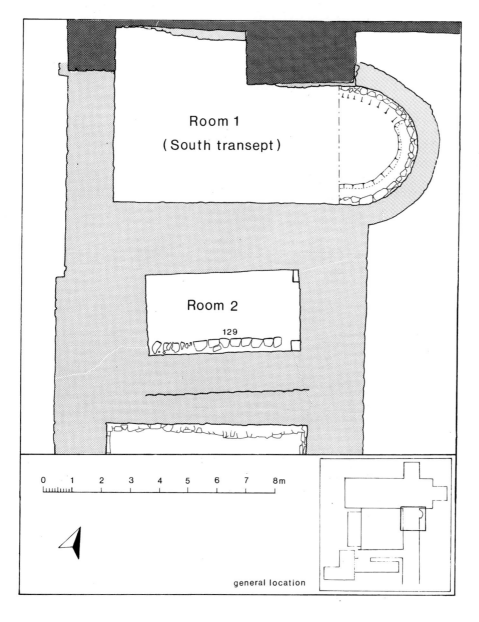

Room 1
(South transept)

Room 2

129

0 1 2 3 4 5 6 7 8m

general location

Illus 18
Plan of Rooms 1 and 2.

STRUCTURES OF THE EAST RANGE

ROOM 1 (SOUTH TRANSEPT) (illus 18)

The foundations of the S and apsidal E walls of the South transept were uncovered in 1936. Thereafter the walls had been partially rebuilt and the interior of the room levelled up with 1.45m of rubble and soils, presumably to echo the floor level of the choir. In 1984 excavation was restricted to the E end of the transept, to avoid disturbing a 20th-century grave in its NW corner. Below the rebuilt masonry the foundations of the S and E walls, each 0.7m wide, survived as single courses of doleritic boulders. There were traces of an associated bedding trench, 0.45m wide and 0.3m deep, cutting the otherwise undisturbed glacial till.

ROOM 2 (SLYPE/PARLOUR) (illus 18; 19)

This room measured 5.4 × 2.7m wide internally. The lower courses of the N, S and E walls, which had escaped the attentions of previous excavators, were built upon disturbed clayey subsoil within which were several disarticulated human bones, presumably redeposited. A thin spread of loosely compacted gravel had been used to level the ground below the W wall and within the adjacent part of the room. Blocks of sandstone, each about 0.4m square and mortared onto the side walls in the NE and SE corners of the room, appeared to be contemporary with those walls and were perhaps the base courses of an arch in the E wall.

Adjacent to the S wall was a line of roughly-faced, mortar-bonded sandstone blocks (129), the single surviving (0.25m high) course degenerating into a few rounded boulders and pebbles towards the W of the room. There was insufficient evidence by which to interpret this stonework with any confidence although conceivably it could have been the foundation for bench seating, which would justify the room's designation as a parlour as well as a slype (RCAHMS 1956, 204). However, the N face of 129 shared the same alignment as the outside face of the N wall of the early Chapter house (see below), suggesting that it was unconnected with Room 2.

Overlying the gravel in the W end of the room was a layer of red sandy clay, probably the bedding for flagstones or floor tiles although nothing remained of the floor itself. Patches of smooth white mortar had been dropped onto the surface of this clay and onto the inside face of masonry 129, presumably when the walls were being plastered or lime-washed.

There appeared to be a wall face within the masonry dividing Rooms 2 and 3 although this may have been a feature exaggerated for display purposes following the 1936–37 excavation. Given the strange configuration of this feature, its interpretation as the day stair (RCAHMS 1956, 204) is difficult to accept.

Illus 19
Room 2; showing the possible foundations for bench seating against the S wall and what may be the bases for an arch in the far corners of the room; from the W.

THE CHAPTER HOUSE (illus 20)

Three distinct phases of development were identified in the Chapter house. Originally the room extended some 3.0m beyond the East range and measured 10.5 × 5.3m internally, giving a floor area of approximately 52.5m^2 (exact measurements were impossible because of wall robbing and rebuilding). At a later stage the Chapter house was extended further to the E, only to be reduced thereafter to the small square chamber whose outline was displayed after 1937.

The W wall was built on sloping ground and laid on a bed of mortar over a thin layer of disturbed, mottled clay. Differing markedly from any other masonry within the range, the bottom courses of cream sandstone resembled a crudely-faced, free-standing wall which, together with a slight eastward alignment, suggested that it had belonged to an earlier structure although there was no other evidence to support this. Alternatively, this may be an example of wall foundations being realigned because of constructional mistakes and alterations, as was the case apparently at Bordesley Abbey (Hirst 1983, 229).

Up to 0.5m of charcoal-rich soils and other deposits that overlay the subsoil had been removed before the foundations of the E, S and N walls were laid. The only surviving evidence of the E wall was a robber trench (1041), 3.1m wide, and a few remnants of the wall's foundations. The S wall, however, was represented by foundations, 2.0m wide, of rubble alternating with layers of clay and pebbles that extended below and to the E of the Period IV E wall. This style of wall foundations was typical of the abbey's primary construction. At the bottom end of the East range mortar, rather than clay, had been used; otherwise the technique was identical. The N wall of the Chapter house, including its foundations, stood to a maximum height of 1.05m, above which was 1930s stonework. Its width could only be estimated as 2.5m because some of its masonry was masked by that of Room 2. However, it is possible that masonry 129 in Room 2 was a section of the N wall's outer face (see above). The difference in level between the two sides of the N wall could be explained by the slope of the ground. Where it extended beyond the East range, the outer face of the N wall had been badly robbed in antiquity. Many constructional details, including the relationship between the N and W walls, were unresolved although the foundations of the N wall were shown to be bonded with clay and a little mortar.

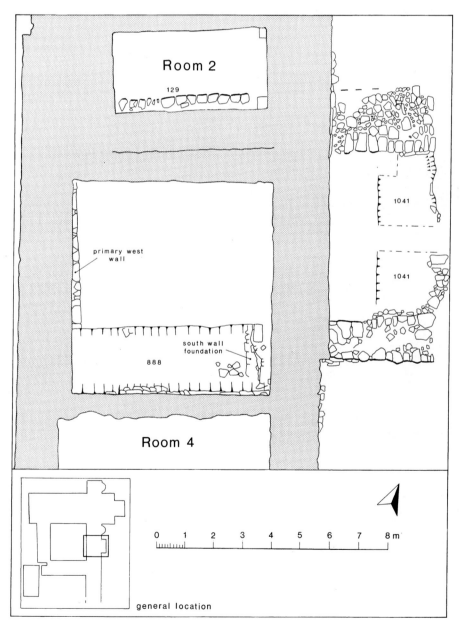

Illus 20
Plan of excavation of the Period II Chapter house.

After its superstructure had been built, the room's interior was raised and levelled, mainly with stone-free soils whose depth increased towards the S to compensate for the slope. There were numerous human bones, many of them juvenile, within these soils, suggesting that there was a cemetery in this area before the Chapter house was built. Above these levelling deposits were thin spreads of fine-textured, mortar-like material, probably derived from the plastering and/or lime-washing of walls. The builders' scaffolding may have been set upon stone or timber base plates for there was no evidence of socket-holes to house the necessary uprights. Similarly, nothing remained of a floor surface, the stone flags or clay tiles presumably having been removed during subsequent alterations.

Entry to the Chapter house would have been through a door in the W wall. Although the floor itself was missing, the drop in level from the cloister alley to the interior of the Chapter house suggests that there had been a short flight of steps inside the door. The space, 1.8m wide, between sarcophagus graves 5, 6, 7 and 8 and the building's W wall was the likely position of those steps.

ROOM 4 (illus 21; 22)

Religious reformers, stone-robbers, 18th-century builders and 1930s excavators had all helped destroy evidence relating to the building sequence within this room: indeed, it is unclear just how much of the surviving fabric of the room was genuinely medieval.

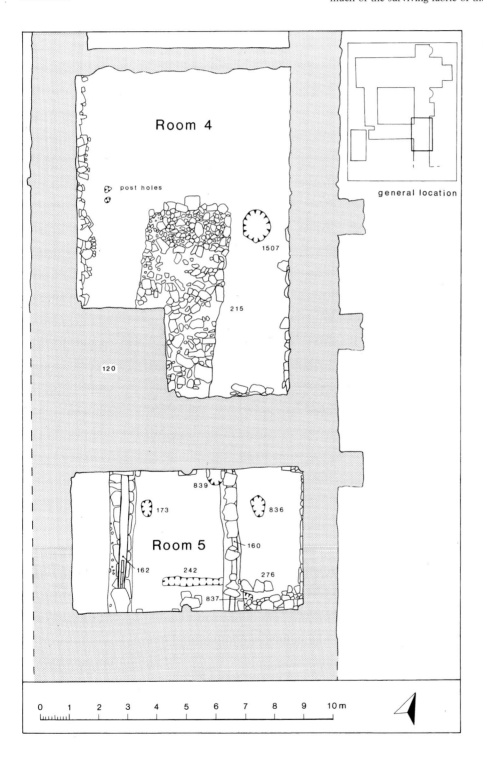

Illus 21
Plan of Rooms 4 and 5.

For example, the surviving portion of the W wall was consistent in style with that expected of 12th-century architecture, yet its masonry appeared to be continuous with the stone platform (120) in the SW corner of the room, below which were found sherds of 16th-century pottery. It is quite possible that the presumed 12th-century masonry had been reused but, without dismantling the walls, it was impossible to reconcile these inconsistencies.

The foundation trenches for the walls were cut into deposits of sand, gravel and small stones, up to 0.3m deep, overlying the gravel and boulders that are thought to pre-date the Augustinian abbey (**2.1** above). Of the primary N wall (and arguably the W wall) only the foundations of large angular sandstone boulders, survived. The thickness (at least 3.0m) of the N wall suggests that this could have been the site of the day stair that led from the canons' dormitory to the cloister. Perhaps more likely, the foundation for this stair was the large platform of clay- and mortar-bonded sandstone rubble (215) in the S side of the room.

Adjacent to the W wall were two stone-lined post-holes (209, 908), cutting the early gravels but covered by primary levelling materials, which were probably settings for scaffolding posts used during the construction of the building. Also cutting the early metalling was a pit (1507), 0.92m in diameter and 0.43m deep, probably too large for scaffolding and too near to the masonry of 215 to have housed a stone pier. Its fill of stone-free sand appears to have been washed in, suggesting that the pit was open for some time, perhaps during the construction of the building.

A strip of yellow-green clay, 1.0m wide, that overlay the levelling deposits on the N side of the room was interpreted as the base of an underfloor drain (similar to 1173 in the East cloister alley), whose course had been truncated.

ROOM 5 (illus 21; 23)

Most of this area was simply stripped down to bedrock before building commenced. However, because Room 5, which measured 8.0 × 4.7m internally, was built astride the old river bank, the gap between the cliff face and the S wall of the chamber had had to be levelled up, using a mixture of stone, gravel, clay

Illus 22
The probable footings of the day stair in Room 4; viewed from the N.

Illus 23
Room 5. Running N–S across the room are the two rock-cut drains 160 and 162; viewed from the W.

and mortar. As well as supporting the upper storeys of the East range, the massive (4.6m thick) wall dividing Rooms 5 and 6 also helped prevent the cliff face eroding any further.

Much of the archaeological record within this room was probably destroyed during the 1936–37 excavation and subsequent programmes of consolidation and rebuilding. The only upstanding medieval masonry to survive until 1984 comprised some of the S and E wall foundations and a few semi-octagonal pier bases, the upper courses of which were modern reconstructions. These piers, located in the corners of the room and midway along its walls, had supported the roof of a two-bayed, quadripartite-vaulted chamber. There had been a flagged floor although only fragments of it survived in the SE corner of the room.

Two rock-cut drains (160, 162) took ground water from the cloister, discharging it into the core of the wall separating Rooms 5 and 6, from where it percolated away. The drains, each 0.2–0.25m wide internally, were lined and capped with mortar-bonded sandstone flags although most of the capstones of drain 162 were missing and its duct reused to accommodate a modern earthenware field drain. It is assumed that two pennies (dated 1913 and 1916) retrieved from drain 160 had been inserted through one of the gaps between the drain's capstones during the 1936–37 excavation. Photographs and drawings from that excavation show a square opening, apparently aligned with drain 162, in the SW corner of Room 4. Although the evidence has been obscured by subsequent masonry consolidation, it may be reasonable to assume that the aperture had a similar function to one found below one of the cloister walls at Butley Priory, Suffolk. There it was interpreted as an inspection point for a conduit that carried water from the cloister roof and possibly from the lavatory (Myres 1933, 254).

There was no obvious pattern to the rock-cut holes dispersed throughout the room and, although some may have been scaffolding sockets, they were certainly not all contemporary. Pits 173 and 836 were filled with materials similar to the levelling deposits on the S side of the room and may have been pre-Augustinian features. Pit 839, adjacent to the N wall, was cut into bedrock and backfilled with three pitched sandstone slabs and loose red clay. The dimensions of pit 837, which was infilled with

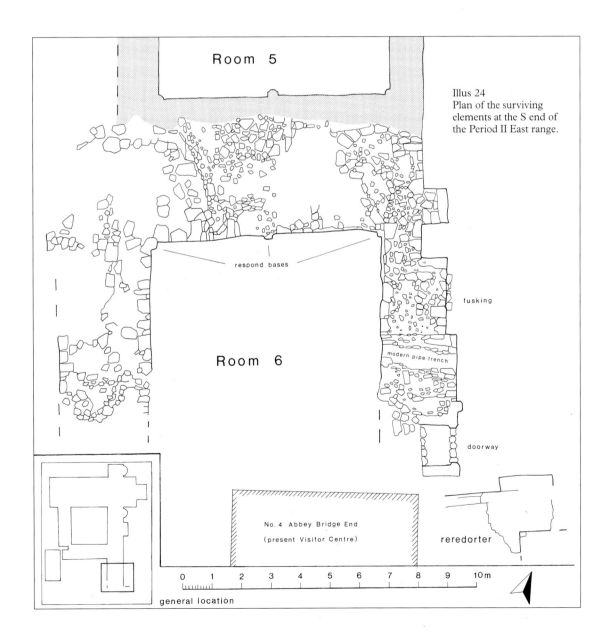

Illus 24
Plan of the surviving elements at the S end of the Period II East range.

red-brown silt, remain unknown for it extended below the S wall. An irregular cut in the SW corner of the room is thought to be a modern feature associated with the rebuilding of the W wall.

Towards the S side of the room were the remnants of a structure that may have pre-dated the main building phase of the East range. These remnants comprised three mortar-bonded sandstone blocks (276), faced on their S side, and a 2.0m-long slot (242), perhaps a robbed section of the same feature. The relationships between these features and the construction trenches for the Room 5 walls are not altogether clear although 276/242 did appear to be cut by drain 160.

ROOM 6 (illus 24–26)

At the foot of the old river bank was Room 6, a large undercroft which had not been excavated prior to 1984 because it lay beneath The Bow. To its S and SE were the remains of the reredorter (illus 24).

The undercroft was two bays (approximately 8.0m) wide and, although at least two bays long, its original extent could not be ascertained because the building was badly damaged at its S end (illus 25). The thickness of the E wall increased from 1.3m to

Illus 25
The S end of the East range. Note the massive walls on the N, E and W sides of Room 6. No 4, Abbey Bridge End (now a visitor centre) stands over the remains of the reredorter; from the NW.

Illus 26
The NE corner of Room 6. Its ashlar-lined walls retain remnants of blind arcading; viewed from the S.

2.6m over the room's surviving length while the W wall was even broader (3.5m) and had been widened still further at a later date. Such massive walls were needed to support the towering height of the East range at this, the lowest point of the abbey.

The wall foundations comprised rafts of large dolerite boulders and sandstone rubble, similar to those used in the Chapter house, although here the bonding material was mortar rather than clay. Each course of the finely-tooled ashlar wall faces was 0.2–0.3m high and built of blocks up to 0.6m long, the very tight joints requiring little or no pointing. Wall cores, however, were of unworked or reused rubble, bonded with a cream-coloured mortar. Within the core of the W wall was a block of fine-grained red sandstone, roughly inscribed into a board used for the game of merelles, or nine-men's morris (**4.7**; illus 87 below).

The highest surviving masonry was the 3.0m-high E wall which was, nevertheless, well below the level of the quadripartite-vaulted ceiling. Evidence of the piers that supported the vaulting survived midway along the N wall of the undercroft and in its NE and NW corners. The latter survived to its full height of 1.23m and still supported some vaulting ribs as well as the blind arcading in the N and E walls (illus 26). Secondary developments had destroyed, or masked, some of the piers although midway along the E wall, behind a secondary E–W cross-wall, a springer was still in evidence. An aumbry, 0.76m long and 0.3m high, was recessed 0.58m into the W wall of the N bay, 1.0m above floor level. Two small areas of flagstones adjacent to the N and W walls were all that remained of the floor. The only visible access to the undercroft was by an inward-opening doorway, 1.16m wide, in the E wall of the S bay. No windows pierced the surviving stretches of the walls.

An ashlar wall, 1.2m wide and surviving as tusking, projected from, and was integral with, the E wall of the range. Being so narrow, it is unlikely to have supported a superstructure and the wall is thought to have been a boundary, defining the limits of another range of buildings.

THE REREDORTER (illus 24)

Only a very brief investigation was possible to the E of No 4 Abbey Bridge End prior to its conversion into a visitor centre. Below post-18th-century deposits of rubble and clay and approximately level with the N wall of the house, was an E–W wall, 1.4m wide and extending 3.3m beyond the line of the East range. The wall's masonry was identical to the 13th-century ashlar of Room 6. There was a southward return on the internal angle but this wall had been damaged during the construction of the house and consequently its width could not be determined.

During operations to underpin the foundations of the house, the quoins of a chamfered plinth and one further course of ashlar were uncovered below the building's W wall, 1.4m from its SW corner. There was an eastward return from the S side of the chamfer and a 1.13m length of walling extending N from the quoins but, otherwise, little else survived.

THE MAIN BUILDING PHASE

THE SW OF THE SITE

The main building phase in this area was preceded by extensive preparation of the steep terrain. This was followed by the building of Structure 8 and Structures 9 and 10.

PREPARING THE GROUND • TERRACING AND FOUNDATIONS

The first stage in the preparation of this part of the site for the main phase of building saw the construction of three, squared blocks of masonry (illus 27) which were to serve a triple function:

a) to support the great W wall of Structure 8 where it proceeded down the steep, stepped profile of the already terraced site, to the river;

b) to give added protection to the W wall where it projected into the full force of the river current; and

c) to receive the main drainage and garderobe outlets for the buildings at the W limits of the site.

PLATFORMS A, B AND C

Three platforms, A, B and C, ran from the S edge of the middle terrace down to the river for a distance of some 11m, with platform C forming the SW corner of Structure 8. Platforms A and B were regular in size and plan: A was 2.3m E–W and 3.0m N–S; and B was 2.3m by 2.8m. However, C was altogether different in that its E face was on the same alignment as A and B but it was wider and its W face was angled obliquely to face upstream. This was originally to ensure the easy passage of the river around the walls of Structure 8 which were to project well beyond the limits of the natural river bank and into the river itself.

The three blocks of masonry were of monumental construction. A and B were both built into the slope and thus required an extensive construction raft of large boulders sunk into the face of the existing upper terrace and the natural bank. Over this foundation course, mortar-bonded sandstone masonry was laid. These heavy foundations acted as revetment against any movement down the slope. They were only partially exposed and, of the two, only B was examined closely. Its foundations were over 1.0m deep and were bonded with clay (2015). They were dug against midden material (2013 type) and appeared to follow the NE–SW alignment of the original river bank.

The upper masonry of A and B stood only about 0.4m high: this was mainly due to the wholesale robbing of all stonework from the abbey buildings which were ultimately covered by The Bow. Platform C projected beyond the line of the river bank and, on its E side, was excavated to a depth of 2.3m. The topmost 0.75m of the face was constructed of narrow, flat sandstone slabs with many small pinnings, forming a crude but dressed finish. The lower courses of the buttress showed no attempt at even crude dressing, being constructed of largely unmortared, more massive and irregular sandstone slabs. The lower masonry also had a distinct

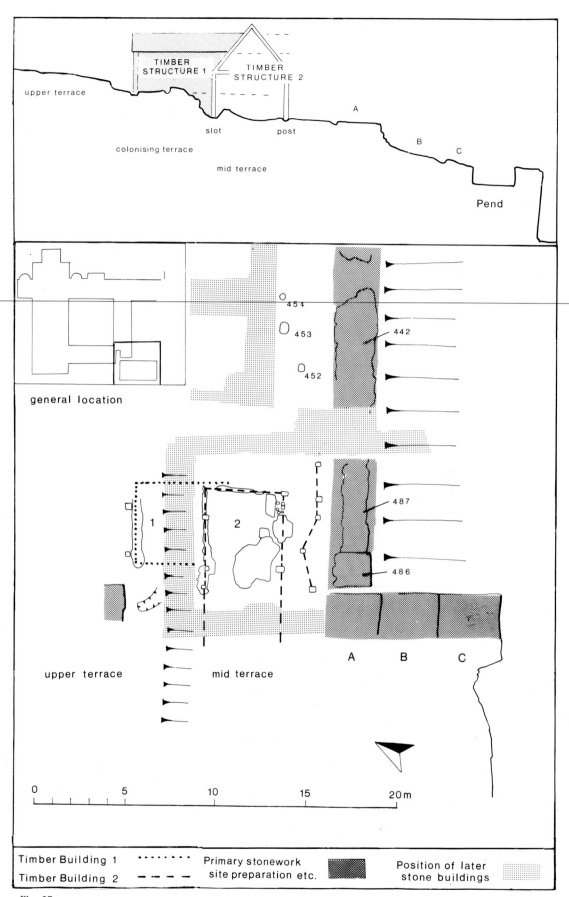

Illus 27
Plan and section of Period II terracing at the SW corner of the site showing the location of the timber structures and Structure 8.

batter to the E, eventually resting on huge boulder foundations. This style of construction is distinct from subsequent Period II building and is only comparable to other 'strengthening' walls such as the revetment walls 487 and 442 (illus 13), both of which were ultimately buried.

The original S end of platform C was obscured by the addition of the massive S wall (378) of Structure 8. However, the original angled W face of the platform was still discernible as a break in build between it and its successor, 2011 (see below).

REVETTING WALL (487) (illus 13; 28)

Once the original W limits of the site were established by the A, B, C platform buttress series, a major E–W revetting wall was constructed (487). This, as in the case of the platforms, served a combination of purposes:

a) the masonry was dug onto the southernmost point of the river bank where a straight E–W line could still be established in order to create a secure naturally founded wall; and

b) the wall supported buildings to the N of the line as well as providing footings for extending S.

The wall had, however, suffered extensive damage by late stone-robbing and further subdivision of the monastic complex (notably Room 11 which abruptly truncated the wall as it proceeded E).

Superficially, the masonry was crude with its visible outer (S) face constructed of large and irregular mixed stones, some water-washed and some crudely dressed. In particular, the N face of 487 was erratic in its course, making the wall appear to vary in width considerably (from 2.5m to a minimum of 1.5m over its entire length of 19.5m).

During the excavation of the Period II pillar base (2017) the true quality of the masonry was apparent. A section across the W end of 487 showed that the irregularities in the N face were due to levelling up from the middle terrace to cover a totally regular straight-sided wall below, set in a foundation trench. The upper irregular stonework was simply intended to

completely fill the construction trench and to bring the upper surface of the wall to the correct height. Once these top two courses were removed, the entire construction was found to be laid against a vertical cut in the natural sand and clay of the colonizing terrace which ran along a straight E–W line 2.0m N of the S face of wall 487. The component layers within the wall were not totally excavated and, of possibly numerous rafts, four were ultimately revealed:

a) the uppermost course of finishing and levelling masonry comprised largely rounded, dolorite boulders with some sandstone for pinning and packing set in a pinkish clay, a maximum of 0.3m deep;

b) a second layer of more random and larger water-washed stones with an overall depth of 0.24m;

c) a flat layer of river pebbles, closely packed to give an almost cobbled appearance some 0.2m thick; and

d) a second cobbling raft, apparently identical to c).

The second cobbling raft (d) was found to run below the E wall of Structure 8 and the uppermost layers ((a) and (b)) sealed a primary Period II post pit (boundary post 3007) – confirmation of the intermediate role of the E–W revetting wall between the primary and secondary phases of Period II.

LEVELLING DUMPS

The extension S of the middle terrace level was carried out to accommodate the massive N–S dimensions of Structure 8 at the S limits of the site – to form, in effect, the SW corner of the abbey complex. This period of extension is characterised by the series of tipped deposits over residual, early Period II midden (illus 14b) down the face of the slope – in particular 2014, a single distinctive dump of smashed sandstone chippings (presumably a by-product of the stone dressing from the building work elsewhere on the site). A similar sequence of events probably occurred with two other later Period II buildings on the site – Structures 9 and 10 – where the terrace revetted by 422 (the E end of 487) was extended S artificially.

STRUCTURAL EVIDENCE

STRUCTURE 8 (illus 28; 29)

Structure 8 was intended to link (at its first floor level) with the cloister while the building had a basement, or undercroft, below. This plan was based on the assimilation of the existing Period II terraces (illus 27) – that on which the abbey church and cloister were built and that under Timber Structure 2, halfway down the slope – within the new building. The two main floors of the block were further complemented by the addition of an alley or pend at a level below the undercroft, at the extreme S end of the building. The creation of the pend was again a reflection of the effort of the builders to utilise the steep slope on the river bank which Structure 8 spanned. An examination of the sequence of levels from the cloister down to the river shows clearly how the three elements of upper floor (S), undercroft and pend could be accommodated. The terrace of Timber Structure 2 lies 3m below the cloister (South alley) and is 4m above the level of the pend which, in turn, stands 4m above the river.

To allow the establishment of an artificial terrace by means of successive tips, two E–W walls were built – the main S wall of the overall structure and the N wall of the pend (378 and 384 respectively). The S wall (378) was to receive the entire combined

weight of the main construction dumps, notably layer 2014, while the N wall (384) was built over the primary tips and revetted the upper sequence (482, 488, 481).

THE GREAT S WALL (378) (illus 30–33)

This section of masonry, still impressive despite only standing to a fraction of its original height, proved to be one of the most interesting and illuminating structures on the entire site. As found, the wall stood to an average height of 4.0m on its S face but could have been in excess of 20m high originally if it shared the same roof line as the refectory.

The wall was constructed of large ashlar sandstone blocks (illus 31), mortar-bonded and of general uniformity, with an average width of 1.4m and an overall length of 10.5m. At its S face, the stonework was built over a substantial timber raft and, to the N, it had foundations of river boulders (as noted in the sondage at the E face of 2005). The use of timber was necessitated by the fact that the wall was built over clays rather than bedrock (compare with the W end of the added Period III S wall) and so the ability of such a construction to spread the weight of the masonry more

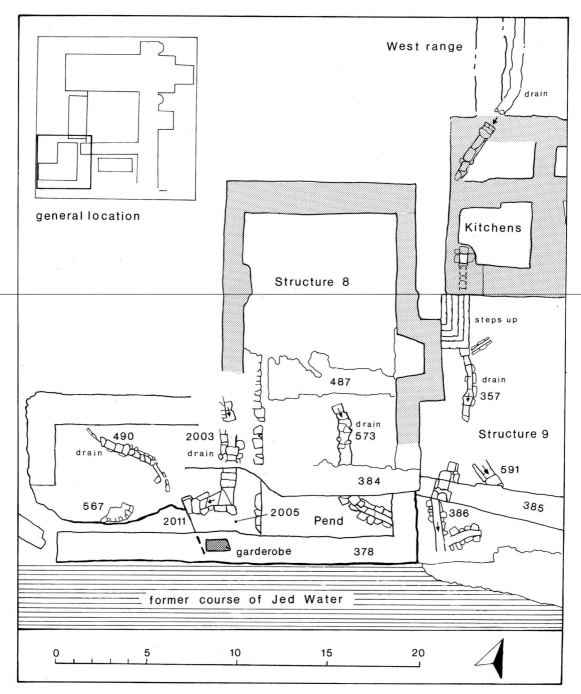

Illus 28
Structure 8 and associated drains.

evenly was vital. It is possible that foundations formed from several components might enable periodic repairs more easily in that a damaged section could be removed and replaced with little disturbance to the rest of the foundations. The timber raft consisted of a single oak beam 9.5m long overlying a series of four projecting cross members which were laid in stone-lined channels 2.75m apart.

The cross members were laid first. The main beam was then laid across them (illus 32), resting in straight sided recesses 0.1–0.12m deep, to form a simple overlapping joint, with the cross members projecting an average of 0.7m beyond the S face of the main beam. The lowest course of masonry was then built directly on to

the main beam and took the form of a simple, angled scarcement (angle some 80 mm from vertical). The main fabric of the wall was then built up from that recessed face (illus 33) over some ten courses to a second scarcement level 2.4m above. This upper scarcement narrowed the wall still further to approximately 1.4m and from this point the wall stood only a maximum of 14 courses.

The relative quality of the surviving wood (oak throughout) at the W end of the wall enabled samples for dendrochronological dating to be taken (from beams 649 and 648) and a date of AD 1258±9 was obtained for beam 649. All the timber (both main beam and cross members) was rectangular in section and, while it was markedly better preserved towards the W of the wall line, decay

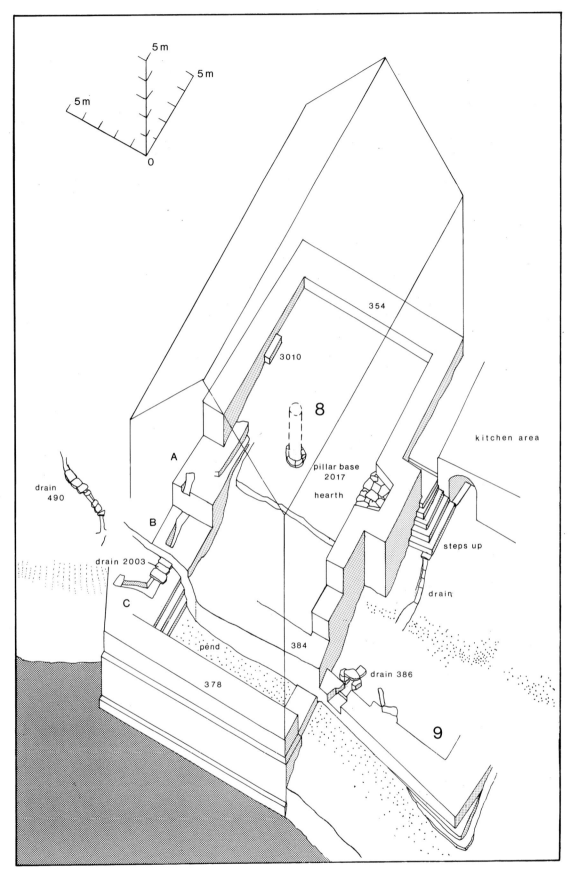

Illus 29
Isometric drawing of of Structures 8 and 9.

Illus 30
The S wall of Structures 8 and 13;
from the SE.

had all but obscured the dimensions and jointing of the E section (beams 650 and 649). Only beam 648 was intact because beam 643, a similarly well-preserved section, was damaged when the textile mill's piped water supply was installed.

Wall 378 was extended W during Period III and was altered within Period II with the construction of a garderobe pit tacked on to its W end: both these developments have obscured the original relationship between 378 and platform/buttress C to some extent. Limited excavation showed, however, that 378 was built across the S end of C, but with no attempt to key the two wall faces together. During excavation, the S wall was found to be slipping back from C, resulting from the partial decay and subsidence within the E half of the timber foundation raft and also due to the simple, butted interface between the walls.

The Timber Raft Beneath Structure 8

Context	Length (m)	Width/ Diameter (mm)	Description
644	9.20	700	main beam
643	1.00	400	cross member
648	1.30	209	cross member
649	1.00	300	cross member
650	1.46	300	cross member

Table 3 Dimensions of elements of the timber raft beneath Structure 8.

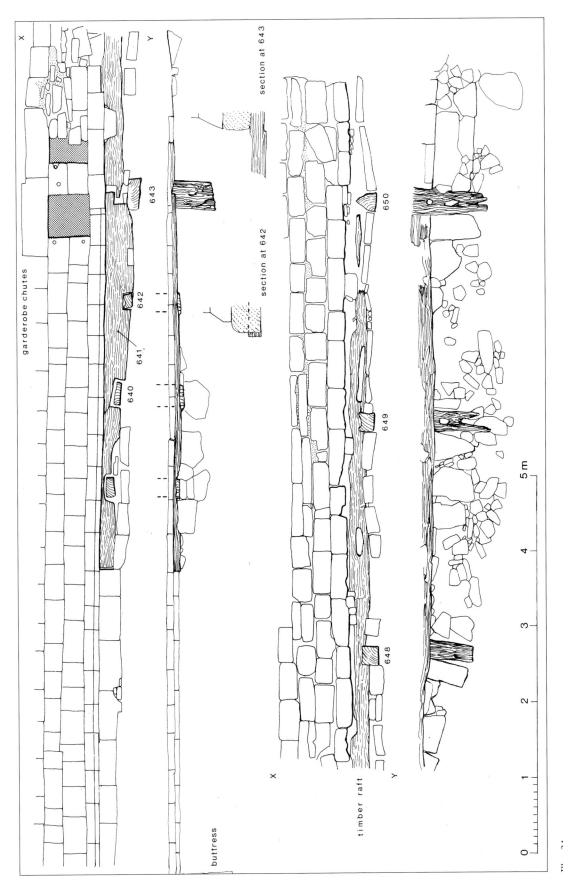

Illus 31
Elevation and plan of the lower courses of the S walls of Structures 8 and 13.

Illus 32
Detail of cross member (648), in a stone setting, supporting the timber raft.

THE N, E AND W WALLS (illus 28; 29; 34)

Virtually all these walls had been extensively repointed after earlier phases of excavation on the site; because of this, much of the detail of their form and construction has been lost.

The N wall closely resembled the S wall in length and breadth. It stood a maximum of four courses high at its N face (a height of 1.2m), diminishing to two courses at its S face (a height of 0.62m).

The W wall ran for some 10m to a point over Platform A. Its S section, ie that part beyond the limits of the middle terrace, was completely missing although it is possible that the sloping W drain (2003) was contained within the width of the W wall. Consolidation of the wall's masonry during the 1930s has made the stump of a possible cross-wall seem dubious. At a point 2.8m S of the internal NW corner of the building, a short section of masonry (3010) projected from the E face of the W wall for a distance of 0.8m. The S face of this possible cross-wall was less certain although it may have reflected a wall some 1.5m wide.

The consolidated section of the E wall ran for 13.5m and stood to a maximum height of 1.02m above the floor of the building and 0.9m at its outer face. Its abrupt termination at such a height was marked by the line of the most recent N wall of The Bow, the construction of which obliterated the S part of the E wall. However, its line was continued up to and beyond the N wall of the pend, culminating in the E threshold of the pend itself and its ultimate junction with the S wall.

The hearth/fireplace in the E wall (illus 29)

The E wall had a recessed hearth halfway along its length – a feature which also helped to stabilise the overall building. This was achieved by the siting of the hearth and flue over a squared platform similar to Platform A in the W wall: its S face was built along the line of Period I revetting wall 487, thus reinforcing the critical break between the terrace under Timber Structure 2 and the extended S half of the building.

The hearth had a flagged surface and splayed sides – 2.3m wide at its mouth, tapering to 1.5m at its back wall. The back wall stands to a height of 0.65m above the paved floor of the hearth although all the masonry involved had been repointed and may have been enlarged. This policy of comprehensive rebuilding (found all over the site) might explain the apparent anomaly of the difference of level between the hearth floor and the interior of the room itself (the main floor surface was some 0.2m above the hearth floor). The narrow trench dug by the earlier excavators along the inside (W) face of the wall and the hearth effectively removed the possibility of ever establishing the reason for this curiosity.

Externally, the buttress formed by the hearth recess was generally simple and unadorned, although a short section of a scarcement survived along its S face.

PILLAR BASE

With the exception of a possible cross-wall (3010) to the N of the undercroft, the surviving evidence as to how the ceiling of the undercroft was supported amounted to a single pillar base (2017) (illus 29; 35).

This rounded structure lay almost exactly in the centre of Structure 8. At its upper surface, it consisted of a rounded, mortar-bonded plinth composed of three or four slabs of pinkish-red sandstone laid flush with the floor, about 1m square. The feature was dug into the two upper levelling rafts within revetting wall 487, to a depth of 0.45m. Large, rounded dolerite boulders were then laid as foundations, set in redeposited natural sands and gravel, over which a raft of smaller, mixed masonry was set in clay. The upper, sandstone, flags were then laid on top of a level, yellow, sandy mortar surface which bonded the stonework.

THE PEND (illus 29; 36)

In order to make most efficient use of the natural profile of the river bank and the terraces, as well as providing a stabilising effect, a narrow passage or pend was constructed at the S limits of the building. To the W, the pend allowed access on to the Period II W riverside terrace and at its E end originally provided an outlet to the river.

The pend ran the entire width of Structure 8 with its E threshold formed by the reduced height of the main E wall of Structure 8; and its W threshold crossing Platform C and its drain via a series of steps. The N wall (384) of the pend ran parallel to the S wall (378) for most of its length (a distance of 7.4m) but turned N as it approached the W end of the passage. This was to ensure a uniform width for the W entrance by making the N wall conform with the angled outer face of Platform C and to permit secure access on to the riverside terrace.

These considerations resulted in a passage with a width of 2.2m

Illus 33
Detail of the S wall of Structures 8 and 13, showing garderobe outlets and timber raft; from the S.

for most of its length which then widened to almost 3.0m at its junction with Platform C; and which narrowed again to 2.0m at its W entrance.

The N wall (384) was of generally crude sandstone construction for most of its length but was much better finished at its two entrances with the use of good, close-fitting ashlar. This shows how visible masonry was harmonised with the general quality of other external masonry.

The wall stood to a maximum height of 3.0m with its lower courses being simply clay-bonded rubble construction. At a height of 1.8m, the wall was mortared and what little survived was of apparently better construction.

By projecting the height difference between the excavated floor of the pend and the level of the floor at the N of the undercroft, the pend could have been over 3.0m in height. A simple, barrel-vaulted roof could have spanned the width of the pend easily as well as binding the N wall of the pend to the main S wall, an important stabilising measure given the vastly different widths of the respective foundations of the two walls.

The reused primary Period II drain (573) found its new outlet to the river via the E entrance to the pend, by means of a well-constructed stone-lined and covered drain. The channel within this feature was 0.35m wide and 0.08m deep – all of which was recessed into the trodden clay and cobble floor of the passage.

THE W DRAIN AND THE ORIGINAL PERIOD II GARDEROBE

Platforms A, B and C provided the foundations for a well-built stone drain (2003) which ran from the middle terrace down to the river (illus 28). The surviving section of the drain was found to be angled downwards, broadly parallel to the original profile of the river bank.

The drain and its outlet into the Jed Water saw two phases prior to its abandonment during Period III (illus 38). The need to alter the original drain seems to have been a result of the construction of a garderobe pit within the width of the angled SW corner masonry. This was achieved by the thickening of the angled face by some 1.5m by the construction of 2011, the Phase 2 outlet wall (see below).

THE W DRAIN (2003)

Phase 1 (illus 37; 38)

The drain was a well-built, mortar-covered, stone channel which rested on angled masonry built over Platforms A, B and C. The bottom of the channel, with the exception of a short section to the N end of Platform B, survived intact from the S edge of the Timber Structure 2 terrace down to the N face of the great S wall 378 – a distance of 5.7m. However, the sides and capstones for the N end of the drain were mostly missing although enough remained to show that the channel itself measured 0.4m deep and 0.45m wide at its N end, enlarging to 0.44m deep and 0.66m wide to the S.

The drain originally ran off due S. The remains of the S end of the Phase 1 channel could be traced for some 0.3m behind the deliberate Phase 2 blocking although the details of exactly how and where the effluent was discharged are unclear.

In Phase 2, the original S outlet was blocked off at a point approximately halfway across the upper surface of Platform C by means of a clay and rubble plug which ducted the flow out to the SW and through the Phase 2 outlet in wall 2011.

The drain, with its capstones, was absorbed in a series of low steps which ran up from the pend surface, onto Platform C then up to the drain via two steps of clay-bonded red sandstone.

Phase 2 (illus 38–40)

A section of fine, yellow, sandstone masonry was butted against the original angled W face of Platform C. The wall was constructed of distinctively dressed, ashlar blocks; some were very large including one which was 1.2m long; outer faces featured fine diagonal tooling.

The wall was excavated to a depth of 3.5m and was found to have been built directly against an artificially dressed edge in the naturally shaley bedrock, creating a neat joint between masonry and bedrock. The outlet for the redirected drain 2003 was marked by a rectangular aperture towards the top of the wall (2011) which was later blocked by Period III work. The outlet measured 0.6m deep and 0.3m wide, thus narrowing the channel from a maximum width of 0.5m (at the E end of the new extension to the drain). Such a device ensured a spouting effect to project effluent away from the masonry.

Illus 34
Structure 8 (Structure 13 is in the left background); from the E. The pend lies towards the bottom left. The steps on the bottom right were associated with Structure 9. To the top left are the remains of an outbuilding contemporary with the manse.

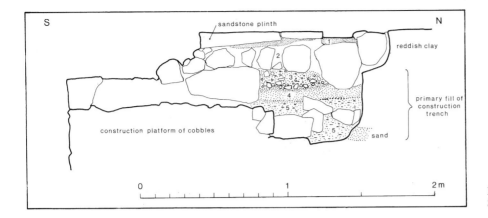

Illus 35
Section across pier base 2017.

Illus 36
The pend leading into Structure 13; from the E. The W end of Structure 9 is visible at the bottom of the picture with drain 386 issuing through its S wall.

Illus 37
The W drain; from the S. The base of the drain can be seen towards the top of the picture. The drain flows out towards the left in the foreground.

The purpose behind building wall 2011 was to create outlets for drain 2003 and a possible garderobe serving the upper floors (S) of Structure 8; and also to create an area of turbulence within the river by deliberately angling the face of the wall into the full force of the current. Such an act would prevent a stagnant pool forming and would help to push the effluent out into the mainstream and away.

This was achieved by creating a 90° angle between the face of the natural bedrock which formed the river bank at this point and the outer face of wall 2011. The bedrock was duly cut back to the N and was also cut vertically over a distance of some 3m, thus providing an appropriate channel for the river to hit the wall with sufficient force.

GARDEROBE (illus 39)

The evidence for a garderobe pit associated exclusively with Structure 8 and located within the width of 2011 was first surmised by the realisation that part of the original W face of Platform C had been retained: it was visible as the E side of the Period III garderobe pit. This face, coupled with the elaborate hydraulics within wall 2011, tends to confirm the presence of a garderobe pit towards the S end of the new outer SW corner of Structure 8. This was superseded by the garderobe within the extended S wall within Structure 13.

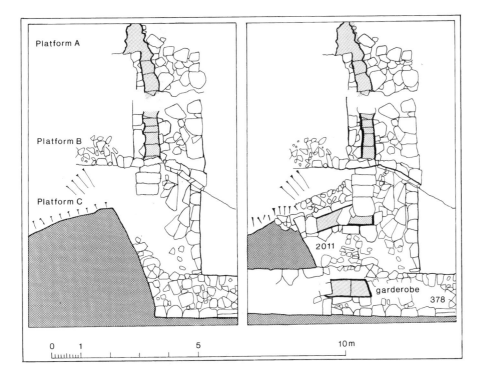

Illus 38
Plans of the W drain, phases 1 and 2.

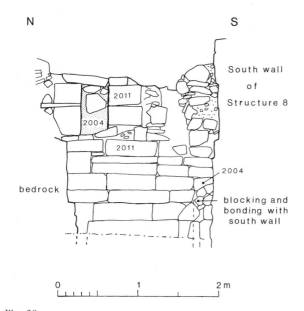

Illus 39
Elevation of the outlet for the phase 2 W drain.

Illus 40
Phase 2 W drain; from the N. The junction between Period II platform C and masonry associated with the W drain (2011) is plainly visible towards the centre of the picture.

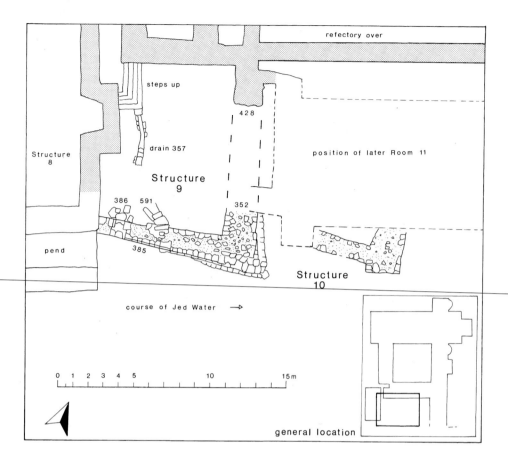

Illus 41
Plan of Structures 9 and 10.

THE CONTINUED USE OF THE PRIMARY W RIVERSIDE TERRACE

The outlet of the primary Period II drain 490 was truncated by the need to cut back the natural N river bank; and the resulting weak point at the corner between the main E–W alignment of the bank and the point where it turns towards the face of 2011 was revetted and stabilised by a short section of rubble masonry (507). The primary route W along the river bank was still a feature of later Period II although its ultimate destination was never ascertained. In due course, this surface was incorporated into the floor of Structure 13; and the need to create more accommodation took precedence over the route along the river to the W.

STRUCTURES 9 AND 10 (illus 41; 42)

Unlike Structure 8, the remaining structures so far identified as being part of the main building phase at the abbey only survive as very fragmentary remains, having been superseded and largely demolished by later building programmes. The creation of a viable route around the S of the site during Period III saw the redrafting of the original riverside elements of the site – the central S area of the site was extended S, thereby pushing the

river further S. This allowed a road to be built over much of what had once been a riverside frontage of distinctive, angled buildings.

STRUCTURE 9

This building or platform appears to have consisted of only two walls, to the S and E, which defined an open area immediately E of Structure 8. The area provided access to the river ultimately from the cloister via a passage between Structure 8 and the kitchen/refectory complex. All that survived of Structure 9 were the upper courses of the S wall and a short section of the E wall. Fuller excavation of these walls was impeded by the presence of later, monastic structures which obscured their full extent. However, enough survived to show its acutely angled external SE corner; and a characteristic stepped outer profile, a feature which suggested that the walls widened considerably as they neared the river.

The S wall (385) (illus 42) was butted against the E end of the N wall of the pend (384) and the visible remains of the S face of 385 ran in a generally SE direction over 11.5m. The wall widened at its upper level from W to E. It stood to a maximum height of 1.15m above the Period III road surface but this may have been due only to the fact that the defining level for the Period III road, which appears to cover much of the S wall, was the threshold of the pend in Structure 8. Towards the SE corner of the structure, the masonry showed the stepped profile. The great stability of this construction technique and the overall obliqueness of the angle of the outer face suggest an original role as a waterfront building. This is largely confirmed by the outlet of a main drain (386) being set in its outer face, and its association with two other distinctively angled structures, one of which did project into the river. This building would be at once strong enough to withstand the erosive effect of the river and would also direct its flow down towards the reredorter.

The masonry in both walls was of bonded sandstone with a simple scarcement at the uppermost surviving level. The build of the walls at the SE corner was of larger, square stones but of rather uneven form – perhaps due to the complete robbing out of an outer angled face in ashlar.

The E wall (352) ran for only 1.6m at its internal face and 4.0m at its external face: its progress N was truncated by both the construction of a Period IV wall (375 – the S wall of Structure 14) and by probable over-digging in previous excavations.

Both walls served as revetment for a series of tips which only survived in the limited area between walls 375 and 385. This material was partially excavated and comprised four main layers of mixed, stoney silt which gave way to a flatter horizon of clean clay sealing a rubble core. The overall depth of the deposit above the rubble core was 0.75m. The lack of finds in these construction levels contrasts starkly with the abundance of material found in destruction horizons (526, 527) which partly sealed them and which predated the building of Structure 14 (**2.4** below).

DRAINS 357 AND 591 (illus 41)

It is possible that drain 591 was the original S outlet for the drain 357 which ran from the cloister. Drain 591 lay at a lower level than the more elaborate drain 386 and had been opened and backfilled. It comprised a short channel running SE and defined by two rows of pitched flat stones with two capstones *in situ* (the southernmost of which was built into the N face of wall 385). The W side of the drain was formed almost entirely from a single massive slab (1.503m long) whereas the E side was defined by a series of four smaller stones laid in a slight curve. This curved side, when viewed together with the alignments of the two surviving capstones, indicated that the drain was turning S when it disappeared at the N face of wall 385. Its abrupt end at this point confirmed that it was an earlier feature, simply built over by 385. Its crude appearance was reminiscent of the primary Period II drains (573 and 490) and, as such, it may have been a temporary outflow for 357 (or an earlier version of the same) which, in due course, was re-aligned in keeping with the carefully considered S face of Structure 9. The channel was a maximum of 0.5m wide and 0.23m deep and was backfilled with the same material as that revetted by walls 385 and 352.

Although it may have had an earlier form (as suggested by the presence of drain 591 and the complex history of most of the drains on the site), drain 357 dated from Period II. It was aligned to serve the W side of the cloister. From the cloister, it passed the probable site of the kitchen and dropped down through an open chute to the terrace defined by Structure 8. From there, it found its outlet via the elaborate construction (386) (illus 43) in the S wall of Structure 9. The entire feature was set in a wide embrasure

Illus 42
The stepped S wall of Structure 9; from the SE. The S limits of the Period II masonry are partially obscured by the Period IV roadway along the edge of the river

Illus 43
Outlet of drain 386; from the S. The drain emanates from the base
of the arched opening, shown at the top of the picture

within wall 385. This comprised a straight-sided recess 0.8m wide
and 0.7m deep at which point the overall width of the feature
narrowed to 0.6m. The only surviving section of the channel itself
rested within this inner section. The channel was roughly square
in section (0.35m high by 0.4m wide) and had a scooped bottom
which was some 0.6m above the bottom of the outer section of the
embrasure. This, coupled with the fact that the bottom of the
channel had been apparently set at a crucial height (there is a gap
below it of 0.2m), suggested that the waste water may have been
projected out beyond the face of the wall via some form of angled
channel or conduit. The details of this were lost owing, in part, to
the fact that the outlet was modified with lead piping during
Period III. There was also some evidence to suggest that the outlet
was a secondary feature within wall 385 in that the nearest stone
from the scarcement level to the outlet had apparently been cut: it
measured only 0.45m, as compared to the rest of blocks which
were up to 0.8m long; similarly, the stone which formed the lower
corner of the outer embrasure had been recut. This possibility
could shed further light on the abandonment of 591 in that a more
sophisticated and efficient method for the final disposal was
required albeit an afterthought once the wall was in place.

STRUCTURE 10 (illus 41)

The presence of another large building to the E of, and on a very
similar alignment to, Structure 9 was marked by a distinctive
fragment of walling (3016). It was not fully excavated, being
almost completely covered by the S access route of Period III and
threshold levels associated with Room 11. Moreover, the W end of
3016 disappeared under masonry from Room 11, thus confirming
it as a Period II feature.

By the end of the excavation, 3016 was sufficiently exposed to
interpret it as the truncated remains of a waterfront revetting
wall, very similar to Structure 9 in terms of alignment and
structural elements. It, too, seemed to comprise essentially a S
and E wall with the suggestion of a reinforced outer face at the
corner of the two walls. The S face of Structure 10 was traced for
6.0m while the E wall ran 2.95m to the N. Both walls were
truncated by the construction of Structure 11. The S wall of
Structure 10 was 1.3m wide for most of its length but thickened
towards the E to 1.7m; the E wall was apparently 2.0m wide
throughout.

2.3 PERIOD III – REMODELLING AND REBUILDING (*c* 1300 – *c* 1480)

The fabric of the abbey was altered many times over four centuries. The church was remodelled before its
original design was fully implemented and it is quite possible that some of the monastic buildings were
modified before the claustral ranges had been completed. However, this could not be confirmed by
excavation because it was difficult to date most of the changes or to explain why they were carried out.

THE EXTENDED CLOISTER

Due to extensive excavation in 1936–37 in the area of the West range, the archaeological evidence for the extended cloister was inevitably fragmentary. The less extensive excavations of 1984 in this area did, however, confirm that the Period II West range was abandoned when the cloister was extended to the W. This development, along with the changes to the refectory, was part of an extensive programme of conversion and rebuilding over the Period II plan. The new layout saw the retention of the Period II W wall (1223) and the demolition of the Period II walls 1212 and 1307 (illus 44). There was then a period of industrial activity in advance of the construction of new walls 1226, 1213 and 1297 which resulted in the Period III plan. Much of

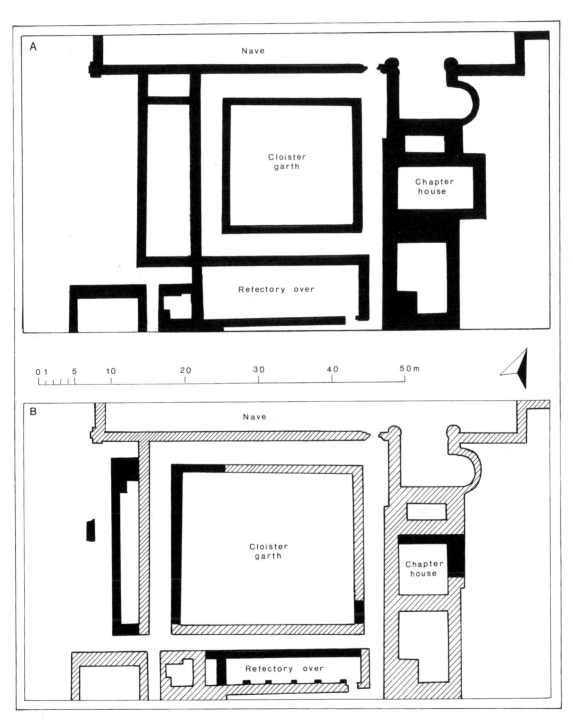

Illus 44
Schematic plans of the primary and secondary cloisters.

Illus 45
a) The W side of the cloister during the 1936–37 excavation; from the N, showing vestigial remains of Period II walls overlain by garden deposits; pier base 1215 is visible at bottom left;

b) the West cloister alley in 1984, with pier base 1215 in the centre; from the N; evidence of plant beds and late drainage channels can be seen to the top of the frame.

the detailed evidence for the sequence of demolition, robbing and rebuilding at the W side of the site did not survive earlier clearance work, as is shown on the photographs of the 1936–37 excavation (illus 45a). Many of the key walls from Periods II and III in this area were almost entirely robbed out with only the N and S extremities surviving to any degree. The construction of the manse and garden appeared to have removed all but the most vestigial evidence of the remodelled West range.

THE EVIDENCE FOR THE CLOISTER

Evidence for the dimensions of the Period II West range relies in part on close examination of the 1936 drawings and photographs (illus 45a, b) which show how walls 1223 and 1226 formed the long walls of a structure or range of structures 20m long and 3m wide.

Little detail from the second West range has survived apart from a blocked entrance (1293) in wall 1226 at a point some 4.5m from the N wall of the building: only the S side of the entrance was excavated but showed it to have been at least 1.0m wide. The blocking and a cross-wall which had removed the N

side of the entrance were all associated with the 18th-century manse.

The precise significance of wall 1227 is not known although it is of similar build and character to Period III walls 1226 and 1223 and is, as far as can be recognised, within the same stratigraphic group as the second West range. Only a very short section of 1227 (5.5m) was exposed, most of which was robbed out, but enough survived to show the presence of a wall running parallel to 1226 and lying 2.5m from it.

THE INDUSTRIAL COMPLEX (1279)

The mortared surface 1230, as well as predating the construction of the second West range, was also cut by a complex of post pits which were associated with a large industrial feature (1279) (illus 46a, b). Wall 1226 cut across the area defined by these distinctive features and thus showed that the activity reflected by these pits and other features occurred before the cloister was moved to the W.

Because of the limitations of the trench, it was impossible to reconstruct the plan of the building(s) reflected by these post settings. The entire industrial platform (which included the post pits) was sealed by a dense layer of ash, charcoal and fragments of burnt stone (maximum depth of 0.13m) – material more likely derived from the industrial function of the complex rather than from its demise (context 1278). The main focus of all the burnt deposits was a lead-lined stone trough (illus 46c) – a large,

rectangular setting of pitched slabs (1.0 × 1.7m), angled in from the sides, which were covered with a thick layer of white lead (up to 0.08m thick). The whole complex could represent a temporary building in use in advance of the extensive remodelling of the cloister. Whereas the precise function of the trough is not certain, its location near the church and adjacent to the Period II cloister could be interpreted as being used in the preparation of some specialised building material, metalwork or paint.

All the pits associated with 1279 had a similar fill, a dark brown, clay loam, stone-free with flecks of charcoal. Most of the pits had packers *in situ* but there was no sign of a post pipe in any. However, the similarity of the dimensions of the series suggests that the maximum timber diameter within the pits was about 0.15m.

THE EAST RANGE

STRUCTURES AND DEPOSITS

ROOM 2 (THE SLYPE/PARLOUR) (illus 47)

If the redesign of the adjacent Chapter house necessitated modifications to Room 2, these changes were not apparent during excavation. However, the unusual configuration of masonry evident within the wall that divided these chambers may be associated in some way with the remodelling of the Chapter house which may, in turn, have affected Room 2.

ROOM 3 (THE CHAPTER HOUSE) (illus 47; 48)

The Chapter house was completely remodelled during Period III. It was difficult to date this renovation with accuracy because of the

lack of surviving architectural detail and because many of the associated artefacts, including a coin of Aethelred II (978–1016), were obviously residual. However, it is argued below (**6**) that this event was probably contemporary with the large-scale remodelling of the claustral area during the early 14th century.

The most obvious aspect of this modification was the expansion of the room to the E, to form a Chapter house measuring 16.0 × 5.3m. Apart from a few foundation stones, the whole of the primary E wall was removed, the resulting robber trench (1041) being 2.1m wide and 0.8m deep. This trench was infilled with debris typical of wall robbing (small rubble, mortar, soils and

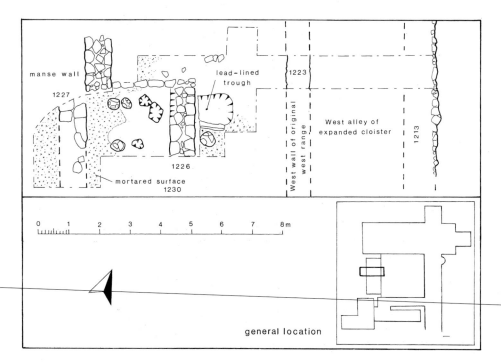

manse wall

1227

lead-lined trough

1223

West alley of expanded cloister

1213

1226

mortared surface 1230

West wall of original west range

0 1 2 3 4 5 6 7 8m

general location

Illus 46
The industrial complex:
a) plan;
b) (below left) view from the S; the lead-lined trough lies towards the centre of the picture while fragments of mortared surface 1230 can be seen towards the left;
c) (below right) close-up of the lead-lined trough; from the N.

gravel), within which were two human skulls, probably from graves disturbed during the Period III building programme. The N and S walls were extended to meet the new E wall and most, if not all, of the original S wall appears to have been rebuilt, perhaps because of damage sustained when the primary E wall was dismantled. Instead of being widened, the extended N wall was stepped outwards although it is not clear if the wall's W section was similarly altered because its masonry was masked by 1930s work. Nothing remained of the new E wall other than at its junction with the N wall. Even its construction trench was obliterated by a Period IV robbing trench (944) which, at 2.3m wide, was perhaps of similar width to the wall itself. However, the surviving foundations, nearly 2.0m below the presumed floor level, comprised sandstone blocks and flags in a clay matrix although the wall itself was mortar-bonded. The primary W wall was demolished and its top surviving course overlain by a spread of mortar, upon which the Period III W wall was built.

The interior of the new building had been levelled with sand and clay containing numerous human bones, presumably from earlier, disturbed deposits within the Chapter house. This levelling material was quite thin over most of the room but 0.45m deep adjacent to the W wall, where subsidence may have been a problem. Three circular post-holes, cut 0.4m into the levelling deposits, may have held scaffolding uprights or, as has been suggested for Bordesley Abbey, a hoist (Rahtz & Hirst 1976, 106). The post-holes were sealed by a thin layer of compact mortar similar to another deposit at a comparable level beyond the later (Period IV) E wall – a rare example of continuity within the stratigraphic sequence on either side of that wall.

The ground level had been raised further with more sand and clay, over which was a layer of mortar, gravel and small stones which survived only at the E end of the room. Similar material found within the refectory or kitchen at Horsham St Faith Priory, Suffolk was interpreted as the bedding for a stone or tiled floor

Illus 47
Plan of the Chapter house in Periods III and IV.

Illus 48
The E end of the Period III Chapter house. The robber trench for the E wall of the building is to the left; viewed from the N.

Illus 49
Plan of the S end of the East range and adjacent structures of Period III.

(Sherlock 1976, 210) – a function it may have served in the Chapter house at Jedburgh.

ROOM 6 (illus 49; 50)

Only major structural damage could account for the radical reorganisation evident at the S end of the East range. There was no sign of failure in the primary masonry of Room 6 and deliberate demolition, rather than a natural disaster, is seen as the likely reason for such a drastic change. Whether the building's destruction was the result of a single assault by an invader or whether its fabric was simply allowed to crumble after suffering relatively minor damage is not clear. Whatever the reason, the upper storeys were dismantled and a partition wall built between the N and S bays of the cellar.

In contrast to the adjacent walls of ashlar, the partition wall was built of clay-bonded rubble, occasionally brought to course. Nevertheless the partition was reasonably well-constructed and nearly 3.0m of its height survived below The Bow. Three squared corbels projected from the S face of the wall, 2.3m above floor level, indicating that the height of the basement had been reduced considerably from that of the original, 13th-century room.

Midway along the same wall face was a small aumbry, 0.4m high, 0.53m long and 0.52m deep. On the opposite side of the wall was a blocked doorway, suggesting that the S side of the wall had been rebuilt at some stage. Unfortunately, shortage of time and the proximity of No 4 Abbey Bridge End prevented a detailed investigation of this area.

MIDDEN

Following the demolition of the upper levels of the building, only the S half of Room 6 was re-occupied: the N bays became new sources of building stone but were otherwise simply abandoned to the elements. Other than a few flagstones in the NE corner, the floor had been removed and replaced by destruction debris which was overlain by 1.0m of amorphous grey-brown to black humic soil. Within this layer there were large amounts of butchered animal bones, significant quantities of pottery (**4.6** below) and two French jettons (**4.5**, nos 45 & 46 below), collectively indicating that this area functioned as a midden between the mid-14th and late 15th centuries.

Because of limited time, most of this midden was removed by machine and only a small fraction of its contents could be retrieved thereafter. Of the bones that were recovered, 90% were from domestic animals (sheep, cattle, pig, fowl/geese) and 8.7% were of fish (all marine), the most common being haddock. The presence of numerous head bones within the assemblage implies that the fish were brought in whole. There were approximately 800 oyster shells but no other edible marine or freshwater shellfish was represented.

Most of the mammal bones were from high-meat joints (upper legs, back etc). The ratio of sheep to cattle bone fragments was 2:1 although, given the size of the bones, beef must have been four times as common on the table as lamb/mutton. The absence of cattle heads and sheep's feet indicates that slaughtering and butchery were carried out elsewhere; the presence of cattle feet may signify that there was a kitchen stock-pot. Most of the sheep bones were from animals in their prime (3 years or less at death), while some were from lambs less than 10 months old; no bovine, however, was younger than 18 months. Pork was not common and wild species were hardly represented although a few bones of duck, woodcock, plover, roe deer, rabbit and hare were recovered. As elsewhere on the site, many of the bones had been gnawed by carnivores and rodents.

None of the other developments post-dating the insertion of the partition wall could be confirmed as being monastic: hence they are included in the account of Period V.

WALL 1114 (illus 49)

Projecting 2.0m from the easternmost buttress of Room 11 were

Illus 50
Room 6, showing the Period III cross wall abutting the primary masonry of the building; from the NW.

the few surviving courses of a wall (1114), 0.9m wide and built of reused ashlar on rubble foundations. This wall was lengthened at some stage, its extension being only 0.36m wide and built of dry-stone sandstone rubble. The area between wall 1114 and its extension and the W wall of Room 6 had been infilled with loose sandstone rubble. Neither the date nor the purpose of this rubble has been established although it may have served to strengthen the W wall of Room 6 or, more likely, supported a passage and steps up to the cloister. Within the rubble was a large sculptured slab, thought to have been a grave-marker of 10th-century date (**4.7**, illus 86 below). A covering of mortar on its front face indicates that this stone had served at least three functions since it had been carved.

ROOM 12 (illus 49; 51)

Outside Rooms 5 and 6 were the remains of a poorly-built structure (Room 12) which, although within an area of considerable post-Reformation activity, is nevertheless believed to be monastic. Time was limited, as was the area available for excavation. Consequently, only a small part of this building was uncovered and its relationships with some of the adjacent structures remain unclear.

After the river had been diverted S (probably in the early 13th century) its bed was levelled with deposits of rubble and gravel which were then cut by the foundation trench for the East range. Thereafter, various materials were washed downhill, outside the East range. Contained within those materials were numerous artefacts including: a cut halfpenny dated 1180–1247 (**4.5**, no 6 below); pottery sherds that conjoined with fragments of the 12th-century straight-sided cooking pot from sewage ditch 928 (**4.6**, no 29 below); and large quantities of ceramics tentatively dated to the 13th century. One of these deposits, a dark, water-laid, organic silt, had lain exposed for 30–50 years (Dr B Moffatt pers comm), before being cut by most of the walls of Room 12 as well as by an earlier, narrow wall (1117) (illus 49) of unknown date, extent or function. Ground water was removed from this area by rubble drains, one of them at least 1.3m deep, although these did not prevent Room 12 subsiding at a later date.

Room 12 measured approximately 8.5m N–S internally but only 2.0m of its width was uncovered, its E wall being beyond the limits of excavation. The few surviving courses of the N, W and S walls,

all of which were built into a terrace of compact red clay, were constructed of sand- and clay-bonded rubble, similar to that of the secondary partition wall in Room 6. The S wall was unique in being faced with reused ashlar. A compact layer of red clay provided a base for the floor, upon which lay deposits of ash and fragments of charcoal.

A buttress built of reused ashlar projected S from the external angle of the S and W walls (illus 52). Integral with it was a doorway of which the threshold and three courses of the E jamb, again of reused ashlar, were intact. The W jamb was missing but, assuming it had abutted the East range the doorway would have been about 1.6m wide. A check on the S face of the E jamb indicated that the door had opened outwards within a recessed arch. There was no evidence of a floor or a metalled surface on either side of the door although such materials would have been easy targets for post-Reformation looters. Running N–S below the threshold was a drain, 0.2m wide, lined and floored with small sandstone slabs but with its capstones missing. Although relationships were difficult to verify, it is thought that the drain was associated with Room 12. The doorway had been damaged, probably in 1937 or 1957, when a dry-stone wall was built against the crumbling cliff face. It may be reasonable to assume, however, that the door led into a (?covered) passage and to steps (perhaps incorporating masonry structures 274, 932 and 936), which gave access to Room 12 and to the monastic graveyard.

At some stage, the building's S and W walls subsided, probably because of the unstable nature of the ground and the poorly-built foundations. Thereafter the building was abandoned, most of its stonework robbed and a dry-stone rubble wall (1049), of unknown date and function, built over its W wall.

WALLING OVERLYING ROOM 7 (THE REREDORTER)

Partially overlying the 13th-century stonework of the reredorter was a stretch of clay-bonded, rubble-built wall, 1.78 × 0.4m (illus 49). Because of a developer's impending activities, only a cursory examination was possible but the resemblance between this wall and those of Room 12 suggests that they belonged to the same building programme.

Illus 51
Room 12; from the W.

Illus 52
The doorway, built of reused
13th-century ashlar, between
Rooms 6 and 12; from the W.

THE S AND W OF THE SITE

This period of building away from the East range is marked by the rationalisation of a proper route around the S side of the abbey, possibly in association with a bridge or ford located near the East range, and the need to replace accommodation destroyed at the S end of the East range. The structures identified from this period are Room 11 and Structure 13 which is traditionally referred to as the Abbot's Hall. It is likely that the subdivision of the refectory and the extension of the cloister occurred at this time as part of a concerted programme to make better use of available space within the original layout – perhaps as a result of the need to reorganize due to a change in the monastic regime, including private lodgings for key members of the community such as the cellarer.

Sufficient architectural detail survived from Room 11 to date it to the late 13th/early 14th century but as yet the dating of Structure 13 is not certain. The problem is further complicated by the fact that Room 11 saw limited re-use after 1559, a period (Period IV) which saw further building within Structure 13, all of which obscured original occupation horizons.

STRUCTURES

ROOM 11 (illus 53–55)

PRIMARY CONSTRUCTION

The evidence of excavation did not support the Royal Commission's conclusion that this building was the infirmary (RCAHMS 1956, 205). Indeed, the infirmary was usually situated to the E of the East range, as is evident at Inchcolm and Kelso Abbeys and at many other monastic houses. Meaningful stratigraphy had been reduced to a minimum by the 1936–37 and 1957 investigations, making it difficult to interpret the building's role or to date its construction, other than by its architectural style which implies that it was built during this period of remodelling.

This undercroft measured 16.0 × 4.7m wide internally and was built against a man-made vertical slope on the lowest terrace of the abbey. The old river bank cut across the S side of the building, the gap between it and the building's S wall being infilled with

sandstone fragments and clay. Contrary to the general topography, the bedrock in this area rose slightly to the E and, consequently, the E wall and most of the N wall stood directly on rock whereas the W wall was built on clayey subsoil. The builders' concern about the stability of the ground manifested itself in five buttresses against the external face of the S wall, the scarcements on them showing many signs of repair. There were two doors in the S wall whilst access to the storey above was presumably from the N.

The assumption that the narrow (0.9–0.95m wide) W gable and perhaps the wider (1.2–1.3m) E gable were secondary insertions within a foreshortened range (RCAHMS 1956, 206) was not supported by the evidence of excavation: there was simply no evidence that this building had ever extended further in any direction. Both gable walls and the N wall (only 0.9m wide but set against the man-made, vertical cliff face) were rubble-built whereas the S wall, 1.4m wide, was of ashlar. The local dark red sandstone was used throughout the building, particularly in the S wall but, although this stone is easy to work, its tendency to laminate has

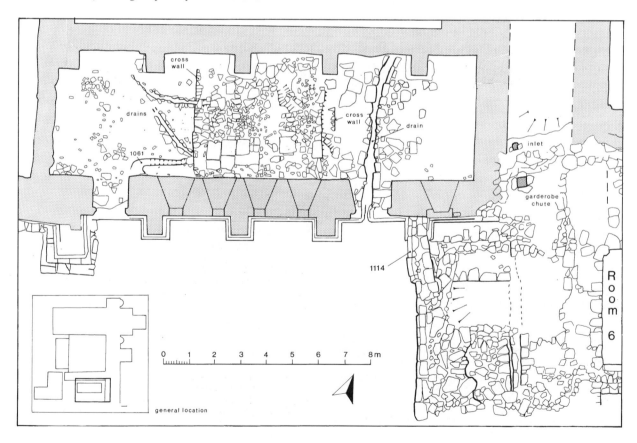

Illus 53
Plan of Room 11, showing the primary rock-cut drains.

Illus 54
Room 11, showing the flagged floor in the central chamber and modifications outside the SE corner of the building.

caused much of the building's masonry to erode badly.

Being on the lowest terrace of the abbey, the undercroft was prone to water seeping downhill from the cloister. Under-floor drains had been inserted to counter this problem although the only drains to survive from Period III were a few rock-cut channels, capped with roofing slates (illus 53), in the E half of the room. Elsewhere within Room 11 the surviving drains and floor surfaces belonged to a later phase of development and no trace of the primary scheme remained.

LATRINE

Projecting from the SE corner of the building were the

foundations of a structure, interpreted as a small latrine (garderobe) tower. Its chute, 0.4 × 0.35m, lined with ashlar, extended 0.5m below the ground surface from where a channel sloped gently towards the S. The latrine was probably flushed through the small inlet located to the N of the chute, the effluent draining away through the rubble infill between Rooms 11 and 6.

There was nothing to substantiate the theory that the five square piers against the inside face of the N wall had provided for a reduced roof span. Although all of the piers had been repaired after the 1936–37 excavation, contemporary photographs show that two of them had stood level with the primary springers in the N wall prior to consolidation. The remaining three had suffered more damage but all were built of finely-jointed ashlar, using the same dark red sandstone as in the S wall.

Illus 55
Room 11, from the W. The remnants of the flagged floor are in the foreground. In the background, the bottom end of the East range has yet to be exposed.

ALTERATIONS TO ROOM 11 (illus 54)

Modifications to this room were numerous. Some of these changes were evidently inter-related although many could not be tied in to any particular phase of development. None could be dated with confidence.

At some stage the floor level was raised with ashy soils, containing large amounts of animal bone and some pottery, which were sealed by a thin layer of orange clay. Cut into this material, at the W end of the room, was a drain which bifurcated into two narrow channels. A few capstones of one of the drains were still intact in 1957 but these had been removed before 1984. Both of these channels and another drain (1061) ran below a flagged floor which measured only 2.5 × 1.3m although an area of small and medium-sized stones further N and E may represent a crude attempt at repair.

Two cross-walls divided the basement into three roughly equal chambers, only the central one retaining a flagged floor (illus 55). Photographs from 1937 indicate that the W partition was rubble-built, was brought to level every three or four courses and stood to the height of the springers in the N wall. By 1957 this wall had been demolished, perhaps because it was not considered medieval, and by 1984 only traces of its foundations remained. The wall was only 0.58m wide and, although it overlapped onto the flagged floor, the two features were probably contemporary. The line of the E partition was traced but it was so fragmentary that its width could not be measured with accuracy. Unless there was a trap-door leading from the upper storey, entry to the central chamber could only have been through this wall because, according to the 1937 photographs, there was no opening in the W partition.

At some point a single stone-lined drain (illus 54; 55) replaced the rock-cut channels at the E end of the room. The threshold of the E entrance was raised to accommodate the drain's course beneath it and, to ensure that the drain's capstones (removed in antiquity) remained covered, the floor surface was also heightened – to a level at least 0.3m above that in the centre of the building.

External alterations included many repairs, especially to the scarcements within the S wall and to its buttresses as well as to the infilling of dry-stone masonry between the E buttress of Room 11 and the W wall of Room 6.

STRUCTURE 13

The structure itself was essentially a large rectangular building added to the W wall of Structure 8 (illus 56; 57). This necessitated the following developments:

a) the abandonment and blocking of drainage complex 2003/2011; b) the re-alignment of the garderobe, now to serve

both Structure 13 and Structure 8; c) the construction of a doorway over the abandoned drain 2003; d) the backfill of the gap between the new S wall of the building (3006) and the recut, angled face in the bedrock; and e) the conversion of Period II drain 490, to act as an outlet for naturally accumulating water from the hill to the N.

THE S WALL (3006)

The wall was of similar build and dimensions to its precursor (378), being of monumental ashlar construction, surviving to a general height of 4.0m and measuring 1.5m wide, and resting on timber foundations.

Closer scrutiny betrayed the separate phasing of the walls (illus 58). 3006 was much better built generally, with more uniform stonework, and was better preserved overall. The relatively weathered appearance of the S face of the earlier wall (378) as compared with 3006 implies that a long period of time might have elapsed before Structure 13 was built, although how much of this differential weathering was also due to inherent qualities within the stone itself was not clear.

The wall had nine courses above the lower scarcement level and a maximum of four above the upper scarcement (the upper line being some 3m above the river level). It was in the different moulding of the masonry within the lower scarcement, despite being on the same line as that in 378, that gave an indication of the two phases of the S wall. One stone had, in fact, both profiles – perhaps evidence of a rapidly abandoned attempt to recut the secondary masonry to conform with the 378 scarcement. The overall build of 3006 was of dressed sandstone blocks (which varied in size), close fitting and mortar bonded.

The foundations of the wall differed considerably from those in 378, being a combination of timberwork, laid masonry and a buttress at the SW corner.

The timberwork consisted of two, long sleeper beams (636, 641) with three cross members (639, 640, 645) over which the lower scarcement masonry was laid (illus 31). The W end of 641 (the Period II sleeper beam) was cut to receive 641 by means of a simple overlapping joint, 0.7m deep. Beam 641 (3.16m long × 0.4m thick) similarly overlapped timber 636 which ran for 2.2m.

Two of the cross members were located more or less halfway along each sleeper beam (639 in 636 and 642 in 641) with the third (640) lying at the junction of the two beams. The cross members were of uniform size, 0.3m wide and 0.13m thick (illus 59). They were all neatly dressed flush with the outer face of the

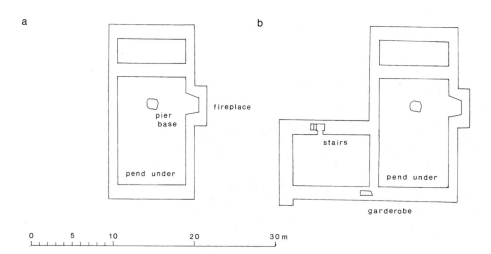

a

b

pier base

fireplace

pend under

stairs

pend under

garderobe

0 5 10 20 30 m

Illus 56
Diagrammatic plan of
Structures 8 and 13.

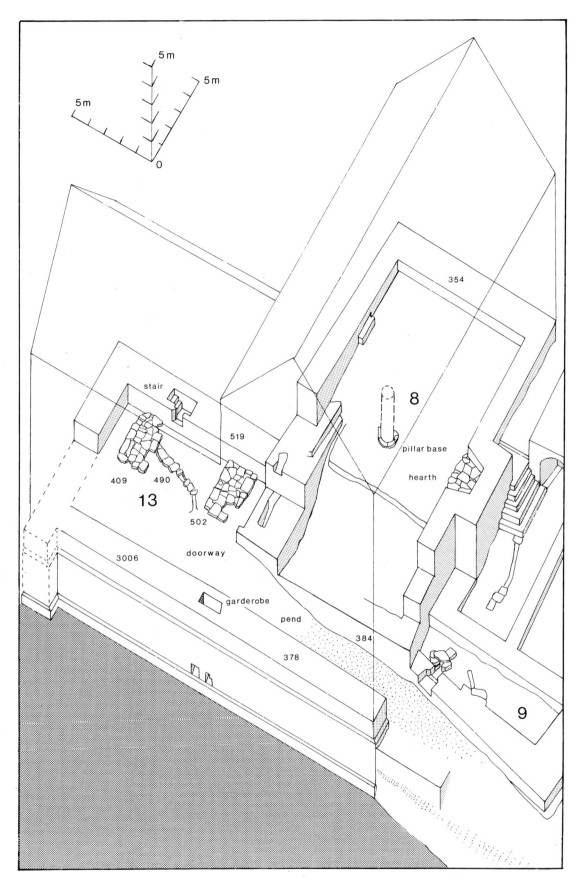

5 m

5 m

5 m

0

354

stair

519

8

pillar base

hearth

409   490

13

502

doorway

3006

garderobe

pend

384

378

9

Illus 57
Isometric drawing of Structures 8, 9 and 13.

main beams and were laid in rectangular channels cut in the bottom of 641. Cross member 639 was laid in a wide and irregular cut in 636 – possible evidence of the reuse of the latter. The overall effect of the Period III timberwork was one of precision and accuracy, an impression which is reinforced by the remarkable state of preservation of the wood.

The westernmost 4m of the wall, however, rested on a single course of very large, roughly dressed, rectangular blocks of sandstone. The limits of these stone foundations coincided with a break in the natural strata forming the river bed at this point

between bedrock and clays. Stone foundations were only laid over bedrock and the more unstable clays received the timber framework.

The buttress, projecting some 0.8m from the wall face, was only partially excavated and stood to a height of 1.06m. The feature reinforced the leading edge of the whole building as regards the flow of the river. Wall 3006 was found not to be built against the surviving face in the bedrock to the N, with the result that the remains of the wall were free-standing. The importance of the buttress was doubtless to provide additional

Illus 58
The S wall of Structure 13, from the SW. This section is an extension of the S wall of Structure 8 but is of superior quality to it.

Illus 59
Detail of a cross member of Period III timber raft; from the SW. The cross member is set into a slot and is laid over a stone pad.

Illus 60
The N jamb of the entrance to Structure 13; from the S. The infilled line of the Period II W drain can be seen within the threshold of the Period III entrance.

support for such a wall, given that its S face had to continue the line of the earlier wall (378) and therefore meant building right out into the river.

THE N AND W WALLS

The W wall was very badly preserved with the southernmost 2.4m of its length completely missing; the remaining 4.7m (at its outer face) stood to a maximum height of only 0.85–1.1m above the floor of the chamber (maximum of four courses) with a width of 1.52m.

The N wall (519) replicated the dimensions of 3006, except in height, standing only to a maximum height of 1.23m above the floor (four to six courses). However, at a point some 3.2m E of the inside NW corner of the room, there was an entrance to an intramural stair with three steps surviving *in situ* (illus 57). The stair consisted of a small recess (0.75 × 0.75m) set in the thickness of the N wall of Structure 13. Its entrance from the basement was defined by a low step (0.2m in height) and two moulded door jambs, creating a doorway (illus 60) 0.55m wide. An iron hinge still survived, attached to the inside face of the E door jamb, showing that the door was hung from the E and opened into the recess rather than the main room. The line of the stair from the entrance threshold was to the W. The room enclosed an area measuring 9.0 × 5.7m and represented an appreciable extension of the accommodation within Structure 8.

THE E ENTRANCE

The threshold of the entrance into the basement of Structure 13 from the E was via the Period II pend under Structure 8 (illus 57). This initially entailed the backfilling of drain 2003 as well as the gap between the Period II river bank and the N face of 3006 – the former with clay and stones, the latter with rubble. Once this was accomplished, the upper masonry from 2003 was extended together with wall 384 (the N wall of the pend) to create a squared section of masonry (516) which formed the N side of a doorway and which still retained part of the N door jamb. This masonry was characterised by the use of a very white, hard mortar faced originally with ashlar which had almost entirely been robbed away. To the S, the surviving masonry had been too badly damaged to retain any detail of the doorway, but the crude dressing-back of 2011 (Period II outer angled face) showed how the door was re-aligned on an E–W axis and appeared to have been about 2m wide. Masonry 516 stood to a maximum height of 0.75m and was 2.4m wide.

THE GARDEROBE AND DRAIN 490 (illus 61)

The Period III garderobe outlet saw a similar re-alignment away from the original angled profile of 2011 (illus 28) to an E–W line. This must have involved the partial demolition of 2011 and its original outflow over which 3006 was built, creating a new pit with three new sides (N, W and S), all on a straight E–W by N–S axis. However, the inside face of the original garderobe pit survived as the E wall of the new one; and showed clearly as an obliquely angled face within what was otherwise a regular rectangular pit. The sides of the pit were vertical and the internal dimensions were a maximum of 1.5m (S face) and 0.6m wide. The bottom of the pit consisted of angled stonework which directed the flow out into the river via two apertures. The latter features were rectangular and separated by a light column of masonry.

Further conversion work was found at the N end of primary Period II drain 490 (illus 57; 61), the primary role of which ended when Structure 13 was built but which was retained, with certain modifications, as a weeper beneath the new building, taking away excess water from the slope immediately to the N. To facilitate this function, a roughly squared sump and associated channel were dug at the N end of the drain immediately adjacent to the inside face of the N wall of

Structure 13. The sump, which could be periodically checked and cleaned out whenever necessary, acted as a trap for silt which might otherwise have blocked the drain. Indeed, the drain would only have been needed if the sump overflowed. Confirmation of this emergency only role for the drain is shown by the fact that no formal outlet into the river for such storm or flood water was built.

THE CONSTRUCTION OF THE S ACCESS ROAD

This development probably coincided with the construction of Room 11 over the partially demolished Structure 10. The orientation of Room 11 over earlier, obliquely-angled masonry and the incorporation of two doorways facing S towards the river suggested that this was part of an overall realignment of the South frontage of the abbey. This also established an access route on the S side of the abbey between its East and West ranges.

The original edges of this new artificial platform were obscured by a late revetment associated with the 19th-century textile mill which lay to the E of the site. However, the monastic river frontage and revetment were probably on a very similar line to the present profile: the later lade with the 18th-century bridge built into its W entrance were likely to have been simply refinements of abbey features.

Illus 61
Drain 490 and associated sump; from the NW. The masonry from the Period II W drain lies towards the top right; and the NE corner of paved area 409 is visible towards the bottom right.

The roadway to the E of the pend comprised a roughly cobbled surface (506, 653) which saw continued use well after the abandonment of the monastic ranges. This was the forerunner of The Bow. A more differentiated sequence of road surfaces was found within the pend where the passage gradually filled up (Period V), due to the narrowness of the route.

Limited excavation to the E of the pend entrance confirmed (on the evidence of the backfill in and around a simple drain or gutter (632, 659) running along the road parallel to the surviving S face of Structure 9) that the road originated in monastic times. This drain, obviously associated with the road, was partly demolished and sealed by midden material from the last phase of activity in the area of Structure 14 (**2.4** below).

A sondage was dug over a narrow, linear feature cut against the upper cobbles and rubble core of the new road (513). This feature (514) proved to contain a lengthy section of lead pipe (illus 62) (3.2m long, comprising two main interlocking sections with a bore of 0.2m). The pipe was damaged and truncated by modern revetment (372), so no indication of its original outflow survived. However, its location and line suggest it was the re-routed outflow for drain 387 which was piped from the Period II outflow (386) down to the new channel 514. Exactly how the buried pipe was linked to 386 is unknown because any visible lead piping would have been robbed out. The bedding trench for the buried pipe was narrow and straight-sided, running virtually the entire width of the surviving road surface. It was 0.48m wide and crudely lined in stone.

Surface 513 proved not to be as regular as was first hoped but it extended as a wide, level surface from the pend up to the East range (illus 64), covering Structures 9 (partially) and 10 (almost entirely) and eventually linking with the thresholds of the doorways into Room 11. This surface also marked the limit of the excavation on the S of the site although a sondage showed the road to be built on a rubble platform (mainly dolerite boulders from the river) which was excavated to a depth of 0.6m below the upper cobbling.

Illus 62
Lead pipe within linear cut 514; from the N. The pipe was sealed by make up for the Period IV riverside road.

2.4 PERIOD IV – LATER REPAIRS AND ALTERATIONS (c 1480–1559)

THE EAST CLAUSTRAL RANGE

ROOM 1 (SOUTH TRANSEPT)

During the 16th century the South transept was divided off from the choir by the insertion of a screen-wall (**8** below). Limited excavation revealed no evidence of other alterations to this part of the church during Period IV.

ROOM 3 (CHAPTER HOUSE) (illus 47)

This period saw the contraction of the Chapter house into a small square building, contained within the width of the East range and resembling the late 15th- and early 16th-century Chapter houses at Cambuskenneth and Glenluce abbeys (RCAHMS 1963, 128; RCAHMS 1912, 106).

The Period III walls were dismantled in stages. Initially, dressed stone was robbed from the N, E and S walls (illus 48); thereafter most of the foundations of the E and S walls were also removed. The footings of the S wall were retained below the Period IV E wall, forming part of the latter's foundations; for different reasons (discussed below) the N wall was only partially demolished. The robber trench (888) for the remaining section of the S wall was 1.5m deep and was backfilled with sand, clay, gravel and other relatively stone-free soils whereas the infill of the E wall robber trench comprised mainly rubble and roofing slates, some of which were complete.

Although shortened on its E–W axis, the Chapter house was widened by some 1.5m to the S to form an approximately square chamber. A new W wall appeared to have been built over the foundations of the primary structure. Other than a few courses rebuilt in 1936–37, the new S wall was represented only by its footings. Because of further 1930s interference, it was impossible to tell whether the Period IV E wall was a new structure or had once formed a partition between the Chapter house and a vestibule. The latter seems unlikely, however, for the wall's insertion had disturbed several stone-lined graves.

There was no indication as to how the Chapter house roof had been supported in Periods II and III whereas during Period IV its weight was borne by a central octagonal pier. The foundations of the pier were set into a pit, 2.0m deep, and comprised ten layers of rafted rubble and clay overlain by two courses of flat sandstone blocks, including a reused sarcophagus capstone. These foundations were sealed with purple-red clay upon which was set the single surviving course of the pier, 0.66m wide and comprising two semi-octagonal components, one of them a modern rebuild.

A purple clay-rich soil covered most of the room, including the capstones of Graves 9, 10 and 11 which had all been disturbed by the insertion of the Period IV E wall. The uniform, plastic texture of the soil suggested that it was a sub-floor layer although no flagstones or tiles were found. Only four graves post-dated the clay's deposition (illus 94): a coffin burial (Grave 14) against the N wall and three similar interments (Graves 15, 16 and 17) cutting the backfilled robber trench 888.

Two stone-lined graves (4 and 5; illus 89, 91) had been disturbed when the pier was inserted (illus 89b; colour VII). The resulting voids were infilled with loose rubble which proved inadequate to the task: the floor subsided on at least one occasion, forcing the pier base to be strengthened and the surrounding area to be levelled with small stones and mortar. Thereafter, all of the graves were sealed with deposits of small rubble, mortar and clay, overlain by red sandy soil and unsorted, mottled clay, up to 0.4m deep. Although post-dating the burials, these were not necessarily post-Reformation deposits; they may simply indicate that by this time interment had ceased within the Chapter house.

Against the exterior of the E wall were the sandstone rubble foundations of two features interpreted as buttress bases. Essentially an extension of the new S wall, buttress 917 measured 2.18 × 1.74m, while the smaller, heavily robbed N buttress (197) measured only 1.3 × 1.49m.

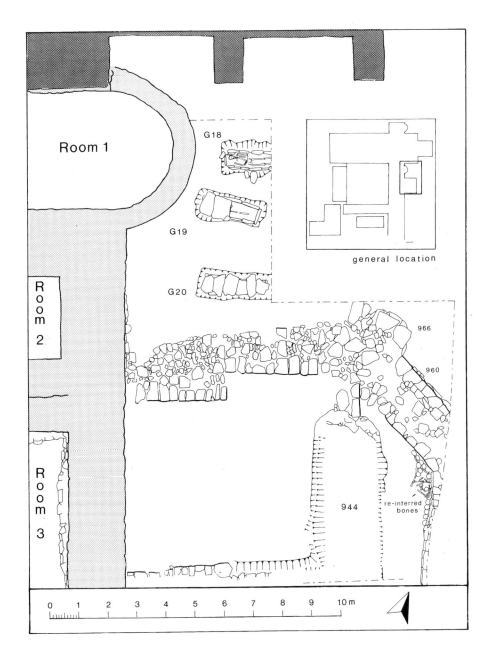

Illus 63
Plan of wall 960, outside the Chapter house.

ROOM 4

There was little evidence by which to date the changes undertaken to the fabric of Room 4, other than those associated with the Period IV remodelling of the Chapter house. Hence these alterations are described within this, the final, period of abbey building.

The N and W walls were completely rebuilt. The primary, sandstone foundations were overlaid with dolerite boulders, gravel and clay upon which were built the Period IV walls, consisting mainly of reused ashlar. Although there was no evidence that the E and S walls had been altered or rebuilt in monastic times, such evidence may well have been masked by the construction of a house that was built on the site of Room 4 in the 18th century (**2.5** below) or by the disruptions caused during the 1930s. Drawings of the 1936–37 excavation show a narrow wall connecting the NE corner of masonry 120 with the E wall of Room 4 but by 1984 only traces of the wall's robber trench survived. It is quite likely that the earlier excavators removed the wall thinking it was a post-monastic structure. However, although this area had been severely disrupted, this wall did appear to pre-date the 18th-century occupation and was probably medieval in date.

The SE corner of the room had been disturbed at some stage, perhaps by stone-robbers, the ground surface being levelled thereafter with dolerite boulders, gravel and sand.

OUTSIDE THE CHAPTER HOUSE (illus 63; 97)

Abutting the NE corner of the Period III Chapter house were two masonry features (960; 966), both robbed to their foundations of clay-bonded, sandstone rubble. Time did not permit either structure to be investigated fully, a restriction compounded by the proximity of masonry 960 to the modern wall that now forms the E boundary of the abbey precinct.

Wall 960 was 1.8m wide at foundation level and ran SE for a distance of 3.0m from the NE corner of the Period III Chapter house. From there its course continued S beyond the Chapter house. Wall 960's foundations differed markedly from those of the Period III Chapter house and, although this area had been heavily disturbed by stone-robbing and landscaping, wall 960 appeared to be the later of the two structures. Against the inside face of the wall were 19 human skulls (illus 97), 124 other cranial fragments and 355 disarticulated, post-cranial bones. Six of the skulls were identified as those of adult males, another nine were adult with male features, one was of an 8–9 year old juvenile but neither sex nor age could be determined for the remaining three (**5** below). The bones were in a similar state of preservation to those within the Chapter house graves, suggesting that these disturbed skeletons had once lain within stone coffins.

There was time only for a very limited investigation of masonry feature 966 and its full extent and function remain uncertain. Possible interpretations include: a buttress for the NE corner of the Period III Chapter house, a wall extending N to the South choir chapel, and an extension of wall 960.

REPAIR AND REFINEMENTS AT THE RIVERSIDE AND CLOISTER

The last phase of building during the active life of the community is generally of crude quality and exemplified by the badly finished masonry of Structure 14 (illus 64). Post-dating an extensive deposit containing general destruction debris and quantities of decorated window glass (**4.10** below), the original open area of Structure 9 was subdivided, firstly by the construction of a S wall (375) on the same alignment as the S wall of Room 11 and then subdivided by two N–S internal walls (409, 440).

WALL 375

Wall 375 was built between the external face of 354 (the E wall of Structure 8) in the W and the inside face of 352 (the E wall of Structure 9) in the E. The construction of the wall and its associated foundation trench (526) truncated the course of drain 357; and a general spread of levelling soils and light rubble (400) was laid in to cover much of the upper surface of walls 385 and 352 where they lay to the S of Structure 14.

The construction trench for wall 375 was fairly regular, measuring 0.55m wide by 0.35m deep and running along the S face of the wall. The fill of the feature (526) also contained demolition debris – quantities of 13/14th-century broken window glass, charcoal and daub, together with 15th-century, green-glaze pottery (**4.6** below).

Wall 375 was constructed mainly of random sandstone blocks. The inclusion of parts of re-used columns, one of which formed the inside face of a possible doorway, suggested that most, if not all, of this masonry has been taken from a demolished building nearby. The lower courses of the wall were of superior construction and ensured stable foundations for an otherwise rather crude structure.

The wall was 8.0m long × 1.2m wide. A short return N at the SW corner, the inner face of which lined up with the outer face of Structure 8's projecting fireplace, effectively squared the corner. This could have meant that either the W chamber within Structure 14 was roofed or that Structure 14 was partially demolished. Otherwise, there seemed little point in building the two walls face to face. Perhaps the degree of reconstruction within 354 (the E wall of Structure 8) belied the true character and scale of the original masonry.

PARTITION WALLS 409 AND 440

The two partition walls – 409 to the W and 440 to the E – were of similar build and dimensions although the latter was extensively robbed. Wall 409, 0.7m wide, ran the entire width of the Structure 14 N–S, a distance of 7.04m. The standing remains of 440 ran for only 2.3m although its line could be traced for a further 1.3m. It was built against the W face of 428, a short section of an earlier, more substantial wall, possibly associated with 352 (the E wall of Structure 9). This wall had been extensively repointed by the Office of Works so that its true character and alignment were impossible to determine. The two partition walls were of crude mortar-bonded construction and, like wall 375, had many re-used moulded stones in their fabric, notably parts of columns.

STRUCTURE 14 (illus 64)

The walls subdivided Structure 14 into 3 chambers – numbered 1, 2, 3 (W–E). Chambers 1 and 2 were roughly 3.0m wide while Chamber 3 was 2.5m wide. Overdigging in previous years had removed all evidence of where the floor of Structure 14 lay. The obvious difference in level between the N end of the overall enclosure and the S (a drop of some 1.1m) suggested that either the

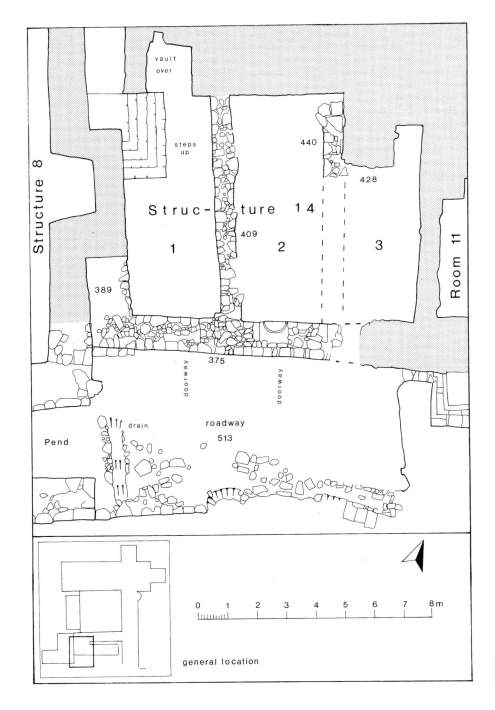

vault
over

steps
up

440

428

Structure 8

Struc-   ture 14

1   409   2   3

389

375

doorway

doorway

Room 11

drain

roadway

513

Pend

0   1   2   3   4   5   6   7   8 m

general location

Illus 64
Plan of Structure 14.

floor was projected across at the higher level or that the rooms had split-level floors. In the likely event that the former was the case, the embrasure noted in the S wall of Chamber 2 must have been a doorway. The opening was only 1.0m wide and a similar narrow doorway could have been located in the S wall of the other two chambers. The function of Structure 14 with its three rooms is obscure, the only certainty being that they post-dated some significant period of destruction at the abbey – on the evidence of the pottery, no earlier than the 15th century. The rooms were probably roofed but their small size, crude construction and late date suggested that they were part of an effort to relocate some key structure in the abbey – be it for storage, kitchen or accommodation – which was too badly damaged to repair or re-occupy.

STRUCTURE 13 (illus 65)

The W part of Structure 13 saw re-use after the whole building

had been damaged to some extent. This was reflected by three associated features: two discrete areas of paving or flagging which fronted onto the robbed remains of a cross-wall, all within walls built during Period III. The two areas of heavy paving were of very similar build and dimensions and were located symmetrically within the W section of Structure 13.

THE PAVED AREAS

The W paved area (409) (illus 57) was built from large sandstone slabs of generally irregular shape but well laid in a roughly rectangular pad. The stonework most probably came from ruined abbey structures and one slab in particular was identified as part of the Period III mural stair (450). This suggested that the walls of Structure 13 were partially collapsed when paving 409 was laid.

The paved area, 3.0 × 1.7m, lay approximately 1m E of 538 (the W wall of Structure 13). This is almost exactly mirrored by the

IIllus 65
Structure 13, from the W, with paved areas 409 and 502 in the foreground and centre. The remains of the intramural stair are visible to the left within the N wall.

area of paving to the E (502) (illus 57) which featured reused stones, covered the same area and lay 1m W of 516 (the E wall of Structure 13). These two platforms stood 3.7m apart and were abutted by the residual traces of some form of cross-wall running E-W across the room and roughly aligned with the face of 516. The evidence for this robbed-out feature amounted merely to two long, narrow bands of yellow mortar sealed by a clean, red clay. Both these deposits were truncated ultimately by the sequence of 'Bows'. When first revealed, the former defined the S edge of a large platform effectively half the area of Structure 13. The platform's upper surface sloped away to the surviving top of the S wall of Structure 13. This represented a drop of some 1.1m.

DESTRUCTION OF STRUCTURE 13

It was the destruction of Structure 13 which allowed The Bow to develop and it was found that this sequence overlaid the partial remains of the building which had been dismantled in a rather measured way. It is likely that the retention of an upper level area and the slope in front of it are associated with the two platforms which were built using stone probably derived from the partially demolished Structure 13.

This evidence reflected the probable use in the 16th century of this part of the precinct as a gun platform; and part of a fairly extensive conversion of elements of the S and E limits of the claustral ranges to form a temporary artillery fortification.

With the creation of The Bow or Horse Wynd in the latter half of the 17th century, the first major building phase of the West range during the post-Reformation period began. There was little doubt that the undercroft of Structure 13 (which later became known as the 'Abbot's Hall') was ruined and reduced to the levels discovered in 1984. This

probably meant that the outline of the lower reaches of Structure 13 were visible for some considerable time while the upper sections were absorbed into the manse outbuildings from an early date.

At some point prior to the creation of The Bow, there was a period when fires were burnt in the area of the two platforms 449 and 502. Several fires were lit in the bottom of the stairwell 450 with the rake out and charcoal debris spread out over an extensive area around 449. This horizon was subsequently sealed by the sequence of roads described in Period V, suggesting that the roof was missing by then.

Illus 66
Buttress base 1215; from the W. The buttress is built into the S wall (1211) of the Period II North cloister alley.

Towards the end of this period, there was evidently an attempt to reinforce the S wall of the church with four buttresses, irregularly spaced and crudely constructed. All four were completely excavated in 1936 and only those W bases, 1215, 1216 and 1225, were excavated in 1984 (illus 66); apart from confirming that they post-dated elements of both claustral phases, no additional dating information was forthcoming. They all featured reused masonry in their build.

2.5 PERIOD V – POST-REFORMATION ACTIVITY (1559–1875)

After the suppression of 1559 the Lords of the Congregation insisted that no harm should befall the abbey church (Watson 1894, 81) and, in common with many Augustinian houses, it survived, albeit modified, as the reformed kirk of the parish (Robinson 1980, 156). Initially, the kirk was housed within the choir (and possibly the transepts) and re-roofed in 1575 with timber from the dismantled refectory (McGibbon & Ross 1896, 99 416). In 1671 it was transferred to the W end of the nave – a common practice in reused Augustinian churches (Dickinson 1968, 66) – where it remained until 1875.

The damage inflicted by the English armies in 1544–5 was probably aggravated by the actions of religious reformers who did all in their power to prevent the re-occupation of abandoned monasteries. Those buildings that could be converted to secular use were often spared, an example being 'the old hall' (?the Abbot's Hall)

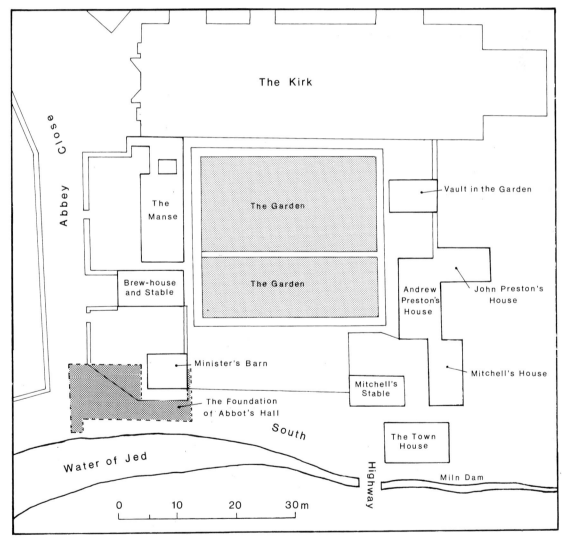

Illus 67
Copy of Winter's plan of the abbey, 1760.

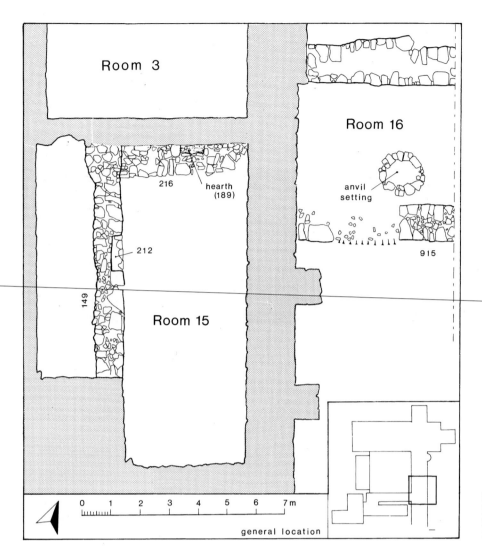

Illus 68
Plan of Rooms 15 and 16, the latter used as a smithy in the 19th century.

at Jedburgh, which is cited in a document of 1671 (Watson 1909, 22). Other buildings were usually stripped of their fittings and dismantled for their reusable building materials, particularly in urban environments where stone was a valuable commodity (Knowles 1956, 383–8). Indeed, oral testimony confirms that building stone was being removed from Jedburgh Abbey as late as World War II.

During the 18th and 19th centuries several houses stood within the claustral area, many of them represented in James Winter's survey of 1760 (illus 67). These included: six buildings overlying or adjacent to the East range; the 'Foundations of Abbot's Hall' towards the SW of the site; and, to the NW of the cloister, the manse in its original, rectangular form. Subsequently, this rather modest building was extended into the impressive edifice illustrated in numerous 19th-century engravings and described in contemporary journals (Kelso 1805). Although the accuracy of such drawings cannot always be trusted, they often present a reasonable portrayal of contemporary buildings. An engraving by W Floyd, published in 1834, depicts three houses in positions identical to those belonging to John Preston, Andrew Preston and Mitchell, according to Winter's survey. The Prestons' houses may have been among the three purchased in 1857 by the Marquis of Lothian whose sole aim was their demolition (Kelso 1857) although, on the evidence of the first edition Ordnance Survey map, Lothian's scheme had not been implemented by 1859. By then John Preston's house had become a smithy, the 'Abbot's Hall' was buried beneath The Bow and the large, L-shaped manse was the only major building standing in the West claustral area.

Most of the buildings illustrated by Winter were at least partially excavated in 1936–37 and/or 1984. Several of those structures, together with other post-monastic features, are described below.

Illus 69
Room 15 (Andrew Preston's house), built over the demolished Room 4; from the N.

THE E END OF THE SITE

OUTSIDE ROOMS 1 AND 2

This part of the site had been subject to stone-robbing and landscaping for several centuries after the Reformation. As a result it was reduced to an area of irregularly-shaped cuts, infilled with miscellaneous materials whose removal demanded a great deal of the excavators' time. To the NE of the Period III Chapter house was a spread of compact red clay – possibly the remnants of a floor surface – within which were 12 coins (**4.5**, nos 9, 10, 12, 13, 15, 16, 17, 18, 19, 22, 30, 31 below), ranging in date from the early 16th to the late 17th century, that may have formed part of a hoard.

ROOM 3 (illus 98)

Adjacent to the N wall were four sub-rectangular pits that cut post-monastic deposits but which were truncated by a 1936–37 excavation trench. Their maximum original dimensions were estimated as 1.5–2.35m × 0.41–0.63m; their purpose was more difficult to assess. The pits resembled graves in shape and in size although their N–S alignment and the complete absence of bones within them would seem to contradict this. Nevertheless, it has been suggested that their orientation may be an indication of the work of religious reformers reacting against earlier burial practices.

ROOM 15 (illus 68; 69)

Overlying the ruins of Room 4 were the remains of a narrower building (Room 15), interpreted as the 18th-century house of Andrew Preston (illus 67). Its N wall lay directly over the foundations of Room 4's N wall; similarly, its S and E walls had probably overlain those of Room 4 although no trace of the later structures survived. The remnants of the N wall, which was plastered on its internal face, had been consolidated in 1936–37, probably because it was thought to be abbey masonry. Within it were the remains of a well-constructed hearth (189), over which were the vestiges of a much cruder fireplace. Whether this signifies periods of abandonment and re-occupation or simply the lowering of standards is unclear.

The W wall (149) was an entirely new structure. Its two surviving courses were built of clay-bonded rubble, faced on the inside with reused ashlar and plastered with a pale cream mortar. The outer face, however, was very irregular and its lower courses had probably been hidden from view, suggesting that the floor of the building was below the external ground level. A recess (212), 1.2m wide × 0.4m deep, situated midway along the inside face of the wall, was too low to be a window and showed no sign of the heat damage expected within a hearth. It is interpreted tentatively as the threshold for a door. At some stage the recess had been blocked with rubble and clay, containing numerous sherds of 18th-century brown and yellow slipware (**4.6** below) and other fragments of contemporary pottery and glass.

Illus 70
Room 16 (John Preston's house), built in the 18th century and converted to a smithy the following century. In the foreground is the circular stone setting for an anvil; from the S.

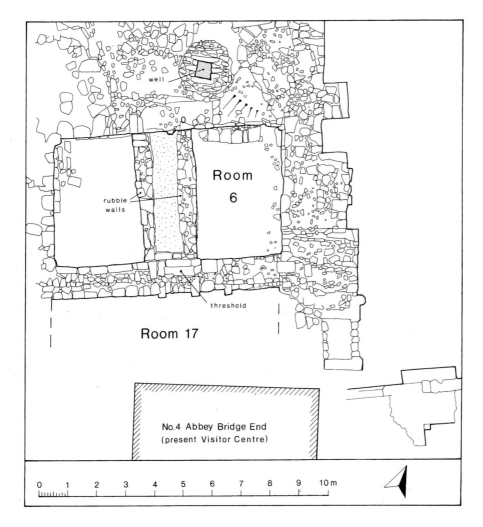

Illus 71
Plan of post-monastic additions at the S end of the East range.

The disturbed clay floor included patches of mortar and, adjacent to the hearth in the N wall, large quantities of coal, ash and other burnt materials. Overlying the floor were destruction debris and the backfill from the 1936–37 excavation, its trenches clearly visible against the walls of Room 15.

ROOM 16 (illus 68; 70)

Room 16, interpreted as John Preston's House (illus 67), was defined on its N by a narrow rubble wall, its foundations comprising the partially-demolished S wall of the Period III Chapter house. The S wall, however, was an enigma. A linear spread of rubble extending the width of the trench, approximately 5m from the N of the building, may have been the infill of the wall's robber trench. Nevertheless, this rubble directly overlay wall 915 (illus 12a) which was 1.1m wide (as was the N wall of the building) and built of tightly packed rubble and compacted small stone chips. Although a prime candidate for the S wall of Room 16, wall 915 could also be interpreted as a pre-Augustinian structure (**2.1** above). The building's W wall is thought to have overlain the E wall of the East range although all material evidence of it had been lost by 1984.

The only indication of a floor consisted of a few patches of cobbles. These were cut by a circular, stone-lined feature, 0.8–0.9m in diameter, which, on the evidence of nearby deposits of coal and hammer-slag and the building's definition as a smithy by the first edition OS map, has been interpreted as the setting for an anvil. This putative anvil setting partially overlay another stone wall (914) that abutted wall 915 and which may have been a primary feature of John Preston's House although its role was far from obvious. Alternatively, this masonry may have been a pre-Augustinian structure (**2.1** above).

ROOMS 6 AND 17 (illus 71; 72)

Operational difficulties and the proximity of No 4 Abbey Bridge End combined to restrict the area of excavation beyond the Period III partition wall in Room 6 to a sondage only 1.0m wide. Overlying the scant remnants of a monastic flagged floor was a deposit of black humic soil, 0.25m deep, containing some cereal grains and large quantities of chaff, perhaps derived from milling. Clay-pipe stems retrieved from this material demonstrated that it was of post-monastic age although more precise dating was not possible.

Although this putative mill appeared to be free-standing with its N wall being the reused Phase III partition wall, the overall dimensions of the building remain unknown. Entry to the first storey was over a very worn, sandstone threshold midway along the top surviving course of the N wall. Two clay-bonded, rubble walls, each 1.4m high and 0.6m wide, which sat directly upon the Phase III midden deposit, were perhaps associated in some way with the adjacent entrance.

At a later, unknown, date the N half of Room 6 was infilled with rubble and clay. Upon this material stood the fragmentary remains of a clay-bonded, rubble-built structure of which only a cursory examination was possible. Nevertheless, the building did appear to occupy a position similar to that of the 18th-century 'Mitchell's Stable' (illus 67). It may also have housed the well that had been sunk through the masonry between Rooms 5 and 6 (illus 71), presumably after the demise of the East range.

Illus 72
The surviving elements of Room 17. The entrance to Room 6 is in the foreground; from the E.

Of the 'Town House', depicted in Winter's drawing, there was no trace. It seems unlikely that there were gross errors in his survey, yet none of the excavated structures could be equated with this building.

Photographs and drawings from the 1936–37 excavation depict a set of five stone steps, built of reused ashlar and rubble, ascending to the E, 1.2m E of Room 5. To the S of the steps were three or four courses of a rubble wall and to its N was the base course of a door jamb. None of these features survived until 1984. The assumption that the steps were contemporary with the 13th-century East range (RCAHMS 1956, 205) is inconsistent with the use of both ashlar and unworked stone within the treads. Furthermore, by overlying the ruins of Room 12, the stair is almost certainly a post-monastic feature, its location suggesting an association with the 18th-century 'Mitchell's House' (illus 67).

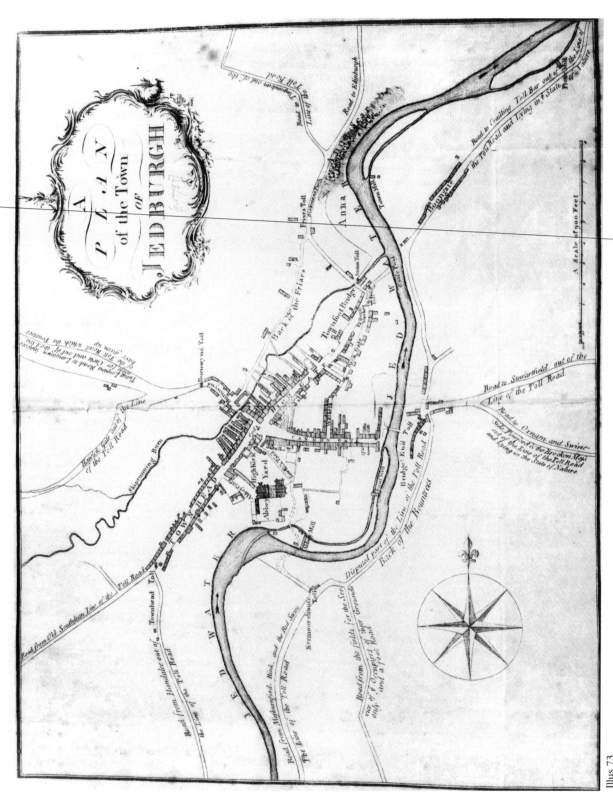

Illus 73
Town plan of c 1775 by John Ainslie.

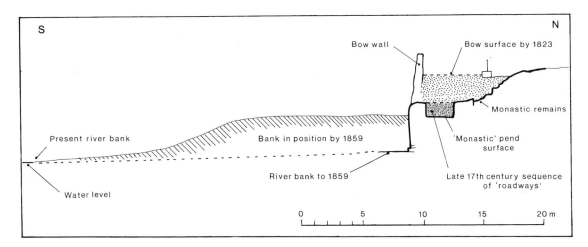

Illus 74
Profile of the post-monastic build-up in the SW of the site.

THE W AREA OF THE SITE

STRUCTURE 13 (ABBOT'S HALL)

It is likely that parts of Structure 13 (known latterly as the Abbot's Hall) were almost entirely removed in the 16th century, well in advance of the development of The Bow which was finally in place by the end of the 17th century.

The nature and extent of what survived from Structure 13 is best shown on two 18th-century maps: one, Winter's plan of 1760 (illus 67) and the other John Ainslie's town plan of *c* 1775 (illus 73). Both show the 'Abbot's Hall' foundations and it is apparent that these only amount to the bottom courses of Structure 13 masonry with nothing surviving of the great E and W walls (307, 354) from Period II.

There is a strong probability that the monastic surfaces up to the line of wall 383 (the N wall of the pend) survived and, indeed, supported the minister's barn yard. Since the upper masonry of Structure 13 was removed, the manse outbuildings were simply built on the Period II platforms and terraces. Most notable of these was the minister's barn and barnyard, access to which was from the W over the footings of the demolished Abbot's Hall.

ROADWAYS WITHIN THE MONASTIC PEND

The archaeological evidence for the period between 1560 and 1700 is mainly concentrated within the build-up of roadways within the monastic pend, first laid out in Period II.

The last 'monastic' surface within the pend survived more or less intact from the 15th to the late 17th century, running along the S of the site. This surface was ultimately raised by 0.2m within the length of the pend to form a good, cobbled road; which, in turn, was sealed by an almost identical sequence of deposits. This comprised soft bedding material, a deep dump of rubble and culminated in yet another cobbled surface. Coins below and immediately above this latest sequence of deposits suggested a single phase of road-building towards the end of the 17th century (**4.5** nos 24, 25 and 32 below).

Within Structure 13, the build-up of a deep, organically-rich deposit over the last surviving monastic surface contained bottle glass dating from the period 1670–1730. This was sealed by a dumped deposit 0.3m deep and was covered by a metalled surface, presumably the 'highway' mentioned on Winter's plan of 1760. Finds from the dumped material included bottle glass dating to between 1720 and 1750. This sequence filled up the pend about halfway and coincided reasonably with the creation of a Horsemarket in Abbey Close in the 17th century and the subsequent traffic to and from it. Despite being progressively infilled, the distinctive bottleneck of the 13th-century monastic pend is plainly visible on the 1775 town plan.

The manse, which had several phases, was originally established towards the end of the 17th century. At this stage, it consisted of a long, narrow, single-storey structure apparently built directly over or within parts of the West range. The building of a new manse for the new church on the S of the Jed Water in 1876 saw the complete removal of the last manse on the site – a large, L-shaped, detached house of several storeys – and the subsequent landscaping of the area.

As with the manse, very little survived of the outbuildings towards the bottom of the site – all having been removed during the successive programmes of site clearance. All that remained *in situ* by 1984 were an area of cobbling and a cross-wall associated with the mid-18th-century barn and barnyard.

To the S of the abbey buildings, the Jed Water was systematically redirected to serve later mills built to the E of the Abbey cloister. In 1770, there was a weir ('the Cauld Back') and a lade adjoining the N side of Abbey mill and leading ultimately to the Snuff Mill before rejoining the river near Canongate Bridge. This general plan persisted until sometime after 1823: by 1859, the river bank to the N, immediately below the abbey, was massively extended and the weir relocated upstream. By then a sluice-controlled, piped water supply served the new woollen mills – the Abbey Mill and Hilson's Mill – and this system prevailed until the mills closed for good in the 1960s.

3

EXCAVATION WITHIN THE ABBEY CHURCH 1990

In 1990 there was limited excavation to determine whether the E end of the 12th-century church was shorter than the surviving one (RCAHMS 1956, 200 & 203). Simultaneously, a trench was opened between the sixth and seventh piers of the nave to establish whether the church had had a temporary W gable.

DETAILS OF THE EXCAVATION

THE PRESBYTERY (illus 75; 76)

There had been so much disruption below the floor of the presbytery that it was difficult to distinguish between those levels disturbed in recent years and those that were contemporary with the monastic occupation. There was a profusion of disarticulated human bones throughout the relatively small, L-shaped trench and, as deep as 0.7m, there were numerous 19th- and 20th-

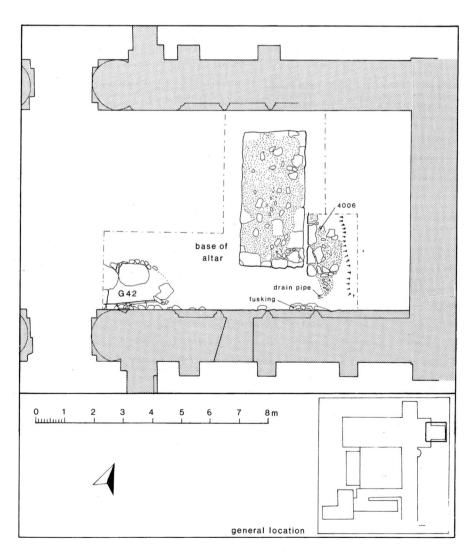

Illus 75
Plan of the principal features excavated within the abbey church in 1990.

Illus 76
Base of altar in the presbytery of the church; from the S.

century artefacts among the disturbed rubble, soils and boulder clay.

Within an E extension of the trench were found the mortar-bonded, rubble foundations (4006) (illus 75) of a wall, truncated on its S side by a modern iron drain pipe. Although its relationships with the side walls of the presbytery were not established, it is conceivable that wall 4006 had spanned the width of the church. However, this wall could have been no wider than the 1.2m of its foundations and hence it is unlikely to have been the original E wall of the church, the surviving E wall being twice its width. It is not clear whether the tusking projecting from the S wall of the presbytery was associated with masonry 4006 or, perhaps more likely, belonged to another phase of the abbey's development.

To the immediate W of masonry 4006 was a rectangular plinth of mortar-bonded masonry (illus 76), 4.4 × 2.3m, that was separated from the N and S presbytery walls by gaps of 0.7m and

1.4m respectively. The location and dimensions of this plinth have led to its interpretation as the base of an altar although its relationships with other structures have yet to be established.

At the extreme SW corner of the trench, adjacent to the SE pier of the tower, was a coffin burial (Grave 43) of probable 18th/19th century date, below which were the fragmentary remains of a sarcophagus burial (Grave 42). These graves are described in more detail in the chapter (5) on burials below.

THE NAVE

A trench, 5.0 × 2.2m, was opened midway across the nave, between the sixth and seventh piers. Numerous 20th-century artefacts were retrieved more than 0.7m below the level of the pier bases, making it obvious that, if there had been a temporary W gable in this area, it is unlikely to have survived into modern times.

4

THE SMALL FINDS

The finds recovered from the excavation reflect activity pre-dating the 12th-century foundation of the abbey to its abandonment in the 16th century and the later absorption of its buildings by the town of Jedburgh. Inevitably, many of these objects were in disturbed contexts, due principally to frequent episodes of rebuilding and clearance. Fortunately, a few key sealed deposits were recovered which reflected critical periods of occupation and the structural sequence of the site.

4.1 BONE AND IVORY
David H Caldwell

CATALOGUE OF ILLUSTRATED PIECES

1 Stylus of turned bone with iron point, used for writing on a waxed table; Chapter house; Period IV.

Similar instruments have been recovered from medieval contexts on several British sites. Harman (1979, 45) lists several. They have been identified as parchment prickers although they are more likely to be styli (Ramsay, 1987, 382–3).

2 Bone, hand-carved pin;
topsoil.

3 Bone handle;
Room 4; modern disturbance.

4 Bone, double-sided comb;
topsoil.

5 Bone, double-sided comb;
outside Room 6; modern disturbance.

A bone tooth from another comb was also recovered from the Chapter house area.

6 Bone cutlery handle, not well polished, with remains of iron tang;
Sewage ditch 918; Period II.

7 Bone plate with bronze rivets. The back is scored longitudinally and stained green from contact with copper-alloy; topsoil.

8 Ivory veneer with circular brown stain (?glue from label); Manse outbuilding and late clearance; modern.

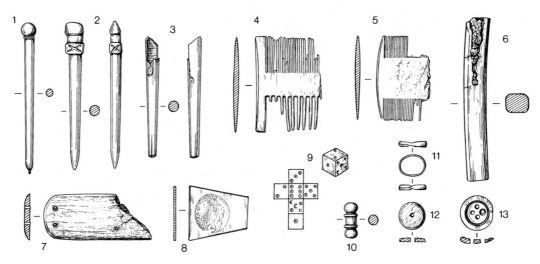

Illus 77
Bone artefacts (scale 1:2).

9 Ivory dice; it has two faces with the value five, one altered from four;
Room 6 midden; Period III.

10 Bone toggle, well polished;
topsoil.

11 Bone ring or mounting;
riverside walkway; Period III.

12 Bone button core;
area of manse; topsoil.

Part of a similar button core was recovered from outside the Chapter house (Period V).

13 Bone button;
Chapter house; modern disturbance.

ADDITIONAL ITEMS OF IVORY AND HORN

THE COMB, PENDANT AND BUCKLE

John Higgitt

(illus 78, colour V)

The following report is a summary of a fuller account of the assemblage published elsewhere (Higgitt 1987, 119–27).

THE COMB

Cut from a single piece of walrus ivory and measuring only 50mm high, 43mm across and a maximum 7mm thick, the comb displayed a superb level of medieval workmanship. Its condition was excellent: only one small sliver was missing although its natural cream coloration had been stained black in places, presumably by chemical attack within the ditch. The twelve larger teeth showed signs of moderate wear, indicating the comb to be more than purely decorative, whereas the 24 smaller ones opposite were effectively unused.

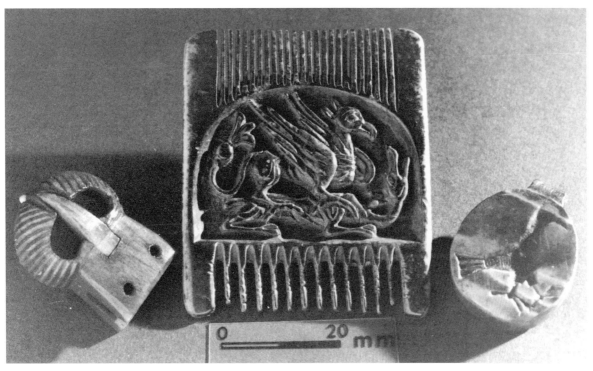

Illus 78
The comb, buckle and pendant, retrieved from ditch 928.

The knight fighting with the dragon has a round-topped, kite-shaped shield and clothing typical of the period between the third quarter of the 11th and third quarter of the 12th century – a time when artistic scenes of combat were very popular. The naturalistic treatment is unusual for a Romanesque piece and may indicate a residual style based on late Anglo-Saxon art or, more likely, influence from the Low Countries. The warrior, a secular figure with no halo or wings, may represent Hercules confronting the guardian of the tree bearing the golden apples within the Garden of the Hesperides. The Labours of Hercules were common themes on Byzantine ivory caskets of the 11th and 12th centuries and appear in western art a little later.

The reverse panel, again given naturalistic treatment, depicts a griffin attacking an animal, thought to be a doe. This is a common theme in Romanesque art, the scene on the comb resembling some of those on capitals in the crypt of Canterbury Cathedral, dated to *c* 1100. Furthermore, the figures on both sides of the comb resemble many of those in contemporary manuscripts from Canterbury, the artists probably being skilled in several different media. Paradoxically, the griffin is sometimes represented as the force of good although the intention here is probably otherwise.

The lack of Christian imagery indicates the comb to be a non-liturgical piece and, being one of the smallest known medieval examples, its use perhaps limited to the beard or moustache of its aristocratic owner. A late 11th- or early 12th- century date of manufacture is thought likely but, because of the wear on the teeth, deposition may have been some time later. Flanders, northern France or England (Canterbury?) are possible places of origin but, given the lack of known medieval ivory-working in Scotland, it is not thought to be local.

THE SEAL PENDANT

The seal-pendant was also of walrus ivory and, like the comb, cream-coloured but stained near-black in places. Its dimensions of 26mm high, 22mm across and 7mm thick may not be primary for its rough edges and lack of inscription suggest it had been cut down from a larger seal matrix and a ?secondary apical tab drilled to allow suspension from a cord or chain. Birds were common motifs on early seals and the subject matter here was expertly carved with fine tools. Its place of manufacture is unknown although it might be British.

THE BUCKLE

Each component of the well-executed and little-worn buckle was of a light ochre-coloured substance, probably horn which was more widely utilised than ivory in 12th-century Scotland. A buckle recovered from Goltho, Lincolnshire was similar in form but was made of bone (MacGregor 1985, 103–5). The Jedburgh piece measured 27mm long by 20mm across the bow with a maximum thickness, including the tongue, of 10mm. The tongue pivoted neatly on a dowel and rested on the bow which was decorated with incised striations.

4.2 COPPER-ALLOY
David H Caldwell

Quantities of scrap copper-alloy, mostly lumps but including some clippings and pieces of sheet metal, were recovered. With the exception of a few pieces illustrated and listed below, these have not been studied in any detail.

CATALOGUE OF ILLUSTRATED PIECES

(illus 79a, b)

PINS

14 Pin with globular head;
    outside Chapter house; Period V.

15 Pin with wound wire head;
    outside Chapter house; Period V.

64 copper-alloy pins were recovered, most of them with wound-wire heads and similar dimensions to those of modern dress-making pins (eg no 15). 11 have considerable traces of tinning and one from a Period V context outside the Chapter house had been bent into a hook. Only one pin (no 14) has a globular head.

LACE TAGS

16 Lace tag.

17 Lace tag.

18 Lace tag.

19 Strip incised with zigzag pattern;
   outside Chapter house; Period V.

20 Lace tag.

21 Lace tag.

22 Lace tag.

MISCELLANEOUS, FERRULES AND BELT MOUNTS

23 Chape from the sheath of a knife or dagger;
   debris from Timber Structures 1 & 2; Period II.

24 Strap-end, still retaining portion of leather;
   Chapter house; Period III.

25 Ferrule, containing substantial piece of charcoal;
   Structure 14; Period IV.

26 Ferrule (?);
   outside East range; modern disturbance.

27 Ferrule (?) with traces of tinning;
   Sewage ditch 918; Period II.

28 Decorative washer or mounting;
   Sewage ditch 918; Period II.

29 Belt mount;
   Timber buildings; Period II.

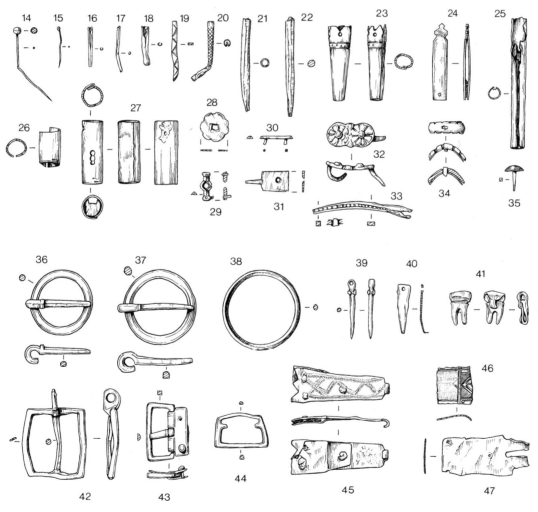

Illus 79
a) Copper-alloy artefacts (scale 1:2).

30 Belt mount;
Chapter house, Grave 16; Period IV.

31 Mounting – possibly a broken hook;
outside Chapter house; Period V.

32 Decorative mount;
surface of The 'Bow'; Period V.

33 Strip decorated with band of pellets; it has two rivet holes, with one copper rivet still in place; outside Room 6; Period III.

34 Mounting, comprising two layers of copper held together by an iron rivet; outside Chapter house; Period V.

35 Tack or stud; the head of a similar tack was found nearby, in a Period V deposit; outside East range; topsoil.

BROOCHES

36 Ring brooch, the pin having a collar;
Chapter house, Grave 15; Period IV.

Silver ring brooches with collared pins can be dated to the late 13th and 14th century on the evidence of those found with Scottish coin hoards (Callander 1924; Metcalf 1977) although the Jedburgh example is from a considerably later (late 15th- or early 16th-century) context. See also no 37.

37 Ring brooch;
Chapter house, Grave 15; Period IV.

38 Ring brooch, lacking its pin;
outside Chapter house; Period V.

39 Brooch pin with collar engraved with saltires;
Chapter house, Grave 6; Period II or III.

STRAP MOUNTS BUCKLES AND ENDS

40 Mount;
S end of East range; Period V.

41 Buckle plate;
Timber buildings; Period II.

42 Strap mount with suspension loop;
riverside road; Period V.

43 Rectangular strap-end buckle with traces of gilding. The buckle plate contains remains of a leather strap; Room 5; Period ?III.

44 Trapezoidal strap mount with spurs;
Room 1; modern disturbance.

At least two other similar mounts are known from Scotland, one from Linlithgow Palace and one from St Anne's Lane, Perth (Thoms 1982, fig 6, no 59).

Others have been reported from sites in England (Allan 1984, fig 191, no 99; Tweddle 1986, no 729) and from France. Two similar strap mounts were found in Southampton; one from a context dated to the 13th/early 14th century, the other from a deposit dated c 1300–50 (Platt & Coleman-Smith 1975, fig 240, no 1725; fig 241, no 1736). Another, from Rougiers in southern France, has been dated to the second quarter of the 13th century (D'Archimbaud 1980, fig 465, no 41).

45 Hasp, perhaps from a book-binding, decorated with geometric design. It retains traces of a leather strap; outside Chapter house; Period V.

46 Part of buckle plate (?) with geometric decoration and traces of silvering;
Room 16; Period V.

47 Part of buckle plate;
Sewage ditch 928; Period II.

48 Strap end(?), all but the terminal was tinned;
Chapter house; Period IV.

49 Buckle;
Manse outbuilding; Period V.

BUTTONS

50 Button, tinned on underside, with trace of gilding on top; machine engraved; topsoil.

Ten other copper-alloy buttons of 19th-/20th-century dates were recovered.

BELL

51 Bottom half of a rumbler bell;
topsoil.

MOUNTINGS, CHAINS, WIRE AND SHEET

52 Part of a mounting;
outside East range; probably modern disturbance.

53 Two fragments of copper-alloy sheet metal with incised decoration and traces of tinning;
Chapter house; Period III.

54 Swivel mount with two suspension loops, one threaded with a length of copper wire;
outside East range; modern disturbance.

55 Length of chain with S-shaped links;
re-use of Structure 13; Period V.

56 Small wire loop;
outside Chapter house; Period V.

57 Piece of folded sheet metal with sheet metal staples;
outside East range; modern disturbance.

The use of sheet metal and staples to repair metal vessels dates back at least to the Iron Age. An example can be seen on a bronze cauldron from Whitehills Moss, Lochmaben, now in the National Museums, Edinburgh (DU 6). However, in this case, the staples may have been intended to stand proud of the surface of the sheet metal and serve as sheaths for a wire or cord.

58 Piece of sheet metal;
outside Room 6; modern disturbance.

59 Piece of sheet metal;
construction of 'The Bow' wall; Period V.

60 Piece of sheet metal;
preparation of SW of site; Period II.

61 Sheet metal patch;
Sewage ditch 928; Period II.

62 Piece of scrap metal with incised decoration; perhaps a trial piece;
Sewage ditch 928; Period II.

63 Piece of a mounting;
Room 6, midden; Period III.

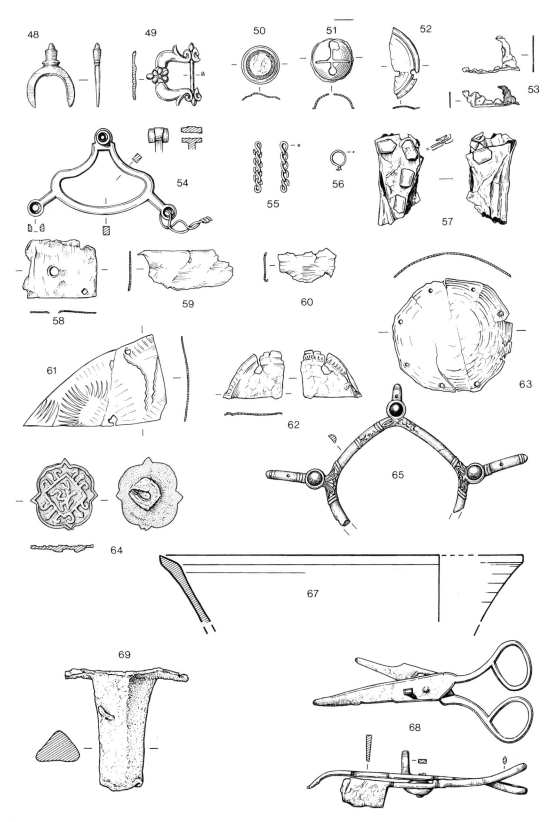

Illus 79
b) Copper-alloy artefacts (scale 1:2).

BADGE

64 Cast bronze quatrefoil badge with stylized rendering of the Scottish royal arms. Although no trace survived, the badge was probably enamelled originally. On the back is a socket, since ripped open, for mounting it.
Outside Chapter house; Period V.

Enamelled badges are often identified as harness mounts. A series of shield-shaped mounts with enamelled decoration has been dated to the 14th century. Several quatrefoil mounts with heraldic decoration are known from England: one example, in the Museum of London and dated to *c* 975, is decorated with the arms of East Anglia; two have been recovered from Billingsgate, London; and another was found in south Yorkshire. One of the Billingsgate mounts (now in a private collection) is similar to the Jedburgh piece, having a crude representation of a lion (*passant* rather than *rampant*) within a fleur-de-lis border. It retains traces of blue enamel and gilding and has a secondary hook attachment held by a rivet through the centre.

DECORATIVE AND INLAID PIECES

65 Mercury-gilded mounting set with two green glass and one blue glass gems and decorated with palmette designs. The style of decoration suggests a 12th-century date. It may be a mount from a book cover.
Chapter house; Period III.

66 Leg and corner mount of a box or casket decorated with strapwork. A reinforcing edge plate, protected by a washer, is riveted to it. The plate was intended to lie horizontally along the base of the object but has been twisted vertically.
Chapter house; Period III; not illustrated.

MISCELLANEOUS: VESSELS, SNUFFERS AND THIMBLES

67 Part of rim of large cast bronze pot of heavily leaded bronze (Cu 59%, Pb 19%, Sn 8%);
Room 6 midden; Period III.

68 Pair of candle-snuffers with remains of tinning. The bottom blade is stamped 66 (or 99). 18th- or early 19th-century.
Manse garden over cloister; Period V.

69 Leg of cast bronze vessel;
Timber Structure 2; Period II.

70 Thimbles;
two from Room 4; both from topsoil; not illustrated.

LACE TAGS • DISCUSSION

Thea Gabra-Sanders

A total of 62 lace tags (or 'chapes') were retrieved from the excavation. All were of copper-alloy sheeting bent into tubes which, with the exception of three incomplete examples, were 11.5–52.0mm in length. Within 15 tubes there were traces of what appeared to be leather.

The typology, based on that of Margeson (1985) and Oakley (1979), is summarised as follows:

Type I tags exhibited a slightly tapered form with the edges overlapping only at the base and with the lace secured by a transverse rivet at the top. There were 42 such examples.

Type II tags were decorated, one of them in a manner similar to that of a post-medieval chape found in Norwich (Margeson 1985, 57–8, no 8, fig 38) and a mid-16th-/17th-century chape from Colchester (Crummy 1988, 13, no 1615, fig 14). Another had a grooved decoration identical to that of a ?17th-century chape from Colchester (Crummy 1988, 13, no 1614, fig 14).

Type III tags were all plain. Three tags could not be categorized.

The earliest known reference to lace tags, which were used for fastening jerkins, hose, jackets and possibly armour (d'Archimbaud 1980, 108), is cited in a London haberdasher's inventory of 1378 (Cunnington & Cunnington 1973, 108). Unfortunately, most of the tags from Jedburgh were found in post-Reformation and disturbed levels although the majority (13) of those recovered from sealed contexts were within the Room 6 midden which is believed to have been in use between the mid-14th and late 15th centuries. Tags from contemporary, or earlier, levels have also been recovered from Northampton (Oakley 1979, 263), Sandal Castle (Goodall 1983, 232) and Crossraguel Abbey (MacDonald 1920, 27).

4.3 LEAD OBJECTS
David H Caldwell

CATALOGUE OF ILLUSTRATED PIECES

(illus 80)

FRAGMENTS AND PIECES

71 Twisted and pulled piece of lead with file or plier grip marks – possibly used as an awl;
Sewage ditch 928; Period II.

72 Strip wound into a ring;
Room 16; Period V.

73 Fragment of lead with crimped edge;
outside Chapter house; Period V.

74 Weight, weighing;
preparation of SW of site; Period II.
A heavier weight (8oz) of similar form from Kirkstall Abbey (Moorhouse & Wrathmell, 1987, fig 71, no 230) has been identified as (possibly) from a clock.

75 Piece of scrap metal with several nail holes punched through it – perhaps used as a cushion or support for other work;
Sewage ditch 928; Period II.

Considerable quantities of scrap lead were recovered. This has not been studied in any detail.

76 Strip of metal formed into a ring;
topsoil.

77 Strip;
Cloister area; Period IV.

78 Sliver;
outside Chapter house; Period V.

79 Fragment, crumpled and partially molten, with nail holes; perhaps a piece of roof furniture;
topsoil.

WINDOW CAMES AND STRIPS

80 Window cames;
preparation of SW of site; Period II.

81 Part of a support for a lead pipe?
Room 4; Period V.

82 Strip, drawn out like a pot handle;
outside Chapter house; Period V?.

83 L-shaped cramp;
Chapter house; Period IV.

84 Strip;
Room 4; Period IV.

85 Strip;
Sewage ditch 928; Period II.

86 Strip;
Sewage ditch 928; Period II.

87 Sliver;
outside Chapter house; Period V.

88 Window came;
Sewage ditch 928; Period II.

89 Window came;
Chapter house; topsoil.

Pieces of scrap lead recognizable as cames were also recovered from many other contexts.

SHEETS

90 Rectangular sheet with a nail hole at one end;
Room 6 midden; Period III.

91 Rectangular sheet with one end folded over;
Room 6 midden; Period III.

These two sheets, together with a similar one from the same context, are comparable to pieces from Kirkstall Abbey. The latter have been described as small rectangular sheets of roughly uniform size, approximately 100 x 50mm with two perforations for nails at one end, the opposite end being folded over (Moorhouse & Wrathmell, 1987 121, fig 72). They appear to be roof fittings. Compare nos 94 and 95.

92 Roof or drainage fitting?
Outside Chapter house; Period V.

93 Piece of lead with copper-alloy adhering to its convex face. Probably part of a cast bronze object with a lead core;
Room 16; Period V.

94 Sheet with countersunk nail hole.
Roof fitting? Compare nos 89–90.
Sewage ditch 928; Period II.

95 Sheet with nail holes.
Roof fitting? Compare nos 89–90.
Outside Chapter house; Period III/IV.

96 Musket ball;
Manse outbuildings, Period V; not illustrated.

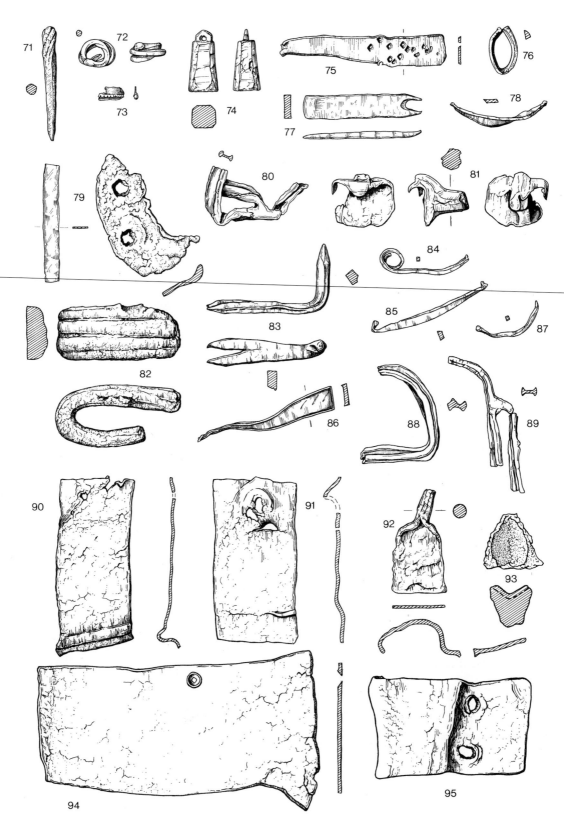

Illus 80
Lead artefacts (scale 1:2).

4.4 IRON OBJECTS
David H Caldwell

Drawings and identification were done largely on the basis of X-rays. Most of the ironwork consisted of nails and fragments of nails. With the exception of horse-shoe nails, these are not reported here.

CATALOGUE OF ILLUSTRATED PIECES

(illus 81a, b)

STAPLE, PLATES AND MISCELLANEOUS TOOLS

97 Staple;
topsoil.

98 Rectangular plate.
Possibly a piece of armour, perhaps for reinforcing plate from a jack.
Chapter house; Period V.

99 Plate with four slots. X-rays indicate that they are lined with another metal, perhaps copper or tin, used to braze other pieces in place.
Outside Chapter house; Period V.

100 Socket;
Room 5; Period V.

101 Tool; this resembles a file in outline although no signs of file markings were discerned on the X-rays;
Chapter house; Period IV.

102 Tool;
S end of East range; Period V.

103 Bar;
Room 11; Period IV.

104 File?
Chapter house; Period IV.

BROOCHES AND BUCKLES

105 Ring brooch or buckle, originally tinned, with some threads of replaced textile (wool?) in the corrosion adhering to it.
Chapter house, Grave 17; Period IV.

106 Ring brooch or buckle, almost completely covered with replaced, unidentified textile. There was a thick layer of insect remains beneath the textile.
Chapter house, Grave 16; Period IV.

107 Buckle, originally tinned, with replaced textile, sometimes of double thickness, on both sides;
Chapter house, Grave 13; Period IV?.

108 Buckle, incomplete and lacking its pin. There were replaced textile, bone and insect remains in the corrosion deposits.
Chapter house, Grave 14; Period IV?.

109 Ring, probably a buckle, lacking its pin;
Timber buildings; Period II.

110 Staple?
Chapter house; Period III.

111 Hinge strap with two nail holes, one with a nail head still in place;
Chapter house; Period III.

112 Reinforcing band;
Chapter house; Period III.

SPEARHEAD

113 Projectile point, with socket and 'wings' at the base of the blade;
Sewage ditch 928; Period II.

This bears comparison with two larger spearheads, one from Oslo (Grieg, 1930, fig 269) and the other from the manor at Goltho, Lincolnshire. The latter can be dated by its archaeological context to before AD 1000 (Beresford, 1987, 186, no 171).

HORSE HARNESS, HORSESHOE NAILS ETC
(illus 81b)

114 Horseshoe with four nail holes on each side and no calkins;
Surface of The Bow; Period V.

There were several other fragments of horseshoes from the same area.

115 Horse-bit and part of mouth-piece;
Timber buildings; Period II.

116 Part of buckle, from horse harness?
Timber buildings; Period II.

117 Horse-shoe nail with fiddle-key head;
Room 4; Period II/III; not illustrated.

Shoe nails of this type are dated by Clark (1986) from the mid-/late 11th century to the mid-13th century but have been recovered from early and mid-14th-century levels in Perth (Ford & Walsh, 1987, 137). A similar nail, also with a straight shank, was recovered from the Period II sewage ditch 928.

118 Horse-shoe nail of 'transitional type' with expanding head with ears;
East cloister alley; Period V; not illustrated.

Clark (1986) dates nails of this type to the second half of the 13th century and the early 14th century. Ford and Walsh (1987, 12) note their occurrence in Perth in the 14th and 15th century. Two more nails of the same type were recovered from the Room 6 midden. One of them had its shank bent back on itself, indicating that the nail had been used.

COFFIN HANDLES

119 Coffin-handle, loop-shaped;
outside Chapter house; modern disturbance; not illustrated.

Three more coffin-handles of similar type were recovered from disturbed contexts.

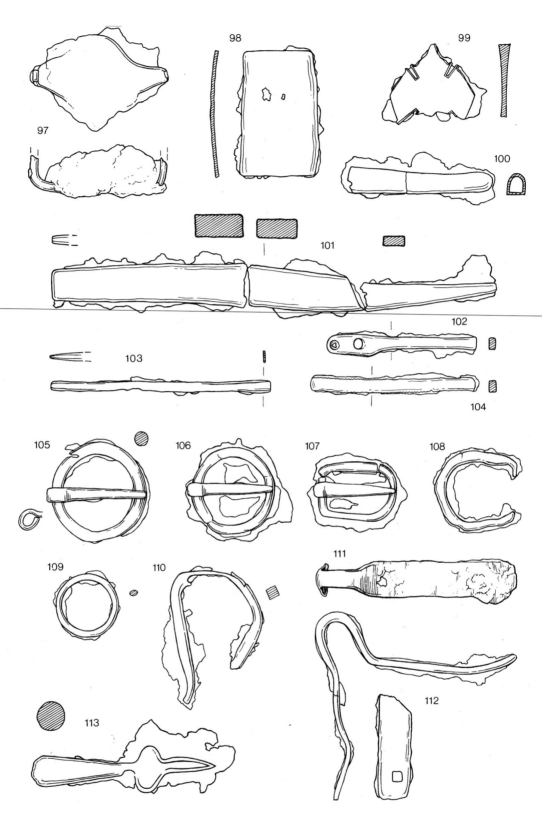

Illus 81
a) Iron artefacts (scale 1:2).

120 Coffin-handles, U-shaped.
   A total of six such objects were recovered from modern
   contexts; not illustrated.

121 Coffin-handle, U-shaped, moulded with knops;
   Room 4; topsoil; not illustrated.
122 Coffin-handle, W-shaped;
   outside Structure 13; Period IV; not illustrated.

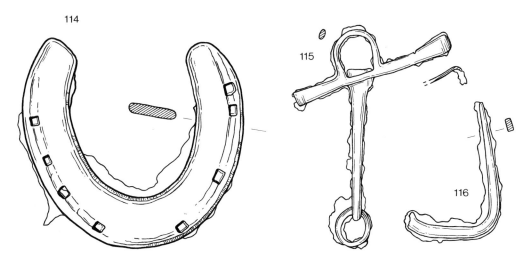

Illus 81
b) Iron artefacts (scale 1:2).

4.5 COINS, TOKEN AND JETTONS
Nicholas McQ Holmes

The numismatic finds from the excavations consisted of 43 coins, one trade token and six jettons. The majority of these predated the monastic occupation of the site; some of the medieval coins were found in disturbed or redeposited contexts; others offer important evidence for the dating of certain deposits on the site.

DESCRIPTION AND DISCUSSION

COINS

The two earliest coins were both survivals in later contexts although each acts as a reminder of other evidence for the early history of Jedburgh. A very worn Roman *dupondius* (No 1) may represent a comparatively modern loss but it is also possible that it was brought to the site by a Roman soldier in the 3rd century AD. Two inscriptions found many years ago in the abbey ruins and now on display refer to military units based at forts on Dere Street. These have been assumed to indicate that detachments from these units guarded some sort of military installation at the crossing of the River Teviot, perhaps as part of the frontier patrol system established at least as early as the reign of the Emperor Caracalla in the early 3rd century (Hanson & Maxwell 1983, 210).

An Anglo-Saxon penny of Aethelred II (No 2) was found in a context associated with the building of the final phase Chapter house. It had clearly been redeposited although other reports of Anglo-Saxon coins found in the vicinity suggest that such items were in local circulation around the 10th century. Many coins of Eadred, Eadwig and Aethelred (of the period 946–1016), as well as later English issues, were found beside the Jed Water, near to Abbey Bridge 'where rubbish from the Abbey and other parts of the town had been deposited' (NSA 1845, 13). Jeffrey (1864, i, 276–77) states that earth tipped on the river bank and derived from E of the existing abbey yielded copper and silver coins, including a silver penny of Athelstan (924–39). A hoard found in a field to the S of the Bongate in *c* 1827 comprised 90–100 silver coins, including issues of Egbert of Wessex (803–39), Athelstan and Aethelred II and one coin of Cnut (1016–35) (RCAHMS 1956, 37).

The coin of Aethelred II, retrieved during the 1984 excavation, belongs to his last issue and is dated between 1009 and 1017, the year after the king's death. A small symbol, shaped like an open-topped box, appears on the reverse, to the left of the cross. This is one of the less common of a whole series of such symbols which occur on Anglo-Saxon pennies, particularly of Aethelred II, and which include pellets, crosses, annulets and letters, singly or in groups. Their function remains unclear although they may have served to identify batches of coins produced by different moneyers.

Six coins dating from the 12th or early 13th century were recovered, of which only two came from stratified contexts. The earliest, a rare cut halfpenny of Henry, Earl of Huntingdon and Northumberland (no 3), was found in the fill of Grave 28 within the East cloister alley. It provides a possible *terminus post quem* of *c* 1136 for the grave although, in all likelihood, the coin was redeposited. Of greater dating value are the two 'Tealby' pennies of Henry II (nos 4 & 5). Neither of them can be ascribed with certainty to a particular class as both are mis-struck but no 4, which was found in the backfill of an early monastic ditch (928), was certainly struck in the decade 1161–70 and probably towards the end of that period. It showed little sign of wear from prolonged circulation and the 'Tealby' coinage was superseded by the short-cross issues in 1180, indicating that this coin was lost by *c* 1180 and quite possibly somewhat earlier.

The second 'Tealby' penny (no 5) was found in a deposit believed to have derived from the same ditch fill which yielded no 4. Accurate identification of this coin has proved impossible, owing to its extremely poor striking and apparent degree of wear. Such details as are visible suggest that it belongs to the latest of the 'Tealby' issues, struck between *c* 1170 and 1180. Poor striking has also complicated an assessment of the coin's period of circulation. Its appearance suggests that it was circulated well beyond the introduction of the short-cross coinage. This is unlikely, however, as the two coinages were easily distinguished and an outdated piece would probably not have survived long in circulation. Hence, the evidence of this coin must be treated with some suspicion because of its provenance, uncertain date of striking and possible misleading appearance. In all probability it was lost either by, or soon after, 1180 but this should not be assumed.

Two cut halfpennies of the short-cross coinage of Henry II (no 6) and John (no 7) and a short-cross penny of John (no 8) are of little archaeological value, the first halfpenny and the two coins of John having been redeposited.

There is a large gap in the coin record after the early 13th century. Neither Edwardian long-cross pennies of the late 13th and early 14th centuries nor 15th-century Scottish billon and copper small denomination coinages were present. Both types are common on sites occupied during these periods; and the negative evidence here is sufficiently striking to suggest that the level of activity at the abbey was considerably reduced during the later medieval period. It is extremely unlikely that the lack of coins of this period is associated with the monastic nature of the occupation because excavations on other Scottish religious sites have produced numerous coins, including types dating from the 15th century. Recent examples include Lesmahagow Priory (Bateson 1982) and Linlithgow Friary (Holmes 1989, fiche 9.5.7).

Of the remaining coins from Jedburgh, 25 are billon or copper issues of the 16th or 17th centuries. Many are from disturbed or unstratified contexts although two concentrations of coins are worthy of consideration. A large deposit of disturbed soils, located to the N of the extended Chapter house, yielded 13 coins, ranging in date from the beginning of the 16th to the end of the 17th century. The earliest was a billon penny of James IV (No 9) which had probably been lost by *c* 1520; an unidentifiable piece, bent completely double, (no 10) may belong to the same period. The remainder comprised five coins from the reign of Mary (nos 12, 13, 15, 16 & 17), two of James VI (nos 18 & 19), one of Charles I (no 22), two Irish issues of William and Mary (nos 30 & 31) and one unidentifiable item (no 43). On the basis of the two latest coins, this material was deposited in the early 18th century and, if it represents an homogeneous deposit, the other coins were minted between 1555 and 1629 and, hence, it is possible that early 18th-century landscaping caused soil to be removed from an area of fairly substantial late 16th-/early 17th-century activity. The James IV penny, however, must be regarded as a survival even in such a context as this.

Most of the coins from this material are of little or no numismatic interest but two are worthy of further mention. The James IV penny (no 9) is unusual in having, on the reverse, a crown initial mark rather than the cross which is normal for Type III of the second issue. This variety was noted by Burns (1887) but it appears to be uncommon. A forgery of a 1557 billon plack of Mary (no 13) is notable for its blundered legends and crude workmanship as well as for the extremely debased metal. There was little chance of its being mistaken for a genuine coin even though they too were often poorly struck. Forgeries of these coins were struck in large numbers and they were frequently imported from abroad, especially from Flanders, but most exhibited greater skill on the part of the manufacturer than this example. In 1572 James VI was obliged to recall all the placks and hardheads issued by Mary and to order a countermark of a heart and star to be applied to each genuine coin. It was perhaps after this that the forged coin, which appears fairly worn, was consigned to a decorative function and pierced for attachment to a chain or cord.

One other area producing a concentration of post-medieval coins was the reused abbey pend at the S end of the site. Various post-monastic metalled surfaces and intervening and overlying accumulations yielded small-denomination coins of James VI (No 20), Charles II (nos 24 & 25) and William of Orange (nos 32 & 33), as well as a Dutch doit of 1680 (no 41) and a redeposited short-cross halfpenny (no 7).

Of the remaining coins, two may be selected for brief mention. A billon lion/hardhead of Francis and Mary (1559) (no 14) was recovered from the fill of a grave (Grave 14) within the Chapter house. The coin was fairly worn and a date of loss prior to *c* 1575–80 seems unlikely; the countermark indicates that the coin was certainly still in circulation in 1572. The grave, however, was a monastic coffin burial although its upper fill was evidently derived from later deposits. A billon half-bawbee of James V's third coinage (no 11), although found in topsoil, is of interest because of its rarity. Bawbees of this coinage are common enough but the halves were evidently issued in much smaller numbers.

TRADE TOKEN

An example was recovered of the only variety of trade token struck for an issuer in Jedburgh. This was a farthing of John Reid, described on the obverse and reverse of the token as a candle-maker and a dealer in spirits, teas and groceries. Undated farthing tokens of this type, which usually bear no design other than the name, occupation and sometimes the address of the issuer, were included by Dalton & Hamer (1916) in their catalogue of 18th-century issues. It seems likely though that many of them date from the early part of the 19th century. The issuing of trade tokens became illegal after 1799, when a drastic shortage of small change in circulation was partially remedied by the minting of regal copper halfpennies and farthings. Issuers often circumvented this by omitting any mention of value from the later tokens. These could thus be officially described as advertising checks while in practice being accepted into circulation within localised areas.

JETTONS

The six jettons, or casting counters, provide a cross-section of the types used in Scotland at various periods. No early English jettons, which are uncommon on Scottish sites, were found at Jedburgh. French jettons reached Britain in large numbers during the 14th and 15th centuries; and the two earliest finds from Jedburgh reflect this. No 45 is of a fairly common type, bearing on the obverse the head of a Moor which appears on jettons of French queens from as early as the 13th century. Feuardent attributes these jettons to the Royal Almonry of France with a probable 14th-century date and, in Rouyer's opinion, Moors' heads were originally references to the Crusades (Barnard 1917, 113). Three jettons of this type were recovered from recent excavations in York (Pirie 1986, 67 & Pl XVI, Nos 211–3); and they seem to have had widespread use in Britain. A somewhat later type of French jetton is represented by no 46 which probably dates from the 15th century. It is of somewhat crude manufacture and may be a copy. Both of these jettons were found in a cellar (Room 6) at the lower end of the East range, within midden material which also contained pottery of 15th-century date. Therefore, the latter jetton at least may be contemporary with the associated material.

Two of the Jedburgh jettons are not what they at first appear to be. No 47 has legends in French, refers to the French king and 'ship of state' and has designs suggestive of the arms of Paris but was made at Nuremberg, Germany. Such jettons were made initially for use in France but they spread widely and are very common in England. They were made in great numbers in the 16th century and possibly later, whilst retaining the antique appearance and lettering as a convention. This example was found in association with later artefacts, within a secondary robber trench for the E wall of the extended Chapter house, and a post-Reformation date for the jetton is, therefore, acceptable.

The designs on no 48 are based on a Low Countries jetton of the Dukes of Burgundy of the period *c* 1487–1507 (Barnard 1917, 188–9, no 7; Barnard 1924, 263–4; Rigold 1981, 120–1, no 15). Barnard (1924, 264–6) identifies pieces similar to this as Nuremberg products of the period *c* 1492–1540; and Rigold ascribes a similar blundered copy (of larger size than the originals) to Nuremberg during the period 1510–1520+. Unfortunately, the context in which the Jedburgh example was found is of no assistance in dating it.

Two jettons, bearing the name of Hans Schultes (no 49) and Hans Laufer (no 50) represent the kind of stock-jettons, or 'Rechenpfennige' produced by most of the prominent Nuremberg manufacturers in the later 16th and 17th centuries. The 'Reichsapfel' and the alternative arrangement of three crowns and three lys are among the commonest designs and large numbers are found in Britain.

It is doubtful whether these jettons can provide much information about human activity on the site. Such a small group, covering a period of up to three centuries, can not be taken as evidence that jettons were used for accounting purposes at the abbey. Stray jettons, particularly of the later period, are common enough among finds from excavations and they are the sort of objects very easily lost or discarded by people who had no practical use for them.

CATALOGUE

COINS

B = Burns (1887)
N = North (1980)
S = Stewart (1967)

1   Roman copper-alloy dupondius, late 1st or early 2nd century AD , possibly of Vespasian. Extremely worn. Provenance: fill of Period II drain in the East cloister alley.

2   AETHELRED II (978–1016): silver penny of last small cross type (1009–17), of the moneyer Aethelnoth at the Lincoln mint.
    obv: +EÐELREDREXANGL
    rev: +EÐELNOÐH-OLIN : symbol [insert] below and to left of cross.

As N 777 and apparently from the same obverse and reverse dies as a coin now in Trondheim, Norway (Mossop 1970, Pl XXI, no 12). Very little wear. Provenance: infill of robber trench (888) for S wall of Period III Chapter house. Hence, associated with Period IV building.

3   HENRY, EARL OF HUNTINGDON AND NORTHUMBERLAND (son of David I of Scotland): silver cut halfpenny, type 1 (*c* 1136–39), of the moneyer Erebald at Corbridge(?).
    obv: +hE[. . . ..]
    rev: EREBA[. . .. .]

From penny as S 8. Generally slight wear but parts of legend flat, probably through poor striking. Provenance: fill of a pit burial (Grave 28) in the East cloister alley.

4   HENRY II (1154–89): silver penny of Tealby (cross and crosslets) type; bust type C–E but probably E (1161–70, probably *c* 1168–70), of the moneyer Nicole at the Ipswich mint.
    obv: +hE[. . .. . ..]
    rev: =NIC[OL]E:[ON]:GIP

Square flan; coin mis-struck to right, resulting in the right part of the bust being missing. Poorly struck in places but apparently little wear. Provenance: upper fill of ditch 928, associated with early Augustinian occupation.

5   HENRY II: silver penny of Tealby type (1158–80); bust type uncertain but surviving features on obverse suggest bust F (*c* 1170–80); mint and moneyer unknown.
    obv: hEN[. .. .. .]
    rev: illegible

Coin struck way off centre on a flan of roughly square shape with three corners cut off; right side of bust missing, reverse legend partly missing and totally illegible. Coin appears fairly well worn. Provenance: midden material washed down slope outside bottom end of East range: possibly came from ditch 928, associated with early occupation of Augustinian abbey.

6   HENRY II: silver cut halfpenny from an English short-cross penny, probably of class 1b and dating from the latter part of the reign (*c* 1180–89). Type as N 963.
    obv: hEN[. . .. .]EX
    rev: +WILLELM[. . .. ..]

Moneyers by the name of Willelm were working at the mints of Lincoln, London and Norwich at this time and the coin could have been struck at any one of these places. The obverse appears very worn but the reverse less so, possibly as the result of differential cleaning. Provenance: a deposit of clay dumped against a ?14th-century wall of Room 12; date of deposit uncertain.

7   JOHN: silver cut halfpenny from an English short-cross penny of class 5b (*c* 1205–10). Type as N 970, of the moneyer Walter at the mint of Canterbury.
    obv: hE[. . .. . ..]EX
    rev: +WALTE[. . .. .]

Fairly worn and slightly bent. Provenance: redeposited (possibly 17th century) on cobbled surface of latest phase of reused pend in the SW corner of abbey.

8   JOHN: silver short-cross penny of class 5c (*c* 1205–10). Type as N 971, of the moneyer Walter at the mint of London.
    obv: hENRICVS REX
    rev: +WALTER.ON.LV

Struck slightly off centre. Slightly worn. Provenance: within residual material within Chapter house.

I   Aerial view of the excavations in progress in 1984.

II   The SW corner of the site during excavation.   III   The East range viewed from the abbey tower.

IV   The E and S sides of the site during excavation.

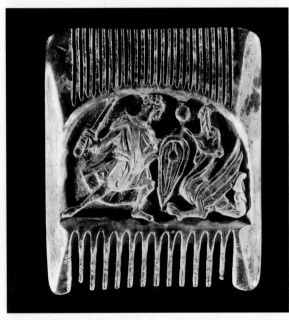

V   The two sides of the comb.

VI   The other objects found in the ditch.

VII   Group A Graves 2, 3 and 4.

VIII   The nave of the church, looking E.   IX   The nave of the church, looking W.

9 JAMES IV: billon penny, second issue, type III (c 1504/5–10). Type as S 133; reverse has initial mark crown, as B p 221, 6h, but lys in first and third quarters; no stops. Slightly bent; slight to moderate wear. Provenance: a post-Reformation deposit to the N of the extended Chapter house.

10 Very thin coin of billon or copper, of diameter 16mm, folded tightly in half. Almost no details are discernible on the exterior surface, apart from what may be the lowest part of a facing bust. The coin may be a billon penny of JAMES IV. Extremely worn. Provenance: as no 9.

11 JAMES V: 3rd coinage billon half-bawbee, type 1a (1539–42); type as S 144. Moderate wear. Provenance: disturbed/modern topsoil.

12 MARY: 1st period billon lion/hardhead (1555–58); type as S 160. Extremely worn, edge much damaged. Provenance: as no 9.

13 MARY: forgery of a 1st period billon plack (1557 issue); type as S 157.
obv: +Z[ ]AD[ ]REGIZ: crowned shield flanked by Z and R
rev: nonsensical legend, the only legible parts of which appear to read ie8[]Z[ ]IVOZO: ornate cross with crowns in angles.

Crude workmanship in an apparently very base metal. Very worn, especially on obverse; pierced at point just above right side of crown on obverse. Provenance: as no 9.

14 FRANCIS & MARY: billon lion/hardhead (1559); dolphins to left, countermarked with heart and stars. Type as S 161. Fairly worn on irregular or clipped flan. Provenance: from the upper fill of Grave 14, probably disturbed.

15 Similar coin to no 14. Provenance: as no 9.

16 Similar coin to no 14. Worn. Provenance: as no 9.

17 Similar coin to no 14 but with dolphins to right. Apparently moderate wear. Provenance: as no 9.

18 JAMES VI: billon plack (1583–90), type 2; S p153. Worn and bent. Provenance: as no 9.

19 JAMES VI: billon hardhead, 2nd issue (November 1588); type as S 200. Struck slightly off centre and very lightly on one side. Probably only moderate wear. Provenance: as no 9.

20 Coin similar to no 19. Surface much corroded; probably moderate wear. Provenance: riverside walk, Period V.

21 JAMES VI: post-Union copper twopence, 2nd issue (1623). Type as S 217. Fairly worn. Provenance: from a post-medieval deposit.

22 CHARLES I: copper turner, 1st issue (1629+). Type as S 235. Fairly worn. Provenance: as no 9.

23 CHARLES I: copper turner, 2nd issue (1632+). Type as S237. Slight to moderate wear. Provenance: from a post-medieval deposit.

24 CHARLES II: copper turner (1663+). Type as S 239 (now reattributed to Charles II). Worn; surfaces partly corroded. Provenance: accumulated material above latest surface of reused pend, Period V.

25 Coin similar to no 24. Worn and slightly bent but apparently of heavy weight for this issue. Provenance: lower cobbled surface of reused pend, Period V.

26 Coin similar to no 24. Fairly worn. Provenance: from topsoil in cloister.

27 Coin similar to no 24. Extremely worn. Provenance: from a post-medieval deposit.

28 Coin similar to no 24. Fairly worn. Provenance: from disturbed/modern topsoil.

29 CHARLES II: copper bawbee (1678). Type as S 244. Worn. Provenance: manse garden, Period V.

30 WILLIAM & MARY: Irish copper halfpenny (1693). Worn. Provenance: as no 9.

31 Coin similar to no 30 (1692–94). Extremely worn and pierced twice. Provenance: as no 9.

32 WILLIAM II (III of England): copper bodle (1695). Type as S 258. Worn; surfaces much corroded. Provenance: accumulated deposit above latest surface of reused pend, Period V.

33 Coin of the same denomination and date as no 32 but type as S 259. Extremely worn. Provenance: riverside walk, Period V.

34 GEORGE II: copper halfpenny, young head type (1729–39). Extremely worn, damaged around edge, surfaces corroded. Provenance: from topsoil.

35 GEORGE II: copper halfpenny (1752). Worn; reverse corroded. Provenance: from topsoil.

36 Copper farthing (1821–60). Highly corroded. Provenance: from 19th-century deposit near edge of river.

37 VICTORIA: silver shilling (1861). Very worn. Provenance: from topsoil.

38 GEORGE V: bronze penny (1913). Very worn. Provenance: contents of disturbed monastic drain.

39 GEORGE V: bronze penny (1916). Very worn. Provenance: as no 38.

40 GEORGE V: silver shilling (1934). Worn; reverse corroded. Provenance: from topsoil.

41 Dutch copper doit of Zeeland (1680)
obv: female figure seated within wicket enclosure: LUC[TOR] ET EME[RGO]
rev: ZEE/LAN/DIA/1680 within wreath

Fairly worn. Provenance: accumulated deposit above latest surface of reused pend, Period V.

42 Unidentified foreign copper coin, of diameter 20mm. Probably a French provincial issue, late 16th–early 18th century.
obv: ? crowned shield
rev: three symbols in a triangle formation

Very worn; surfaces corroded. Provenance: from a post-medieval deposit.

43 Unidentifiable copper disc; very thin, diameter 16–17mm. No details distinguishable on either side. Provenance: as no 9.

TRADE TOKEN

44 Copper farthing trade token of John Reid, Jedburgh (late 18th or early 19th century). Type as Dalton & Hamer (1916) Roxburghshire, 1. Slightly bent and pierced near edge; moderate wear. Provenance: from topsoil in cloister.

JETTONS

References are to Barnard (1917)

45 French copper jetton of diameter 21mm (Mionnet scale 5); probably 14th century.
obv: +AVEMARIA:GRACIA – A Moor's head to right
rev: +A/VE/M/AR – bowed cross of two strands fleurdelissee, enclosing a lys

Type very similar to Barnard 113 and pl IV, no 12. Moderate wear. Provenance: from Period III midden material in Room 6.

46 French copper jetton of diameter 26.5mm (Mionnet scale 7); probably 15th century.
obv: X AVE MARIA.GRACIA – heater shield of France-modern
rev: long cross of three strands fleurdelissee with quatrefoil in centre, enclosed by tressure of four arches; fleuronnee at each angle; annulet between two pellets in each spandrel.

This appears to be a badly worked and slightly mis-struck version of Barnard 118–9 and pl VI, no 47; perhaps a copy. Fairly worn. Provenance: as no 45.

47 German copper jetton of Nuremberg, of diameter 24.5mm (Mionnet scale 6–7); 16th century or possibly later.
obv: VOLGUE:LA:GALLEE:DE:FR – single-masted ship at sea with flag and streamer fore and aft above
rev: crown VIVE:LE:BON:ROY:DE:FRAN – a lozenge of France-ancient (shown as four lys) within a granulated inner circle; in each spandrel is a trefoil between two annulets.

Slightly bent; moderate wear, especially near edge. Type similar to Barnard 210 and pl XXIX, no 8 but smaller with slightly abbreviated legends. Provenance: from post-Reformation robber trench in Chapter house area.

48 Copper jetton of Nuremberg, of diameter 34mm (Mionnet scale 10); probably from the first half of the 16th century.
obv: nonsensical legend, blundered and partly illegible. Naked woman standing, slightly draped with a veil, holding in right hand a wand or sceptre and in left hand a funnel-shaped watering-pot, known as a 'chantepleure', from which water is falling; various flowers ('marguerites') around.
rev: nonsensical legend *MVNBE *MVNNEMV-_VNDE*_DE ; round-based shield of the arms of Burgundy, surmounted by a crown; various symbols in field.

Somewhat mis-struck in legends and fairly worn. Type similar to Barnard 188–9 and pl XXIII, no 7, but larger. Barnard (1924, 264–66) attributes these derivative 'Venus-penny' jettons of Nuremberg to the very late 15th or 16th century. The 'chantepleure' disappears from the design c 1540. Provenance: late occupation of Structure 14, Period V.

49 German copper jetton of Hans Schulters of Nuremberg; diameter 24mm (Mionnet scale 6–7); c 1550–74.
obv: Reichsapfel: nonsensical legend BOMDIBOA-.....BADMIBOAMIA
rev: HANS:SCHVLTES[:N]ORMBER: – three lys and three crowns arranged alternatively around a rose.

Fairly worn with surface corrosion deposits. Provenance: from an area of post-monastic disturbance outside the lower end of the East range.

50 German copper jetton of Hans Laufer of Nuremberg; diameter 23mm (Mionnet scale 6); c 1607–45.
obv: +GOTES+SEGEN+MACHT+REICH – three open crowns and three lys arranged alternatively around a rose within an inner circle of rose-pattern.
rev: +HANS*LAVFER*IN*NVRMBER – Reichsapfel within double tressure of three curves and three angles set alternatively, all within an inner circle of rose-pattern.

Similar to Barnard 222 and pl XXXIII, no 82 but slightly smaller and with different legends. Little wear. Provenance: riverside walk, Period V.

4.6 CERAMIC MATERIAL
George Haggarty & Robert Will

The ceramic material comprised more than 1100 sherds, the earliest perhaps dating from the first quarter of the 12th century. The assemblage has been extensively examined by Eoin Cox and the fabrics categorized employing the same criteria used to catalogue the pottery from the 1975/76 excavations at Kelso Abbey (Cox 1984, 381–95). This research has formed the basis of the present report. Of the range of fabrics found at Jedburgh, some bear close comparison with those retrieved from Kelso.

Because of widespread disturbances over much of the site, this report has concentrated on several contexts that are, on the evidence of their stratigraphical locations and on the basis of associated coins and jettons, chronologically secure. The two principal contexts that were examined were ditch 928 (illus 11; 12), infilled in the second or third quarter of the 12th century (although some later material was recovered from soils that had slumped into the top of the feature), and layers of midden material deposited in a basement (Room 6) at the S end of the East range, probably between the mid-14th and late 15th centuries.

DESCRIPTION AND DISCUSSION

The pottery can be divided into four main categories: Scottish East coast white gritty ware; coarse redwares; late medieval green glazed wares; and imports.

WHITE GRITTY WARE

Much has been written about the Scottish East coast white gritty ware, particularly about the problems of tracing the location(s) of its manufacture, its distribution and its dating (Brooks 1980; Cox 1984; Haggarty 1984; Crowdy 1986). The white gritty-type wares recovered from Jedburgh Abbey can be tentatively sub-divided into two main groups: a general white gritty ware; and an easily identified local variation which accounts for approximately 30% of the total assemblage.

General white gritty wares

Many of the jugs within this group have a slight orange-pink hue, the result of a red slip. The slip is overlain by a clear lead glaze which sometimes includes specks of copper, giving a dappled red and green pattern (illus 84, no 80). Many of these sherds were decorated with a variety of incised designs.

Local white gritty wares

The presence of this local material tends to support the view that a white gritty-type ware was produced in the Tweed valley from the mid-12th century (Haggarty 1984, 397; for a description of these wares see Cox 1984). In general, the vessels produced from this fabric were distinctive, straight-sided pots with flat bases and pronounced rilling on the sides. Extensive fuming on the bases and sides of the vessels has led to their being interpreted as cooking pots.

Geologically similar fabrics have been found at Berwick, Hawick and the Hirsel near Coldstream, while typologically similar vessels have been found at other locations, including Elgin, Inverness, Aberdeen and Edinburgh. Hence, although the fabric may be specific to the area, the vessel forms are not.

The white gritty fabric also occurs in a reduced state and, although it has been termed 'Reduced Gritty' by Crowdy (1986), it is merely the method of firing, deliberate or otherwise, and not the clay source that is different.

COARSE REDWARES

Another important type of pottery was represented by a group of sherds, composed of various coarse, gritty, red fabrics, which pre-dated the white gritty wares (above). Although no complete profiles were recovered, the fuming on the vessels suggests that they too were cooking pots. The geological evidence suggests that some of these fabrics are of local or Northumbrian origin while some are similar to material retrieved from a kiln of possible 12th-century date at Newcastle (E Cox pers comm).

These redwares are uncommon in Scotland although a few sherds from an apparently early, but undated, drain at Kelso Abbey may be of similar origin (Cox 1984, 394) to those recovered from Jedburgh. One of the sherds from Kelso (ibid, illus 21, no 51 (fabric 6)) has the same type of cross-hatched design as does no 26 (illus 82) from Jedburgh. The possibility that there was a pre-white ware tradition, linked to production sites south of the border, may be an indication that the site of Jedburgh Abbey was occupied immediately prior to the arrival of the Augustinian canons in c 1138.

LATE MEDIEVAL GREEN GLAZED WARES

Late medieval to post-medieval green glaze, which has been discussed elsewhere (Haggarty 1980), occurs in both oxidised and reduced forms. Caldwell & Dean (1981) have identified at least one production site for this material at Throsk, near Stirling, although there must certainly have been other kilns elsewhere producing this type of ware. The Jedburgh examples appear to have more in common with northern English material, for example bung-hole cisterns, than with Scottish forms such as those retrieved from the 1977–78 excavation at Stirling Castle (Haggarty 1980).

Some of this pottery was found within disturbed contexts, probably as a result of large-scale demolition, stone quarrying and intermittent post-monastic occupation of the site. A substantial amount of this material was also recovered from a midden within Room 6 which, although stratigraphically secure, represents deposition from the mid-14th to the late-15th century.

IMPORTS

Scarborough-type wares are represented by eleven sherds. All other non-Scottish earthenware comprise a mere six sherds from unidentified sources. German stonewares are represented by three sherds of Seigburg and Langerwehe wares, one sherd of Frechen ware and two conjoining sherds from a Martincamp flask of late 15th-/early 16th-century date. A near complete fragmented, yellow tin-glazed drug jar, of small Albarello-type shape and possibly Anglo-Dutch in origin, was also recovered from the excavation.

18TH–20TH CENTURY WARES

This assemblage represents a wide range of objects from both Scottish and English factories as well as from potteries working on a much smaller scale. The material comprises mainly roof tiles, drainage pipes and domestic wares, the latter represented by plates, dishes, cups, storage jars, bottles, flagons and tea pots. No porcelain or other fine quality 18th-century wares and only a few small fragments of tin-glaze and slip wares were recovered.

Unfortunately, because of the similarities in the produce of many factories and the small size of the sherds retrieved, only a few fragments can be attributed to specific potteries. For example, white earthenware, being common to most 19th-century potteries, is particularly difficult to ascribe to a specific kiln site and, without a maker's mark or a distinctive pattern, they cannot be identified. Similarly, some types of red earthenware vessels, although peculiar to Scotland, may have been produced at a number of different sites.

CATALOGUE OF ILLUSTRATED POTTERY

LOCAL COARSE REDWARES (illus 82)

1 Cooking pot: everted rim; reduced grey interior; burning on both surfaces; topsoil.

2 Cooking pot: everted rim; heavily burnt around the rim; Period II, occupation of timber structures.

3 Cooking pot: everted rim; smoke blackened; as no 2.

4 Cooking pot: flattened rim; reduced grey core; pronounced rilling; as no 2.

5 Cooking pot: rectangular rim; Period IV, riverside surfaces.

6 Cooking pot: everted square rim; smoke blackened around the rim; as no 2.

7 Cooking pot: everted rim; reduced grey core; slight smoke blackening; as no 2.

8 Cooking pot: everted rim; thumbed pie crust decoration around the rim; slight smoke blackening on the interior; as no 2.

9 Cooking pot: everted square rim; sooting around the interior; as no 2.

10 Cooking pot: everted rim forming a lip on its inside; slight burning; as no 2.

11 Cooking pot: everted rim; reduced grey core; as no 2.

12 Cooking pot: upright square rim; thumbed decoration on the top and bottom of the rim; reduced grey core; Period II, midden from timber structures.

13 Cooking pot: everted rim; heavily burnt to grey/black; Period II, occupation of timber structures.

14 Cooking pot: everted square rim; smoke blackened; Period II, midden from timber structures.

15 Cooking pot: rectangular rim; heavily reduced and burnt; Period II, occupation of timber structures.

16 Cooking pot: everted rim; reduced core; Period IV; Chapter house.

17 Base angle: flat base with pronounced rilling; reduced core; smoke blackened on interior and exterior; as no 15.

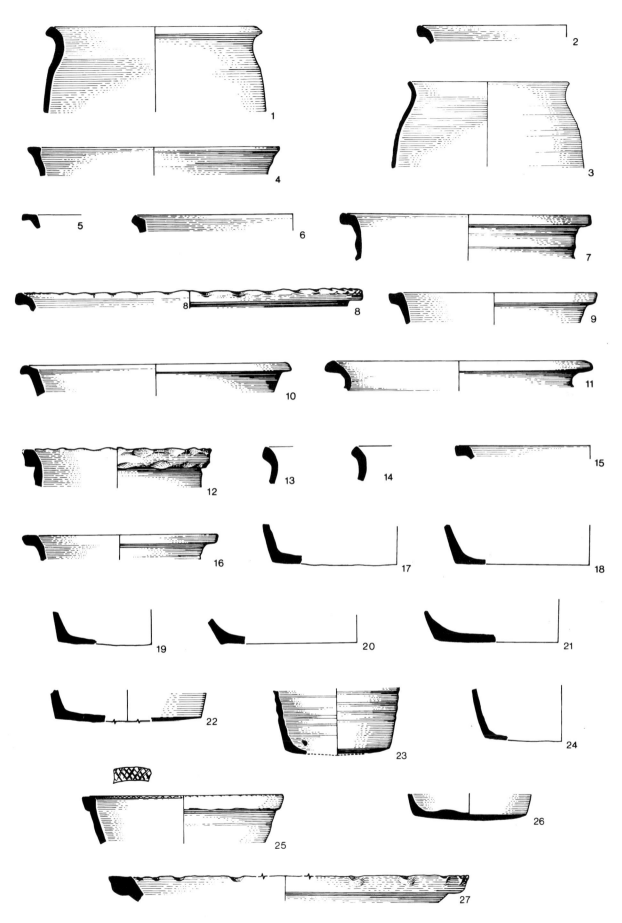

Illus 82
Pottery: local coarse red wares (scale 1:3).

18 Base angle: flat base; reduced grey core; splashes of clear glaze on the exterior;
Period IV; Room 12.

19 Base angle: flat base; reduced grey core;
Period IV; Chapter house, fill of Grave 17.

20 Base angle: sagging base; score/notch on the underside; smoke blackened;
as no 15.

21 Base angle: flat base; reduced core; scored on the interior;
as no 13.

22 Base angle: flat base; heavily burnt on exterior;
Period ?III; outside East range.

23 Base angle: straight sided cooking pot; sagging base; smoke blackened on exterior; pronounced rilling;
Period II; fill of sewage ditch 928.

24 Base angle: straight sided cooking pot; pronounced rilling; splash of clear glaze on base;
Period II; fill of sewage ditch 928.

25 Cooking pot: square rim; cross-hatched design along the top; reduced core;
Period V; Room 17.

26 Base angle: sagging base;
Period II; fill of sewage ditch 928.

27 Cooking pot: everted rim with thumb decoration around the rim; heavily reduced core;
Period V; Room 6.

LOCAL WHITE GRITTY WARE (illus 83)

28 Cooking pot: rounded rim; reduced core; smoke blackened;
Period II, midden from timber structures.

29 Cooking pot: complete profile of straight sided cooking pot;
Period II; fill of sewage ditch 928.

30 Cooking pot: everted rim; burnt black;
Period II, occupation of timber structures.

31 Cooking pot: everted rim; slight burning;
as no 30.

32 Cooking pot: rounded rim; smoke blackened;
Period ?II/III; outside East range, fill of Grave 18.

33 Cooking pot: everted rim; reduced core; smoke blackened;
Period II, preparation of SW of site.

34 Cooking pot: rounded rim from a globular pot; smoke-blackened;
as no 30.

35 Cooking pot: flat rim from a globular pot; smoke blackened;
as no 30.

36 Cooking pot: square rim;
as no 2.

37 Cooking pot: club rim;
Period II/III; redeposited midden material outside S end of East range.

38 Base angle: flat base; smoke blackened;
as no 30.

39 Base angle: flat base; smoke blackened;
as no 30.

40 Base angle: flat base; smoke blackened;
as no 30.

41 Base angle: flat base;
Period V; outside Chapter house.

42 Base angle: flat base; reduced core; smoke blackened;
as no 30.

43 Base angle: reduced to grey; smoke blackened;
as no 30.

44 Base angle: slightly sagging base;
Period II/III; redeposited midden material outside S end of East range.

45 Cooking pot: everted rim; reduced core; yellow/green glaze;
Period II; Chapter house.

46 Cooking pot: square rim;
Period II, drain fill.

47 Decorated body sherd: reduced core; dark green/brown glaze; inscribed line decoration;
Period ?; upper fill or slump at top of sewage ditch 928.

48 Decorated neck sherd: reduced core; dark green/brown glaze; decorated with three cordons;
Period ?; upper fill or slump at top of sewage ditch 928.

49 Decorated body sherd: reduced core; inscribed cross decoration;
Period II/III; redeposited midden material outside S end of East range.

50 Decorated body sherd: reduced on interior; incised linear decoration;
Period ?II; Room 5.

51 Cresset, or spike, lamp: ceramic lamps are rare in Britain and most of the known examples are of 11th- or 12th-century dates (Jennings 1981, 21). A glazed example from Inverness has been dated tentatively to the mid-14th century (Wordsworth 1982, 367).
Period II; fill of 12th-century sewage ditch 928.

52 Cup/flask: rounded rim; green glaze; heavily burnt;
Period II/III; redeposited midden material outside S end of East range.

53 Jug: club rim; reduced core;
Period ?III; disturbance below Room 12.

54 Everted rim sherd;
topsoil.

55 Cooking pot: club rim with cordon; reduced core; splash of clear glaze;
Period ?III; disturbance below Room 12.

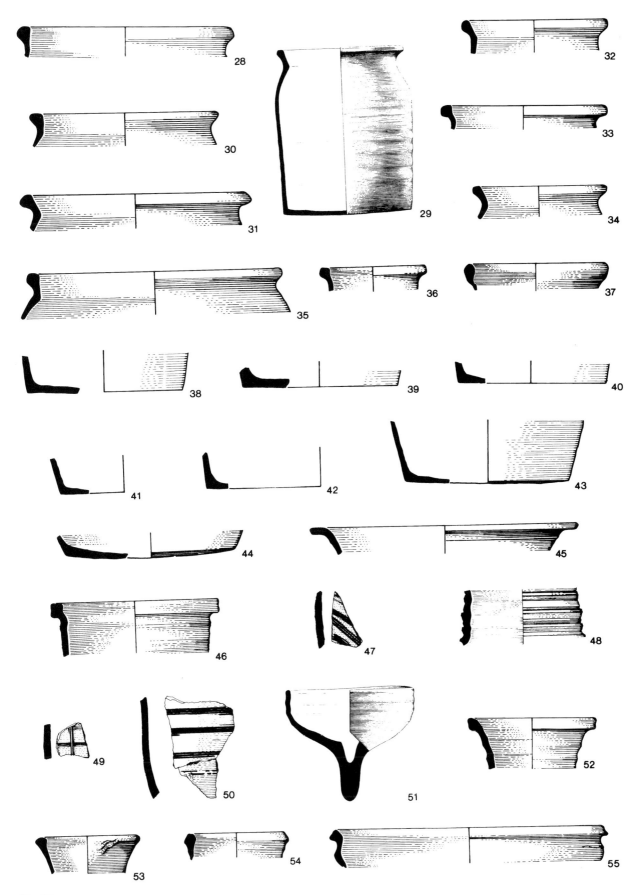

Illus 83
Pottery: local white gritty wares (scale 1:3).

Illus 84
Pottery: miscellaneous decorated vessels (scale 1:3).

MISCELLANEOUS DECORATED VESSELS (illus 84)

56   Jug: club rim with scar for grooved strap handle; sandy fabric with a reduced core; green glaze;
Period ?III; disturbance below Room 12.

57   Decorated body sherd, possibly from a face mask jug: incised design; white gritty fabric with reduced core; thick green glaze;
Period IV; Room 12.

58   Sherd from tubular spout: white gritty fabric; yellow/green glaze on exterior;
Period IV; Chapter house.

59   Sherd from pipkin leg: pointed hole into leg; white gritty fabric with reduced core; light green glaze on exterior;
topsoil.

60   Jug: square rim with scar for strap handle; green glaze on exterior;
Period III; occupation of Structure 8.

61   Base angle: redware with reduced core; purple slip with green glaze;
Period IV; Chapter house.

62   Small jug/flask: rounded rim; redware with reduced core; green/brown glaze on interior; very finely made;
Period II; fill of beam slot in Timber Structure 2.

63   Body sherd with attached rod handle: redware with reduced core; purple slip with green/brown glaze;
Period IV; Chapter house.

64   Decorated body sherd: incised parallel line design; redware; orange/brown glaze;
Period ?; upper fill or slump at top of sewage ditch 928.

65   Decorated body sherd: incised wavy line design; redware with reduced core; green/brown glaze;
Period ?; upper fill or slump at top of sewage ditch 928.

66   Body sherd with terminal for grooved strap handle; green/brown glaze;
Period ?; upper fill or slump at top of sewage ditch 928.

67   Jug: club rim with possible lid setting; highly decorated cordon with continuous thumbing and vertical incised line design; green/brown glaze;
Period III; Room 6 midden.

68   Decorated jug neck with scar for strap handle: (very similar to 67) pronounced cordon with thumbed band and incised vertical design; green glaze on both sides;
Period III; Room 6 midden.

69   Pipkin leg: a hole has been pushed into the fabric on the interior; orange/green glaze on both surfaces;
Period III; Room 6 midden.

70   Sherd from a bridge spout with rim: applied decoration survived as scars beneath the spout; green/brown glaze;
Period III; Room 6 midden.

71   Plain strap handle: incised line decoration; brown/green glaze;
Period III; Room 6 midden.

72   Plain strap handle: incised line decoration; brown/green glaze;
Period III; Room 6 midden.

73   Plain strap handle: brown glaze;
Period III; Room 6 midden.

74   Grooved strap handle: green glaze;
Period III; Room 6 midden.

75   Plain strap handle: green/brown glaze;
Period III; Room 6 midden.

76   Base sherd: base 90% complete; splash of clear glaze;
Period III; Room 6 midden.

77   Upright jug rim: possibly lipped for a lid; green glaze;
Period III; Room 6 midden.

78   Base angle: heavily reduced; green glaze;
Period III; Room 6 midden.

79   Base angle: heavily reduced; green glaze;
Period III; Room 6 midden.

80   Complete profile of jug: flattened rim; decoration of horizontal incised bands; strap handle with incised decoration; orange fabric with reduced areas; brown/green glaze on exterior;
Period III; abandonment of Structure 9.

4.7 STONE SCULPTURE
Dennis Gallagher

DESCRIPTION AND DISCUSSION

THE CROSS-SHAFT FRAGMENT

The fragment of a cross-shaft (illus 85a, b), with its deep confident carving and firm moulding, is an example of late Bernician work of the 9th or early 10th century. The form of the spiral vine scroll on Face A is derived, in its general form, from the earlier work of the Hexham school (Cramp 1974, 135) and may be compared with another fragment of vine scroll ornament, also from Jedburgh, which has been described by Cramp (1983, 270). However, Face A is unlike that fragment in its details: it lacks

Illus 85
Stone sculpture 1: cross-shaft fragment: a) Face A; b) Face B.

the distinctive fruit clusters typical of Hexham and is a product of a more generalised Northumbrian school. The trilobed berries, the lack of leaves and the tendency towards overlapping foliage elements are derived from the deep, tangled foliage seen on work from Jarrow and Rothbury. A cross-shaft from Norham, dated by Cramp to the second quarter of the 9th century, has the same stylistic treatment of the vine scroll and would seem to provide a closer link, geographically and historically, with Jedburgh (Cramp 1978, 12 and pl 1.7; Cramp 1984, 208–9 and pl 203, 1157–9). However, the Norham shaft has a complex design: a form closer to that of Jedburgh is found on a simpler cross-shaft fragment from Hulne Priory, dated by Cramp to the first half of the 9th century (Cramp 1984, 193–4 and pl 188.1033–7).

The simple, two-strand plait interlace on Faces B and D is found on other pieces from Jedburgh. It is used on two fragments of probable 10th-century date, originally perhaps part of a cross-shaft but now reconstructed as the sides of a tomb cover (RCAHMS 1956, 208–9 and pl 260; Cramp 1983, 283–4; Sharratt & Sharratt 1985, pl 99). A similar form of simple plait occurs on the sides of another Jedburgh fragment, of late 9th- or early 10th-century date, which is illustrated by Cramp (1983, fig 118 a–b). This same piece has one wide face which, although at present facing a wall and not easily viewed, is very similar to the interlace of Face C.

THE DOUBLE-SIDED CRUCIFIXION SLAB

The slab (illus 86) had been reused within a late medieval rubble infill to the SE of Room 11 which, together with its incomplete state, makes its original function difficult to ascertain. Furthermore, the top of the slab is missing and its original form remains unknown. Although use as an item of furniture or similar fitting cannot be ruled out, it was more likely a grave marker. The figures on Face B were probably meant to be viewed upright, which would make the slab an erect, rather than recumbent, monument.

Only a few such grave markers have been found *in situ*, some of which were recovered from the 1920s excavations at Whitby Abbey (Cramp 1984, pl 247, 1370). The Jedburgh slab is similar in size and cross form to that from a recently-excavated, round-headed grave marker of 11th-century date from Newcastle (Cramp 1984, pl 249, 1376). Crosses with narrow V-shaped arm pits were common in Northumbria during the 11th century (Cramp 1984, 8), the concentric ring decoration being a common motif of the period and found on a similar form of cross from Corbridge (Cramp 1984, pl 238, 1349–51). The stone may, however, belong to the general Celtic tradition of crosses seen on Pictish monuments and continuing in southern Scotland on slabs such as that from Kinneil (Hunter 1967, fig 9).

Illus 86
Stone sculpture 2 (face A): probable
10th-century grave slab, depicting
Christ in majesty.

The iconography of the slab may best be interpreted as that of the Last Judgement. If the pyramidal forms on the lower panel represent flames then the right of the scene could show the saved and the left the damned. The figure on the extreme right raises his arms in adoration, a comparable pose to that of King Edgar on f.2b of the New Minster Charter (BL Cotton MS Vespasian A. viii) who gazes upwards towards Christ in Majesty. The upper panel apparently shows Christ on the cross with arms outstretched in the manner of contemporary, triumphal crucifixions. Alternatively, the scene may be of Domesday with Christ being revealed simultaneously with the cross – a frequent theme in early medieval Christian thought and one which is described in Cynewulf's Domesday, where '. . . The lofty cross, set upright as a sign of sovereignty, will summon the crowd of men into His presence . . .'

The occurrence of this image in literature has been discussed by Bailey (1980, 162–70), with particular reference to the Viking sculpture of northern England. A slab from Addingham, Yorkshire (Bailey 1980, fig 40) has a simpler form of the Jedburgh scheme of iconography, with two figures under the cross. A closer parallel may be found on a grave-marker of late 9th-century date from Lindisfarne which can also be interpreted as depicting Domesday (Bailey 1980, pl 48; Cramp 1984, pl 21, 1132–4). A cross-shaft fragment from Lindisfarne, of late 9th- or early 10th-century date, has also been interpreted by Cramp as depicting the Day of Judgement (Cramp 1984, 195–6 and pl 1050–51). This fragment, like that from Jedburgh, has a basic composition of Christ in Majesty accompanied by the Cross and with secondary figures. Cramp has noted the 'rather lumpy figure style' with 'wedge-shaped heads' and has compared the Lindisfarne fragment with sculpture from sites in south-west Scotland, such as Barochan (Allen & Anderson 1903, 3, 454–7) and Cambusnethan (Allen & Anderson 1903, 3, 461–2). The Jedburgh slab is cruder in execution than that from Lindisfarne and, whilst in the same sculptural tradition, is likely to be a little later in date. Its grooved technique may be loosely connected with the Viking-period sculpture of the Solway basin (Bailey 1980, 223–9).

The upper figure of Face B appears to be standing on the head of the lower figure. The latter has a leg held at an angle that bears some resemblance to squatting, bound figures found in Viking-period sculpture from northern England, eg from Gainford (Cramp 1984, pl 63, 297). The panel may represent Christ crushing evil.

FRAGMENT OF INTERLACE

This fragment (which is not illustrated) could belong to a monument with a face of several planes, as is found on late Pictish slabs such as that from Cossins (Allen & Anderson 1903, 3, 216). Two of the faces bear fragmentary decoration, one consisting of two rings with diagonal strands crossing what may be a spiral, bordered on one side by flat-band moulding the other decorated with a three strand plait and bordered on one side by flat-band moulding. However, the rebated surface suggests an architectural fragment, perhaps part of a door jamb or a fragment of furnishing, such as a screen or bench end. The probable closed circuit interlace of Face A can be compared to similar examples of Bernician work, such as the cross-shaft fragments from Lindisfarne (Cramp 1984, pl 189, 1044; pl 190, 1050), and are likely to date from the late 9th or early 10th century.

THE MERELLES BOARD

The merelles board (illus 87) was recovered from Room 6, the construction of which may be dated by its architectural details to the mid-13th century. The discovery of merelles boards incised on stones which were reused in medieval walling has led to the suggestion that the game was popular among medieval masons (Robertson, 1966, 322), although there is no particular reason why the occupants of a building could not have used such stones, which would be freely available during the building campaign, for this purpose.

Merelles is a game for two players in which each player attempts to place three of his own counters in a line, thus gaining one of his opponent's counters. The game of merelles, or nine-men's morris as it was also known, is of ancient origin (Shirreff 1953, 111–15): a similar board game has been found on Viking sites in Scotland, eg Buckquoy, Orkney (Ritchie 1977, 198–9). The name, merelles, derives from the Old French, merel, or counter; the word morris being a further corruption of that word. It is thought that the game was introduced to Britain from France in the 11th century and boards have been found in a late 12th-century context at Castle Acre Castle (Hinton 1982, 260). A number survive on the stonework of monasteries; there is an undated example on a step at Furness Abbey (Kelly 1926, 227); and others on the cloister benches at Gloucester and Salisbury Cathedrals (Micklethwaite 1892, 325).

Two other merelles boards have been recorded in Scotland, both from monastic sites. One was incised on a foundation stone in the N wall of the 13th-century nave at Dryburgh Abbey (Robertson 1966, 321–2; Richardson & Tabraham 1987, 8–9), a context similar in date to the Jedburgh board. The other example was found reused in post medieval walling at Arbroath Abbey (Robertson 1966, 322–3).

Illus 87
Merelles board carved in stone; found within the core of the W wall of the East range.

CATALOGUE

1   Part of a cross-shaft (illus 85a, b)

Dimensions: max height 270mm × max width 210mm × max depth 95mm

Stone type: creamy medium-grained sandstone, probably Carboniferous. Stained reddish purple.

Condition: broken, but unworn.

Provenance: unstratified within the South cloister alley

Description: a tapering shaft, edged by a single roll moulding.

Face A: One volute, and part of another, of a spiral scroll with short curling tendrils and trilobed berries.

Face B: Simple two-strand plait.

Face C: A turned pattern of interlace with breaks and diagonal strands (cf Cramp 1984, xxxiv; fig 16C).

Face D: Two-strand plait, as Face B.

2   Slab (illus 86)

Dimensions: max height 725mm × max width 465mm × max depth 170mm

Stone type: cream-coloured sandstone, probably Carboniferous.

Condition: broken and worn.

Provenance: reused within a dry-stone wall between Rooms 8 and 11

Description: Two faces with carving survive, although they are incomplete. The carving is partly in a grooved technique, with incised details, and partly humped, the latter being confined to the figural details.

Face A: In the centre is a crucifixion within a square panel. A frontal Christ has arms rigidly outstretched and a wedge-shaped head with incised features. The feet rest on the lower frame of the panel. Details on hands, feet and loincloth are indicated with incised lines, similar lines appearing on the sides of the torso and head. These may represent ribs and beard; they also serve to emphasise relief. The groove behind the head has been widened to form a halo which is decorated with radiating incised lines.

The cross on which the figure of Christ is superimposed has V-shaped arms terminating on the edge of the panel. Incised, double concentric circles decorate the field between each cross arm; each is compass-drawn and has a prominent centre point. Six single incised circles form a horizontal row above the panel.

Below the panel there is a figural scene. On the extreme left is a head, with incised features, which is apparently detached although it may be connected with the limb outstretched above it. Below the head is a circular form, possibly another head, and, to the right, a standing figure with outstretched arms. The sides of the torso have incised lines, similar to those on the figure of Christ, and two lines demarcate the legs from the torso.

To the right of this figure are three tall pyramidal shapes decorated with inscribed lines. Under the two right-most pyramidal shapes, and extending towards a damaged area further to the lower right, is a limb, the details of the hand indicated by incised lines. Two figures occupy the right side of this panel. Both have facial features and hands indicated by incised lines. One of the figures, of which the lower part is missing, leans diagonally to the left with an arm outstretched. Of the figure on the extreme right, only the head and arms survive. Its head, which has incised features, is uplifted and gazes towards the figure of Christ. The arms are raised and the details of the hands are drawn with incised lines.

Face B: Two figures survive on this face, one apparently standing on the head of the other. Both have facial features drawn with incised lines. The upper figure, which is frontal with arms outstretched and downturned, has a halo decorated with radiating incised lines and may represent Christ. The lower figure has a frontal head which is slightly inclined to the right. The body appears to be in profile with bent arm and upturned leg, both perhaps bound behind the back, although damage to the figure and adjoining fields makes interpretation difficult. The area surrounding the figure has been dressed smooth and has no border.

3   Fragment, possibly architectural (not illustrated)

Dimensions: max height 145mm × max width 170mm ×
max depth 140mm

Stone type: creamy coloured, probably Carboniferous sandstone.

Condition: broken and worn

Description: The fragment consists of a main face of two panels, one of which is rebated, a smoothly dressed face and another bearing slight remains of decoration.

Face A i: A fragmentary interlace design, consisting of two rings with diagonal strands crossing what may be a spiral, bordered on one side by flat-band moulding.

Face A ii: A panel rebated 30mm from Face A i, decorated with a three strand plait and bordered on one side by flat-band moulding.

Face B: Smoothly dressed with no decoration.

Face C: Badly damaged, but with a narrow rectangular field of ornament, possibly interlace, bordered by flat-band moulding.

4   The Merelles board (illus 87)

Dimensions: 24mm × 23mm

Stone type: fine-grained red sandstone.

Provenance: core of the W wall of Room 6

Description: one face crudely incised with three concentric squares linked by a line on each side.

4.8 WINDOW GLASS
C Pamela Graves
(illus 88)

The excavation yielded a substantial amount of window glass (about 270 fragments) – one of the largest collections from a Scottish monastic or ecclesiastical site. Most other Scottish material was deposited in museums during the last century although it is still available for comparison (Graves 1985).

Examples have been identified of both standard manufacturing processes: the cylinder process which produced broad, sheet glass; and the spun process which produced discs. However, it has not been possible to equate either method, by context or decoration, with any particular date-range. No evidence has been found of a production site for medieval Scottish glass. White glass may have been brought in from England where there is both archaeological and documentary evidence for production; coloured glass was probably imported from continental Europe. Coloured glass from the Rhineland was imported to Hull and Newcastle via the Hanseatic ports (Knowles 1936, 47, n2). The Exchequer Rolls for Scotland record imported window glass from the 14th century onwards at Blackness, Dundee and Leith; customs accounts imply that the cargoes were supplied by Flemish, Gascon and Lombard merchants (eg Burnett 1880a, 222; Burnett 1880b, 621). There can be little doubt that window glass was imported in this way during the 13th and possibly the 12th centuries.

At Jedburgh, there are very few examples of coloured glass: three pieces of green and turquoise-blue pot

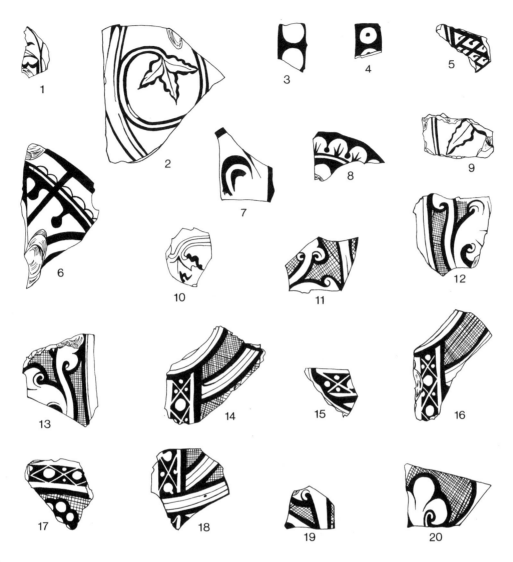

Illus 88
Painted window glass (scale 1:2).

metal; and only one fragment of flashed ruby. The majority of fragments are now opaque through weathering and prolonged burial in the soil although much of the original paintwork can still be discerned. This is mostly grisaille glass: predominantly white, painted with a paste of metal (iron and lead) oxides mixed with gum arabic and sometimes ground glass. When fired, the enamel turns red-brown although against the light it appears black.

LOCATION, DISTRIBUTION AND DESCRIPTION OF GLASS

THE CHAPTER HOUSE AREA

The variation in design reflects the residual nature of many of the deposits in this area. Only three pieces had cross-hatching which was widely spaced and very crude in execution. The majority of fragments were found within the backfilled robber trench of the E wall of the Period III Chapter house. These included a portion of naturalistic ivy leaf on a curling stem (no 1), dated to between the late 13th century and c 1330. The same design is found on fragment no 2 from Room 6 and on nos 9 and 10 which were retrieved from disturbed levels. This sort of grisaille might have filled the background to geometric shapes enhanced with colour, as at Chartham parish church, Kent. The panels of grisaille might alternate with heraldic, figural or narrative glass in band windows, as at Merton College Chapel, Oxford (c 1289–1328), York Minster Chapter house (c 1285) or the nave aisles at York Minster (early 14th century). There were beaded borders of ubiquitous 13th- to 14th-century design (eg nos 3 and 4), which may have acted as decorated fillets to geometric patterns set on the grisaille. A small piece painted with lozenges in reserve (no 5) may be from a border; although similar designs have been used as detail on architecture or furniture in figural and narrative glass, eg pegged tiles on roofs. Both nos 6 and 9 (the latter from a disturbed level) may have been details from an architectural canopy, perhaps the cusped underside. The paint on no 7 has chipped off; originally the curves would have extended as lines representing the folds in hanging drapery of the 13th or 14th century. Nos 6, 7 and 8 are all consistent with a banded glazing scheme.

ROOM 6

Of the painted fragments, several had cross-hatching and one very large piece (no 2), coloured yellow-brown by corrosion but originally white, had a complete ivy leaf on curling stem. This piece is dated to between the late 13th century and c 1330 and can be compared to nos 6, 7 and 8 above (Westlake 1881, pl LXXXV).

THE W AND SW AREA

The deposits in this area represent the demolition of Structure 9, possibly in advance of the erection of Structure 14. This, the largest assemblage (91 fragments) of glass from the site was retrieved from a complex series of tipped deposits infilling the area around the Period IV S wall of Structure 14.

The earliest of these tips contained several examples of fleshy foliage and trefoils of varying size (nos 11, 12 and 13). There were also a number of pieces sharing the same fine cross-hatching and portions of curving line, suggesting the stalks of trefoils, in conjunction with a linear stickwork pattern of lozenges, triangles and circles (nos 14, 15 and 16). Fragment no 17 has a cluster of berries on a cross-hatched ground beside the stickwork border pattern. This kind of grisaille is earlier than the naturalistic ivy forms found in the Chapter house, and would have formed lancets in patterns similar to those still visible at Salisbury Cathedral (c 1220–58) or York Minster (c 1250).

Fragments of the same type of trefoil, with thin lines or spurs at the junction of head and stem, were found in tipped deposits both pre-dating (no 20) and post-dating (nos 18 and 19) the main building phase of Period II.

DISCUSSION

The largest assemblage, from the SW part of the site, had the greatest proportion of plain or opaque glass to painted fragments. The cohesion of the stylistic evidence suggests that all the fragments from this area came from the same window or from a range of similar, contemporary windows. The carefully executed painting, with very fine details in the cross-hatching and stickwork, suggests high quality workmanship. Indeed, the quality surpasses that of any other grisaille known in Scotland, with the exception of material excavated from Elgin Cathedral and Spynie Palace, Moray (Lewis forthcoming). It is not known if there were indigenous Scottish glass-painters in the 13th century. However, there are stylistic parallels between a lot of Scottish grisaille, such as material from Cambuskenneth Abbey (Augustinian) and the Border houses of Melrose Abbey (Cistercian) and Coldingham Priory (Benedictine) and glass found in the north of England at the Abbey of Newminster (Cistercian) and the Priories of Brinkburn (Augustinian), Durham Cathedral (Benedictine) and Tynemouth (Benedictine). The precise, controlled paintwork on the Jedburgh pieces is similar to some of the material from Rievaulx Abbey (Cistercian).

There are two significant features of the Jedburgh grisaille: the fleshy foliage (eg nos 12 and 13); and the foliage stems crossing over the stickwork border on at least five fragments (eg nos 14, 15, 16 and 18). Rather than uniformly tight trefoils, the broad leaves are reminiscent of the curling acanthus leaves found in richly coloured borders at York Minster (late 12th century) (O'Connor & Haselock 1977, 324) and at Beverly Minster (1230s) (O'Connor 1989, 66–8, pl XIVb–g). This hybrid acanthus/trefoil form is seen in grisaille reset in the Chapter house vestibule at York Minster and in material excavated from Hickleton parish church, South Yorkshire (Graves forthcoming). There are also parallels in French grisaille, particularly glass from Saint Jean-aux-Bois (Day 1909, 142–45, fig 119). The second significant feature is the interlace of stem and stickwork fillet. At Salisbury, bands of coloured glass have scrolled foliage growing through them and crossing over in a similar manner (ibid, 142, fig 115). In French windows the fillets interlace although the foliage appears to grow beneath the fillets, seldom crossing over them.

There may have been a limited use of colour integral with the overall geometric design in these windows; perhaps with discrete panels of historiated coloured glass.

Stylistically, this glass appears to date from the period between the late 12th century and c 1260; excavation suggests that this material is derived from the destruction of Structure 9. The earliest date for the installation of the glass might be taken from the single fragment (no 20) retrieved from a tipped deposit pre-dating the main building phase of Period II. Structure 9 was built during Period II (1138–1297) and it is likely that this glass was installed during the middle of that period and that no 20 is an intrusive stray from the building's construction.

The glass from the East range contrasts with that from the W area of the site. One or two stylistically indeterminate fragments may have been contemporary with the glass from the W area although the varied designs imply band windows of the late 13th or early 14th centuries, with a far greater use of colour and figures. This would be in keeping with the importance of the Chapter house as the hub of the monastic community, where activities of central importance to the religious life took place. It is perhaps significant that the Chapter house of York Minster, perhaps the most renowned Augustinian church in the north of England, was glazed in this way. How far such considerations would influence a Scottish house in the midst of the Wars of Independence is uncertain. Furthermore, a survey of excavated and intact window glass does not seem to indicate a distinctive Augustinian form of glazing.

It is certainly not unusual to find evidence for glazing of different types and dates in different buildings within a monastic precinct, for each room had a specific purpose and relative importance. Finally, the nature of the bias in the excavated material from Jedburgh may be explained by post-destruction activity: the best glass might be sold and the poorest stripped of precious lead, as at Rievaulx (Knowles 1936, 46). A limited amount of coloured glass debris might be taken away for re-melting as cullet or for enamel.

4.9 VESSEL GLASS
Robin Murdoch

The great majority of the fragments recovered from the excavation were from liquor bottles (the term 'liquor' is preferred as a generic term as such vessels did not always hold wine). An examination of fragments showed that deposition differed markedly between the E and W sides of the site. A comparison of date distribution is outlined in Table 4 below.

There was some activity in both areas around 1700. The West range had considerable material from throughout the 18th century but almost nothing later than 1850; whereas very little of the East range assemblage dates from before the last quarter of the 18th century and over half of it post-dates 1850.

Small percentages from around 1700 do not necessarily represent modest activity, for very few bottles *per capita* were in use. Where there is a wide date range within a particular context this might suggest redeposition, perhaps resulting from the clearance of a wine cellar. Early wine cellars frequently had earth, sand or clay floors which would make the clearing of breakages difficult. It was also common to partake of a libation in the wine cellar, no doubt with an occasional inebriated catastrophe ensuing. The concentration of material, dated *c* 1775–*c* 1850, around the East range reflects the reuse of that area for housing in the 18th century.

The Vicinity of the East Range

(65 Datable Items)

Period	Percentage
Around 1700	6
1775-1825	38
Around 1850	18
Late 19th/20th century	38

The Vicinity of the Abbot's Hall

(95 Datable Items)

Period	Percentage
Around 1700	13
Solid 18th century	77
Around 1850	8
Around 1900	2

Table 4
Date distribution of vessel glass in the vicinity of the East range and the Abbot's Hall.

Very little amber or black glass was represented in the Jedburgh material although this is not unusual in a Scottish context, the latter probably reflecting the loyalty to claret north of the Border when England had turned to port in the early 1700s.

The early material was almost certainly manufactured in Leith. If, as seems likely, the Scottish industry suffered a recession in the early 18th century, bottles may have been imported thereafter from Newcastle although the hazardous journey over the Cheviots may have allowed Leith to retain its position as a distribution point.

4.10 LEATHER
Clare Thomas

Of the 180 pieces of leather retrieved, the majority were scraps with neither stitched nor cut edges although a few were identified as shoe fragments.

SHOES

Shoes form a small but important part of the assemblage. One almost complete sole survived, as did two foreparts and two seats. Uppers include the quarters of an ankle-boot, the front of the vamps of two other shoes and three heel-stiffeners.

All of the fragments are of turnshoe construction, where a single piece acts as outer sole and insole. The sole is joined to the grain-to-flesh stitching channel of the lasting margin of the upper by an edge-flesh channel, stitch length 4–8mm. The sole is stitched with the flesh side out, then turned inside out.

There is no evidence to suggest that rands (thin strips of leather) were enclosed between sole and upper to strengthen the seam. Fragments of uppers were stitched to each other with butted edge-flesh seams. Top edges and vertical edges of latchets were oversewn. Heel-stiffeners were attached by tunnel-stitching which could also be used to attach a lining. Three sole fragments have traces of tunnel-stitch holes for the attachment of clump repair soles.

SOLE STYLES

One sole (from Grave 10) is almost complete, with a long seat and a gently curved forepart ending in an oval top which is inclined inwards slightly. This was a very common medieval shape of sole, of 12th- to 14th-century date. It corresponds to Perth High Street Type 3, which came predominantly from contexts dating to the second half of the 13th century (Thomas 1987). Other parallels include material from Weoley Castle,

Birmingham (13th century) and the Custom House site, London (early to mid-14th century) (Oswald 1963, 132; Tatton-Brown 1975, 154–58).

UPPER STYLES

Within Grave 10 was part of a probable upper of one-piece design with a large fragment comprising vamp and quarters. This was the most common medieval way of cutting uppers, and dates from the 12th to the 14th century, as is exemplified at Perth High Street (Thomas 1987, Types A and B). No other evidence survived to suggest styles or methods of fastening.

MISCELLANEA

Miscellaneous items included two semi-circular fragments, one of which was probably part of a fastening. Two strips which had been folded once, and stitched where their edges met, were almost certainly bindings, perhaps for the top edge of a shoe or for the edge of a piece of clothing.

A large proportion of the leather consists of torn scraps with neither cut nor stitched edges. These 'scraps' might have been part of recognizable objects before deterioration and should not be regarded simply as waste from leather-working. The only definite suggestion of leather-working is a thick triangular offcut. This was characteristic waste from cutting-out of soles. As such, it could indicate the manufacture of new shoes from new leather or cobbling – the repair of old shoes and the manufacture of new shoes from reused leather.

4.11 TEXTILES
Thea Gabra-Sanders

Fragments of textile and cord were retrieved from the outer surface of the coffin uncovered in the choir of the abbey in 1990. The textile had been nailed to the coffin and decorative metalwork placed over it.

DESCRIPTION AND CATALOGUE

The textile had not been conserved before inspection and was still covered with clayey soils and sand and had fragments of wood and metal adhering to it.

At first sight the textile appeared to be a simple woollen one although a closer inspection revealed evidence of a yarn of cellulosic fibre which was once part of the material but which had since degraded. Microscopic examination showed that the remaining fibres were of wool, mostly red-brown in colour with a few coloured blue-green. Staining was so extensive, however, that the dyes cannot be identified without chemical analysis.

One basic weave – tabby (plain) weave – was represented and the fragment was woven from Z-spun woollen yarn in a single system. There was no evidence of a selvedge so it is uncertain whether the woollen yarn was warp or weft. The material was very matted on both sides.

The fragment of cord, retrieved from beneath a handle plate, was also degraded and very brittle. It comprised three loose strands which retained their original grey-brown coloration but which were no longer plied. Microscopic examination showed the fibres to be of cotton which, being a vegetable fibre, rarely survives on archaeological sites except under unusual conditions.

The cabled cord was plied from three Z-twisted strands, each strand consisting of approximately five S-plied yarns.

CATALOGUE

The systems are termed 1 and 2 as neither warp nor weft could be identified. In general the higher the thread count the finer the fabric.

1 Fragment of red-brown wool cloth, measuring 100 × 55mm and of tabby (plain) weave. System 1: Z-spun woollen yarn; 14 threads per 10mm. System 2: neither spin nor weave identified; approximately 15 threads per 10mm.

2 Fragment of cabled cotton cord, 30mm long and retaining its natural shade of grey-brown although it was degraded and very brittle. Originally twisted from three Z-twisted strands, each strand of 2mm width and consisting of approximately five S-plied yarns (?3Z?5S2Z).

DISCUSSION

Covering the lids of coffins was common until the 19th century, various materials such as cambric, baize, cotton velvet, Geneva and Utrecht velvet being used (J Litton pers comm). Thereafter French polishing became more fashionable.

The outer coverings of coffins recovered from the burial vaults of Christ Church, Spittalfields, London and dating between 1729 and 1859 were mostly of plain woven wool with a raised nap (Janaway 1990, 38) and, in all probability, originally dyed black.

4.12 CLAY TOBACCO PIPES

Dennis Gallagher

The Jedburgh assemblage can be divided chronologically into two groups. The first, and largest, group consists of pipes dated 1630–1730, the second predominantly from the period 1850–1950. There was a small amount of material from the early 19th century.

DISCUSSION

1630–1730

Scottish pipe-making during the first half of the 17th century was dominated by the monopoly of William Banks of Edinburgh, whose pipes were common throughout southern Scotland, many being found during excavations at Smailholm Tower, near Kelso (Gallagher 1988, 257–8). The number of pipes from Jedburgh predating 1660 is small but there was at least one bowl made by Banks. Holland was another major source during this early period and Dutch material has been found at Berwick (Davey 1982, 95) and further inland at Kelso (Gallagher 1987c, 281), although none has been identified from Jedburgh. There was a small amount of material from Newcastle/Gateshead, the main area of production in north-east England, and similar numbers have been retrieved from other Border sites.

After 1660 the main suppliers continued to be from the Edinburgh area although the new Glasgow industry was slowly establishing a foothold in the Borders. Several of the Jedburgh pipes are the work of Patrick

Crawford who was recorded as a pipe-maker in 1671, when he was working in Pleasance, Edinburgh. He was dead by 1696 although his widow continued to make pipes marked P/C until at least 1698 (Gallagher 1987a, 10). The Jedburgh bowls include three examples of the various stamps used by Crawford. One of these is a stamp of the highest quality and may reflect Crawford's close ties with various Edinburgh pewterers, whose hallmarks it resembles.

There was, however, a lack of care in the finishing of his pipes and, although all the Crawford bowls were burnished to give them a superficial appearance of high quality, the use of worn moulds, worn basal stamps and careless milling indicate that they were second-grade products.

The Crawford pipes are replaced chronologically by those marked D/M, which may be the products of David Montgomery of Tranent. Like Crawford, he supplied pipes to the Company of Scotland in 1696–7 although his produce was uncommon in the Edinburgh area. A bowl, marked D/B, typologically similar to Montgomery's, may be a product of David Banks of Leith who was recorded as active in 1705–06 (Gallagher 1987a, 11). Glasgow pipes are represented by a bowl of James Colquhoun and perhaps by one of John Aitken (Gallagher 1987b, 51–2).

The Jedburgh assemblage demonstrates the development of Scottish bowl forms. The typical mid-17th-century biconical shape of the William Banks bowl was superseded *c* 1660–70 by a taller bowl with narrow neck and S-shaped front profile. After *c* 1690 larger capacity bowls with straighter sides became popular. The precise mechanism of the trade in pipes to the Borders is unknown although they were probably bought by consumers through the local burghs rather than direct from Edinburgh.

POST 1800

During the first half of the 19th century the Borders were supplied mainly by makers in Edinburgh and Leith. The Jedburgh assemblage contains examples of the work of Thomas White, the most prominent of Edinburgh makers of this period. White's business finally closed in 1870 (Gallagher 1987d, 27) and the market was shared by smaller Edinburgh/Leith manufacturers and by the Berwick factory of Charles Tennant. After 1900 the main pipe manufacturers represented in the Border area are Charles Tennant and William Christie of Leith.

5

HUMAN BURIALS
Richard Grove

As well as two graves uncovered in the E end of the church, a total of 41 burials and over 5,000 disarticulated bones were excavated from within the East range or adjacent to it. One part-skeleton, retrieved from ditch 928, is thought to be a 12th-century lay burial, 26 graves appeared to be monastic and 15 post-dated the Reformation. Of the probable monastic inhumations, five were from the East cloister alley, three were located in stone-lined graves to the NE of the Chapter house and 17 were unearthed within the Chapter house. These comprised 12 stone-lined graves and five coffin burials.

A full account of all the human remains is contained within the archived site record.

A number of the monastic burials had been disturbed and their bones lost, displaced or damaged as a consequence. Most of this damage took place during the final re-organization of the Chapter house. The rebuilding of the E wall disturbed four graves, three of which (Graves 9, 10 and 11) were foreshortened and their skeletons replaced in disorganized states with some elements missing and miscellaneous bones from elsewhere added. The insertion of the Period IV central pier disturbed the two skeletons within stone-lined graves 4 and 5 although the disarticulated bones were replaced. In common with other graves, the relocated bones were in much better condition than those still *in situ*.

Another Chapter house grave, 8, was disturbed by a later coffin burial (Grave 13) and two others outwith the building had also suffered during later developments, Grave 28 in the East cloister alley and Grave 18 to the NE of the Chapter house.

PRESERVATION OF SKELETONS

The conditions dictating the state of preservation are complex. In general, the style of burial and the subsequent disturbance have the greatest influence although duration of burial is obviously an important factor. The latter point was demonstrated by the states of the post-Reformation skeletons which survived better than those from monastic levels. However, there were exceptions to this: in particular, the articulated remains within coffins and sarcophagi were in a much worse condition than the disarticulated bones recovered from earlier levels in the Chapter house. Many of the stone coffins survived intact, thus allowing airborne bacteria prolonged contact with the skeletons inside, whereas in Grave 18, where the sarcophagus had collapsed inwards covering the corpse with soil, the skeleton was well-preserved. In all but one case (Grave 18) the bones within sarcophagus burials were soft, eroded and cracked, and frequently discoloured grey or even black. The worst affected were those bones in contact with damp coffin bases.

Teeth tended to survive even when the jaw had rotted, probably because of their high mineral content. Foot bones also survived well, particularly in Graves 2, 4, 5, 7 and 13, having perhaps been protected by leather shoes (although the shoes from Graves 9, 10 and 11 seemed to offer little protection).

The condition of remains within wooden coffins was consistently poor. The bones were often crushed, probably by the weight of soil following the inward collapse of the coffins.

AGE AND SEX

The poor condition of the majority of skeletons restricted the number of criteria available to estimate the sex of individuals and their age at death (Brothwell 1981; Genoves 1969; Krogman 1962). In particular, the more fragile bones of the skull and pelvis, which provide the most reliable and greatest number of criteria, rarely survived intact. It is clear, however, that all the monastic burials were of adults, most of them being aged by means of their teeth although it was difficult to age individuals beyond 50.

PATHOLOGY

The condition of the skeletal remains has an obvious influence on the extent to which bones and teeth can be examined for evidence of disease. Even minor damage to the surface of bone can obscure pathological change and hence many skeletons exhibited no signs of disease.

Dental diseases were common. Out of a potential total of 736 teeth (including the third molars) from 23 individuals, 351 teeth were still in their sockets. However, although most would have been lost *ante mortem*, it is apparent that only an incomplete picture of dental diseases is possible.

Ten of the 17 individuals with some teeth surviving had carious lesions whereas the three which had almost complete dentitions (in Graves 2, 18 and 27) had none. Calculus was visible on skeletons within Graves 1, 3, 8, 13, 15, 18, 19, 20, 26 and 27 although its extent is often difficult to estimate because it chips off easily.

The most common post-cranial diseases were degenerative. The formation of spurs of bone (osteophytes) on vertebral bodies becomes increasingly common from the third decade of life (Nathan 1962, 258) and are frequently used as manifestations of age. For want of more reliable indicators, this method was used to age the corpse in the early ditch 928. Other degenerative diseases included: the formation of Schmorle's nodes (Schmorle & Junghanns 1971); those, such as osteoarthritis, that affect the synovial joints; and periostitis. There was one probable case of gout, perhaps caused by lead poisoning.

5.1 MONASTIC BURIALS

WITHIN THE CHAPTER HOUSE

The lack of meaningful stratigraphy, caused by the proximity of grave cuts to each other, made it difficult to work out the complete sequence of burials within the Chapter house (illus 89a, b). Without doubt, Grave 1 (illus 89b; 90) belonged to the building's initial phase of development (Period II) and several other graves certainly post-dated its final (Period IV) remodelling. However, although most of the remaining burials appeared to pre-date the Period IV developments, none could be assigned to a specific phase of the building's evolution. All seventeen graves were oriented E–W and most were found within the limits of the Period IV building.

PERIOD II

GRAVE 1 (illus 89b; 90)

The insertion of the Period IV E wall destroyed the W half of this grave which was situated directly below Grave 12. Its crude sarcophagus resembled those of Graves 2, 3 and 4 (described below) although it was situated at a level 0.7–0.8m beneath them.

Almost the whole skeleton survived although the bones were disarranged and most were damaged, having been re-interred together with some bones from at least two other individuals and a single fragment of a leather shoe. The individual was probably male, approximately 1.76m (5' 9") tall and aged 45+ at death. Degenerative change was evident in several of the vertebrae, there was slight osteophytosis in the limb bones and dental health was poor.

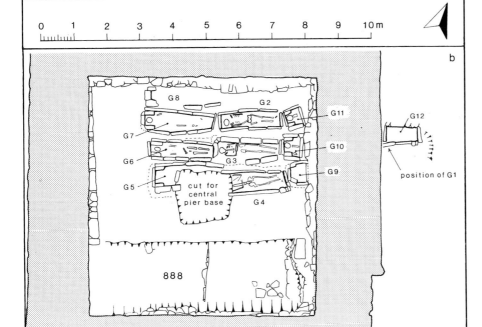

Illus 89
Chapter house burials: a) plan of stone-lined graves with capstones;
b) plan of burials showing central pier base and grave covers removed.

PERIODS III–IV

Of these graves, 11 contained stone sarcophagi and five retained evidence of wooden coffins. The stone-lined graves (illus 91) were divided into three groups:

A Three graves (2, 3 and 4) of simple construction, situated to the E and NE of the Period IV central pier.

B Four, more elaborately-constructed graves (5, 6, 7 and 8), to the W of group A.

C Graves 9, 10, 11 and 12, to the E of groups A and B. Similar in construction to the group B graves, these had been disturbed by the insertion of the E wall of the Period IV Chapter house.

Illus 90
Grave 12, overlying Grave 1; from
the S.

Illus 91
Partially excavated graves
within the Chapter house; from
the N.

Also described here is pit 1064 which perhaps represents the remains of one or more disturbed burials.

GROUP A – GRAVES 2, 3 AND 4

This group (colour illus VII) consisted of relatively simple sarcophagi constructed of the easily laminated, dark red sandstone that constitutes the local bedrock. The coffins were built of two or three panels per side and single stones at each end, all with smooth internal faces but with markedly coarser exteriors. The stones were bonded with mortar although some clay was also used in Grave 3.

GRAVE 2

Internally the sarcophagus measured 1.8m long, 0.3–0.35m deep and, although having a distinct curve, it was 0.44m wide over its entire length. This was the only coffin, other than that of Grave 12, to have a stone base, neither of which was pierced. The base of Grave 2 comprised two large slabs and one small stone. All of the 70mm-thick lining stones were intact but only three capstones were *in situ*, the fourth having collapsed inwards.

The skeleton was very badly decayed, the skull vault and a few foot bones being the only elements to survive reasonably intact. The skeleton was probably that of a male, 1.72m (5' 7.5") tall and, on the evidence of tooth wear, aged 25–35 years at death. There was no indication of pathological change. Nearby was some black organic matter, probably the decayed remains of an unidentified textile.

GRAVE 3

The sarcophagus was 1.87m long, 0.35m deep and narrowed from a maximum 0.5m width at the shoulder to 0.32m at the feet. The sides, each comprising three panels, had been forced outwards causing the five capstones to break and collapse into the coffin. There was a head-stone but the E end-stone was simply the head-stone of Grave 10.

Although the majority of the skeleton was recovered, most of the bones were worn and damaged. In contrast, the teeth were in good condition, all but one being recovered. The morphology of the skull indicated that the corpse was that of a male, 1.80m (5' 11") tall, whose age at death was calculated as 35–45 from tooth wear but in excess of 45 years from the severe osteophytosis evident on some of its vertebrae.

GRAVE 4

The insertion of the Period IV central pier severely damaged the W end of this grave (illus 89b) and neither its original length nor its maximum width could be determined although it appeared to narrow to a minimum of 0.48m at the feet. Each side consisted of two unequal-sized slabs. Although cracked, the two furthest E capstones were still *in situ* whereas the remainder had collapsed into the grave.

The overall condition of the skeleton was poor although the footbones were well-preserved. Part of the skull had been disturbed and subsequently replaced during alterations to the building. Of the 27 teeth recovered, only one was still within its socket. Tooth wear suggests an age of 45+ at death. Features within the skull and the morphology of the pelvis indicate that the corpse was that of a male, the stature of whom is estimated as 1.82m (5' 11.5"). There was evidence of degenerative disease in some of the limb bones.

GROUP B – GRAVES 5, 6, 7 AND 8

These four sarcophagi, located towards the NW of the room, were constructed of the same hard, pale sandstone as the abbey's primary buildings. Other characteristics distinguishing these graves from those of group A were superior workmanship, mortar-bonded masonry, thicker lining stones and the use of internal, lateral head-stones.

GRAVE 5

The E end of the grave had been disturbed by the insertion of the Period IV central pier and by Grave 4 although enough survived to indicate an internal length of 2.08m and a width of 0.6m, reduced to 0.4m within the lateral headstones. Two capstones were *in situ* at the head end; the other three were dislodged. Although varying in length, the lining stones were of uniform thickness and height, those on the N side of the grave being intact while those to the S were badly damaged.

The skeleton had been badly disturbed, the only bones left *in situ* being the skull and the left humerus. Disarticulated bones, replaced from below the chest to a position near the head, were in better condition than those that remained in place. Ageing and sexing were made difficult by decay although the bones were robust which is a male characteristic. The body's stature is calculated as 1.76m (5' 9"). Within the grave fill were numerous scraps of leather, some of which were identifiable as shoe fragments.

GRAVE 6 (illus 92)

The sarcophagus, measuring 1.8m long and narrowing from 0.5m at shoulder level to 0.35m at the feet, was defined by four stones per side, single end-stones and lateral head-stones. All five capstones were undisturbed and intact and the coffin fitted tightly into a trench the sides of which may have respected earlier, adjacent graves.

Much of the skeleton had decayed although the lower limbs were reasonably intact and the foot bones were comparatively well preserved, protected within leather shoes. The length of the right tibia gave an estimated stature of 1.71m (5' 7") and the wear on the few surviving teeth allowed for an age estimate of 25–35 years at death. It was not possible to sex the individual.

GRAVE 7 (illus 92)

A grave cut was discernible only on the S side of the coffin and the relationship between this and neighbouring burials remains unclear. Internally the coffin measured 2.04m long and 0.6m wide at shoulder level, narrowing to 0.34m at the feet and 0.29m within the lateral head-stones. The four stones on each

Illus 92
Group B Graves 6 and 7; from the N.

side of the coffin and the five capstones were all undisturbed.

Unlike the remainder of the skeleton, the foot bones were well-preserved, protected by leather shoes of which a single fragment of a left sole remained. There were no surviving skeletal criteria to determine the sex, stature or age at death of the individual.

GRAVE 8

Positioned between Grave 7 and the N wall of the building, this interment had been badly disturbed when a coffin burial (Grave 13) was inserted directly over it. The only intact structural elements were the head-stone, the lateral head-stones and two slabs on the S side of the coffin. The outline of the sarcophagus was not clear and its length and width could only be estimated as 1.9m and 0.55m respectively.

A few disarticulated bones had been replaced into the W end of the sarcophagus; the remainder of the skeleton appears to have been forced into the coffin of adjacent Grave 14. The skeleton appears to have been of a male, approximately 1.72m (5' 7.5") tall and, according to tooth wear, aged 21–25 at death although the extent of sutural closure suggests he was older.

GROUP C – GRAVES 9, 10, 11 AND 12

These graves which were similar in style to those in group B had all been disturbed by the insertion of the Period IV E wall. With the exception of Grave 12, the sarcophagi had been shortened and their disarticulated skeletons replaced thereafter.

GRAVE 9

Truncated to a mere 0.4m in length, the sarcophagus had a maximum surviving width of 0.55m, reduced to 0.3m between its lateral head-stones. Unusually, the lining stones were roughly tooled and the single trapezoid capstone, replaced over the shortened grave and mortared to the lining stones, had been smoothed only on its under side.

The skeleton had suffered considerably from damage and decay and, except for the vault of the skull, it was completely disarranged. The only visible indication of sex was the prominent nuchal crest and, on this criterion alone, it is assumed to be male. There were several fragments of leather shoes and, attached to some of the bones, pieces of a woollen garment.

GRAVE 10

A blocking stone had been used to reduce this grave's length to 0.47m; its width decreased from a maximum of 0.58m to 0.32m between the lateral headstones. The two surviving capstones had probably been re-bonded onto the masonry of the sarcophagus lining.

Most of the post-cranial bones could be paired and together with the skull and the remains of the axial skeleton constituted an almost complete skeleton. The corpse had been that of a male, approximately 1.7m (5' 7") tall. On the evidence of tooth wear, the age was estimated as 25 years at death whereas the degree of suture closure within the bones suggests the age to be greater. All the bones were damaged and decayed although some pathological change was still evident.

Among the loose bones were several which did not come from the original occupant, including two badly decayed skulls from individuals tentatively aged 25–35 and 33–45 at death. These are thought to have originated from other graves (perhaps including Grave 12) disturbed during the Period IV rebuilding programme. Also present were bones from three juveniles, one about 7 years and another about 11 years at death, which may have originated from (pre-Augustinian?) levels disturbed during building operations.

Within the grave fill were several leather objects including a near complete sole from a left shoe, a substantial part of an upper, part of the vamp of an upper and numerous miscellaneous fragments. Several of these items belonged to shoes of types that were common between the 12th and 14th centuries (**4.10** above).

GRAVE 11 (illus 93)

It is not clear whether the odd alignment of the sarcophagus (being oriented somewhat N of E) was an original feature or the result of disturbance during the Period IV remodelling. Its shortened length was 0.44m and its width 0.5m, reduced to 0.24m between the lateral headstones. A single capstone was mortared to the lining and another had been reused as a blocking stone.

The skull and possibly the left humerus were *in situ*; otherwise the skeleton was completely disarticulated and in a poor state of preservation. Fragments of leather shoes and textile were also found within the grave. Enough evidence survived to suggest that the individual was male, about 1.76m (5' 9") in height and aged 25–35 at death. There was no indication of pathological change.

GRAVE 12

The W end of the sarcophagus had been destroyed by the construction of the Period IV E wall and the capstones had all been removed although the remainder of the coffin was reasonably intact. The sarcophagus, which had been foreshortened to a mere 1.26m, retained part of a sandstone base, an unusual feature at Jedburgh and shared only with Grave 2.

The human remains were from at least three individuals and it was not possible to reconstruct an accurate picture of any of them. It is quite possible that the original occupant had been disturbed during the Period IV developments and replaced in another grave (Grave 10?) and that Grave 12 was disrupted again in 1936–37 and some stray bones placed within it.

PIT 1064

Pit 1064, to the immediate S of Grave 12, was contemporary with the Period IV rebuilding programme. Its dimensions, 1.36m N–S × 1.35m E–W (the latter measured from the Period IV E wall, below which it extended) and its infill, which contained bones from at least four individuals, suggest that the pit was a robbing trench for two adjacent graves. It is conceivable that some of the secondary skeletal elements within Grave 10 were derived from these putative graves.

COFFIN BURIALS 13, 14, 15, 16 AND 17

Graves 15, 16 and 17 (illus 94; 95), which cut the backfilled robber trench 888, clearly post-dated the Period IV alterations, as did Grave 14 which had disturbed contemporary sub-floor levels. The remaining coffin burial (Grave 13) could not be linked stratigraphically with others in this group although its location, directly above Grave 8, strongly suggests that this, too, was a late interment. Coffin outlines, often distorted by soil pressure, were represented by thin dark stains.

GRAVE 13

Most of underlying Grave 8 had been destroyed by this burial, adjacent to Grave 14 and to the N wall of the Chapter house. The gaps between the rectangular coffin, 1.9m long and 0.45–0.5m wide, and the edges of the grave pit were infilled with small stones. The skeleton was completely disarranged and poorly preserved: only one portion of a badly decayed skull and damaged fragments of long bones and foot bones survived. Over half the teeth were present, their wear suggesting the age at death to be 45+ years.

Illus 93
Group C Graves 10 and 11,
their sarcophagi foreshortened
by the insertion of the E wall of
the Period IV Chapter house;
from the E.

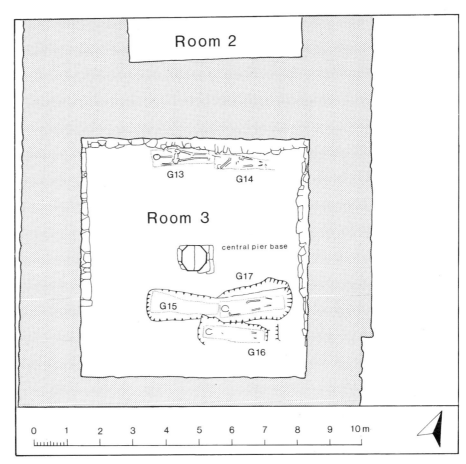

Illus 94
Plan of Period IV coffin
burials in the Chapter house.

GRAVE 14

The coffin was 1.8m long and approximately 0.45m wide although its W end was severely distorted by the later interment of Grave 13. Also present were an incomplete iron buckle with some associated textile, five iron nails (some with fragments of wood attached) and a worn Francis and Mary coin, dated 1559 (**4.5** above). If the coin's deposition was contemporary with Grave 14 the burial would appear to date to the period immediately after the abbey's suppression.

The general condition of the skeleton was very poor, particularly those bones which had been disturbed. The vault of the skull was *in situ* and still intact although very eroded. It was difficult to tell which of the remaining bones were derived from the original occupant and which came from the underlying Grave 8.

Illus 95
Coffin burials in the S side of the Chapter house; from the S.

GRAVE 15

Within the grave pit, which was cut into the backfilled robber trench 888, were the remains of the coffin, defined by a dark stain, 59 iron nails and numerous small fragments of wood. The coffin measured 2.05m long and tapered from its maximum width of 0.64m at the head to 0.32m at the feet. The SE corner of the pit had been disturbed by Grave 16 although its chronological relationship with adjacent Grave 17 was unclear.

Most of the skeleton was badly decayed whereas the skull, which displayed clear masculine features, was reasonably well preserved. According to the evidence of tooth wear, the individual was aged 25–35 at death although poor dental health may have distorted the record, resulting in an under-estimation of age. There was slight evidence of pathological change to the skeleton.

Adhering to some of the bones were fragments of textile, including silk embroidered with gold and silver thread, and two copper-alloy ring brooches, one with a collared pin (**4.2** above). Silver brooches of similar design have been dated to the late 13th and 14th centuries (Callander 1924; Metcalf 1977) although the examples from Jedburgh must be considerably later.

GRAVE 16

Within a grave pit only 0.16m deep at the excavated level were the distorted remains of the coffin, measuring 1.86m long, and 21 iron nails, some with wood attached.

Only two fragments of the skull, one with clear masculine features, and a few fragments of the post-cranial skeleton could be identified. Dark staining on the bones had presumably resulted from the decomposition of the coffin and/or clothing. Associated with the latter was an iron ring brooch or buckle, almost completely covered with textile.

GRAVE 17

Situated to the immediate E of Grave 15, the pit for Grave 17 accommodated a rectangular coffin, 1.96m long and 0.46m wide. Nearby were 37 iron nails, some with wood attached.

Although still partially articulated, the skeleton was in a very poor condition, having been crushed by the collapse of the coffin. An age of 25–35 at death was estimated from the wear on the 16 teeth recovered. Associated with the skeleton was a circular iron ring brooch or buckle with some unidentified textile attached.

DISCUSSION OF CHAPTER HOUSE BURIALS

The sequence of burials

With the probable exception of Grave 1 which was sealed by the mortar spread associated with the Period III floor, none of the graves within the Chapter house can be dated with any certainty to the earliest phase of the building. However, Graves 9, 10, 11 and 12, which were cut by the Period IV E wall, and Graves 4 and 5, disturbed by the insertion of the central pier, can all be said to predate the final reorganization of the Chapter house, whereas coffin burials 14, 15, 16, 17, and probably 13, all post-date that development.

The similar constructional styles of the sarcophagi of groups B and C suggest continuity of burial practice while the cruder central group, A, could fit at either end of the chronological sequence. It may be tempting to believe that the simple coffins of group A belonged to the earliest graves and that the burial sequence radiated outwards thereafter: this seems more logical than to leave a gap (conveniently grave-length) between groups B and C. However, the relatively poor quality of these sarcophagi may point to a decline in constructional standards that is evident elsewhere in the abbey: for example, in the secondary cross-walls of Rooms 6 and 11. The friable, local stone used for the group A sarcophagi is associated mainly with 14th-century building work although it would be unwise to date these graves solely on this evidence.

The difficulty of interpreting stratigraphic relationships, rendered unreliable by constant redeposition, was compounded by the close proximity of the graves to each other and by the similarity between their infills and the materials into which the graves were cut. However, one element of the stratigraphic record did support the cruder graves being the later of the two types. In the NE corner of the room a layer of loose pale brown soil and stones overlay two group C graves (10 and 11) as well as Graves 2 and 3 of group A although this material appeared to be cut by another group A burial (Grave 4) as well as by coffin burial 14.

The late 15th-/early 16th-century reconstruction of the Chapter house necessitated repairs to several graves although there were no graves in the E end of the Period III building to be disturbed. It is not clear whether the skeleton in Grave 12 had been removed during the Period IV rebuilding or during the 1936–37 excavation. If the former, a likely destination for the remains was the foreshortened Grave 10, wherein were found three adult skulls. However, if the third skull was derived from adjacent pit 1064 it is difficult to understand why the sarcophagus that was presumably within it had been removed in its entirety whilst that of adjacent Grave 12 remained almost intact.

There were few clues to the status of the graves' incumbents; certainly none could be identified with confidence as an abbot. Indeed, several of the skeletons appeared to be of young men: individuals that were unlikely to have been senior members of the monastic community. This may be an indication that the Chapter house was the final resting place of some of the abbey's benefactors or, more worrying, that current techniques for dating skeletons are unreliable. In some cases the bones were too badly decayed to allow sexing. None, however, was positively identified as female whereas lay folk of both sexes were buried in the Chapter house of Melrose Abbey after 1215 (RCAHMS 1956, 283).

Dating the burials

The absence of grave markers and the paucity of diagnostic artefacts did little to help date any of the Chapter house burials. The last such burial at the Augustinian Priory of St Andrews Cathedral was in 1416 (RCAHMS 1933, 237) and as early as 1346 at the Cistercian abbey of Fountains (Gilyard-Beer 1970, 46). Thereafter abbots were usually interred within the church. The typology of the graves at Jedburgh provided minimal assistance towards the interpretation of the burial sequence and even less towards absolute dating. It was evident that the sarcophagus burials pre-dated those in wooden coffins, yet burials within long-cist type coffins spanned an enormous period, from the Bronze Age until the 17th century and even later on the Isle of Lewis (Henshall 1956, 269).

Most of the grave goods were in poor condition and hence unreliable indicators of date. In this respect, the leather fragments were of limited value. Some were derived from shoes of a type extremely common between the 12th and 14th centuries; others were undatable. Even the reasonably intact leather sole, the date of which falls between the mid-13th and the mid-14th century (**4.10** above), was found within a grave (10) which included elements of at least three skeletons. Shoes were usually associated with laymen, rather than with canons who tended to wear sandals although, according to a late 13th-century register, a wide variety of footwear was in use at the Augustinian Priory of Barnwell, Cambridge (Clark 1897, ixxx). These included: leather shoes (perhaps worn over gaiters in summer), gaiters with leather soles and knee-length leather boots. This miscellany of footwear may be difficult to reconcile with the accepted image of monastic life but such variations may simply reflect different local traditions of dress.

OUTSIDE THE CHAPTER HOUSE

Three graves (illus 63; 96), presumed to be monastic on the evidence of typology, were excavated to the NE of the Chapter house. These burials were within sarcophagi similar to those of groups B and C in the Chapter house although here the standard of masonry work was slightly lower. Several other graves had been disturbed by the insertion of wall 960 (illus 97) although nothing survived of their coffins or burial pits.

THE GRAVES

GRAVE 18

The furthest N of these three burials, Grave 18, extended beyond the E end of the trench, leaving only 1.6m of its length uncovered. Each side of the coffin comprised four roughly cut, unmortared slabs (a fifth is assumed to have lain beyond the limit of the trench), a thin headstone and two lateral headstones. One of the four exposed capstones had collapsed inwards; a fifth may have been dislodged by a later interment.

Not all of the skeleton was exposed and hence its length could not be measured. The bones which remained *in situ* were in good condition, having been protected by soil following the collapse of the coffin. The individual was clearly male and the degree of tooth wear suggests an age of 30–35 years at death. There were numerous signs of degenerative change throughout the skeleton.

GRAVE 19

The grave pit measured 2.6m by 1.0m and contained a sarcophagus, 1.85m long and 0.45m wide. The two capstones that were *in situ* were mortared to a lining consisting of five stones per side, E and W end-stones and two well-cut lateral head-stones.

Unlike those within adjacent Graves 18 and 20, the skeletal remains were sparse and in very poor condition. However, the shape of the skull suggests that the incumbent was male and aged 33–45 at death although his very poor dental health suggests he was older.

GRAVE 20

This was a relatively crude sarcophagus, measuring 2.0m long, narrowing from 0.5m at the head to 0.28m at the feet and contained within a grave pit, 1.0m wide. The coffin comprised five slabs per side, end-stones and internal lateral head-stones. Six roughly-fashioned capstones were wedged with small fragments of stone and bonded to the lining with small quantities of mortar.

Despite interment in a sarcophagus, the skeleton was reasonably well preserved. The skull was identified as that of a male, 1.79m (5' 10.5") tall who died at the age of 33–45 although the loss of several molars *ante mortem* suggests that this is an underestimation. There was evidence of degenerative change within several vertebrae and within some limb bones.

WITHIN THE EAST CLOISTER ALLEY

Of a total of five graves in this area (illus 15), two were sarcophagus burials, one retained evidence of a wooden coffin and two were simple pits.

THE BURIALS

SARCOPHAGUS BURIALS

GRAVE 24

This grave, which abutted the W wall of the alley, had been truncated during the 1936–37 excavation, its length being reduced to 0.5m. The end-stones had been removed and single slabs of sandstone were all that remained of each side of the sarcophagus. The skeleton had been removed, probably in 1936–37.

GRAVE 25

The sarcophagus which had been disturbed, probably during the 1930s excavation, measured 2.03m in length, narrowing slightly towards the foot end. Two (of three?) lining stones survived on each side and the head-stone was still *in situ* whereas the E end-stone and all but one of the capstones were missing. The skeleton had been removed, probably in 1936–37.

COFFIN BURIAL

GRAVE 28

Only 1.15m of this grave's length remained, its W end having been destroyed during the 1930s. Although the outline of the coffin could not be defined, two iron nails and a fragment of wood at the edge of the pit and two more nails within the grave's infill implied that there had been one. Also within the infill were fragments of copper and lead and a coin of Henry of Huntingdon, minted between 1136 and 1139 (**4.5** above), which may have been residual.

Only the pelvis and limb bones remained articulated although some of the hand and foot bones were recovered from the grave fill. The individual was male, aged 35+ at death and of estimated height 1.79m (5' 10.5"). There was evidence of pathological change in some bones.

Illus 96
Sarcophagus burials (Graves 18, 19 and 20) outside the East
range. Grave 19, in the centre, is overlain by a post-Reformation
burial (Grave 37); from the N.

Illus 97
Re-interred burials against the W face of wall 960; from the N.

PIT BURIALS

GRAVE 26

The W end of this grave, which measured 2.0m × 0.5m, was overlain by the W wall of the alley, indicating either that the burial pre-dated the Augustinian occupation of the site or that the wall was a secondary structure.

With the exception of the vertebrae and ribs which had decayed almost completely, the skeleton was very well preserved. The incumbent was male, about 1.67m (5' 5.5") tall and, on the evidence of tooth wear, 21–25 years at death although the

morphology of the pubic symphases suggests he may have been a little older.

GRAVE 27

This rather irregular pit was only 1.55m long and, to accommodate a corpse of 1.63m (5' 4") height, its head had been placed in an upright position at the W end of the grave. The burial was not fully excavated.

Most of the skeleton survived although the majority of its bones were damaged and worn. The individual was probably male; the age at death was estimated from tooth wear as 25–35 years. Some pathological change was evident.

WITHIN THE CHURCH

GRAVE 42 (illus 75)

Adjacent to the NE pier of the South presbytery chapel was a stone sarcophagus, badly damaged by an overlying post-monastic coffin burial (Grave 43). The remains of the sarcophagus consisted of: four neatly cut sandstone flags on its S side; recessed internal head-

stones; and, overlying the latter, the sole surviving capstone. There was no evidence that the coffin had had a stone base.

There were a few disarticulated bones within the grave fill although it was not clear if any of these had belonged to the original incumbent.

5.2 NON-MONASTIC BURIAL

GRAVE 38

There was no evidence of a coffin associated with this burial, or possibly re-burial, within the 12th-century sewage ditch (928) outside the East range. Although the rib cage was relatively articulated, the body had not been oriented. It is not clear whether

any of the other bones found within the same context had been part of this skeleton.

The individual was probably male and aged approximately 20–25 at death. There was no evidence of pathological change to any part of the skeleton.

5.3 POST-MONASTIC BURIALS

Other than a single coffin burial within the presbytery of the abbey church and several possible N–S grave cuts in the Period V Chapter house (illus 98), all of the post-monastic graves that were uncovered were situated to the NE of the Chapter house. The assumed date range is based on the mutual similarities of the graves (all were simple pits with no evidence of coffins, shrouds or burial goods) and the state of skeletal preservation which was generally good. Some of these burials disrupted earlier, monastic graves. Two (Graves 21 and 22) were overlain by a spread of clay (possibly the remnants of a floor surface) within which were coins and other artefacts of late 17th-century date whereas the remainder were overlain by various disturbed, undatable deposits.

Age and sex distribution were much more diverse than within the monastic population. Three of the skeletons were of children, one of them under one year old; by contrast, on the evidence of tooth wear, only one individual had reached the age of 45 years by death. Dental disease was common, as were degenerative diseases, particularly among the older individuals.

OUTSIDE THE EAST RANGE

GRAVES 21–23 & 29–40

GRAVE 21

The W end of this grave had been disturbed, leaving a shallow pit, 1.5m long and 0.45m wide. The skull, the right clavicle, the vertebrae down to and including the 10th thoracic and some of

the hand and foot bones were missing although the remainder of the skeleton was in good condition. The skeleton was of a female of estimated height 1.64m (5' 4") who died aged 20 –25 years.

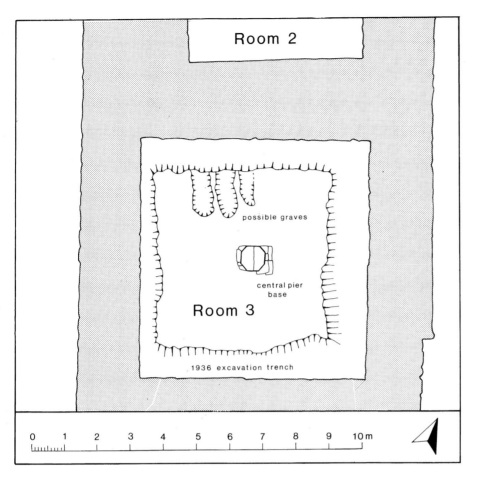

Illus 98
Plan of possible post-Reformation burials, truncated by a 1930s excavation trench, in the N side of the Chapter house.

(Within plan: Room 2; possible graves; central pier base; Room 3; 1936 excavation trench; scale 0 1 2 3 4 5 6 7 8 9 10 m)

GRAVE 22

Only the central area of this grave pit survived. The skeletal remains comprised a few vertebrae, ribs and some miscellaneous fragments, all of them damaged. The appearance of the innominate bones suggests that the individual was male and, on the evidence of degenerative disease on the vertebrae, he was over 30 years at death.

GRAVE 23

This shallow pit, measuring only 0.5m × 0.3m, had evidently had been disturbed at some time. Within the pit and scattered around its periphery were the partial remains of a child, aged 1 year at death.

GRAVE 29

The grave was so badly disturbed that its outline was not clear and the condition of the bones was so poor that only a few could be identified as belonging to the original skeleton. It was not possible to sex the individual. On the evidence of tooth wear, death did not come until at least the age of 45.

GRAVE 30

The remains comprised only the vault of a skull and it is questionable whether this was the original grave or merely a displaced fragment of a skeleton. The skull was of an adult and possibly male.

GRAVE 31

The grave extended beyond the E limit of the trench and the skeleton below the knees remains unexcavated. The exposed

bones were in a good state of preservation and evidently belonged to a female, 1.59m (5' 2.5") tall who died at the age of 20–25.

Evidence testifying to the poor health of this young adult included tooth decay and various pathological changes to the skeleton, including porotic superior surfaces on both orbits, possibly caused by iron-deficiency anaemia.

GRAVE 32

Most of the grave lay beyond the trench edge, the skeleton below the pelvis remaining unexposed. The excavated bones were in good condition although many were damaged. The individual was male, approximately 1.67m (5' 6") tall and, on the evidence of tooth wear and the morphology of the pubic symphysis, aged 25–35 years at death. Many areas of the skeleton showed signs of degenerative change.

GRAVE 33

The outline of the grave pit was difficult to discern although it was believed to extend beyond the limit of the trench. The bones that were recovered comprised a fragmented skull, a few vertebrae and the disarticulated left arm excluding the hand bones.

Stature was impossible to estimate whereas tooth wear suggests the age at death to have been 21–25 years. The skull had masculine features whereas the width of the atlas vertebra was typically female. There was no indication of pathological change to the skeleton.

GRAVE 34

The lower part of the grave pit and the lower limbs of the skeleton remained beyond the trench edge. The skeleton was clearly male, its height estimated as 1.8m (5' 10.5"). Age at death was estimated from tooth wear and from the morphology of the pubic symphasis as 21–25 years.

GRAVE 35

The whole of the pit, measuring 1.85m long and 0.55m wide, was exposed and almost all of the skeleton was recovered. The individual was male, approximately 1.74m (5' 8.5") tall and aged 25–35 years at death according to the evidence of the innominate bones. There was evidence of degenerative disease in many areas of the skeleton, including the elbows, knees and feet and the absence of pitting within the left orbit suggested iron-deficiency anaemia.

GRAVE 36

This grave, aligned approximately NW to SE, was cut into the inside face of the N wall of the Period III Chapter house. The grave pit measured 1.95m long and narrowed from 0.8m at the shoulder to 0.35m at the feet.

The skeleton, in excellent condition, was of a male, approximately 1.74m (5' 8.5") tall, who died at the age of about 25, according to the evidence of tooth wear and the morphology of the pubic symphasis. There were signs of mild degenerative disease at various points in the skeleton and there had been some pathological change, probably secondary,

caused by a traumatic incident to the left elbow.

GRAVE 37

This pit burial had damaged the sarcophagus of the underlying Grave 19, removing two of its capstones, but it was, in turn, disturbed by Grave 32 which removed the skeleton's lower limbs. The skeleton which was in very good condition was of a male of estimated height 1.67m (5' 5.5") who died, according to the evidence of tooth wear and the morphology of the pubic symphasis, aged 21–25 years. There were some signs of degenerative changes in some bones.

GRAVE 38

The only part of the skeleton to be exposed was the skull which appeared to be that of a male, aged 25–35 at death.

GRAVE 39

Only the W half of this grave was exposed. Within it were the skull, a few vertebrae and some other disarranged bones of a child aged approximately 4 years at death.

GRAVE 40

This partially excavated grave contained the fragmentary remains of a child, aged under 1 year and possibly newborn.

WITHIN THE CHURCH

GRAVE 43

Lying directly over monastic Grave 42, this burial contained a coffin constructed of timber planks enclosing a box made of lead sheets, 1–2mm thick. Later disturbances had removed the lid and upper sides of the coffin although the surviving elements were quite well preserved. Overlying the coffin's timber exterior was a covering of textile (**4.11** above) and sheets of copper-alloy beaten into shell-like patterns. Within the coffin was a fully articulated skeleton in an excellent state of preservation and still retaining some hair which, together with the style of the coffin, suggests a

comparatively recent (?late 18th-/19th-century) date for the burial.

On the N side of the grave was a massive dolerite boulder which had been chipped and partially cracked, either during this interment or that of the underlying Grave 42.

Within the remaining area of the trench were numerous other burials, none of which was excavated. Most, if not all of them, had been disturbed.

6

DISCUSSION OF THE EXCAVATION RESULTS

It was a relatively simple task to divide the excavation results into pre-Augustinian, early monastic, later monastic and post-Reformation phases. The findings from Period II, the major building phase, were subdivided into those associated with the temporary accommodation of the canons and/or the builders (in the mid-12th century) and those related to the construction of the original claustral ranges (from the late 12th to mid-13th century). However, for three centuries after the completion of this programme the abbey underwent numerous alterations and repairs, many of them difficult to place within neatly-defined periods. Nevertheless, two principal stages of rebuilding are postulated. In Period III (c 1300–c 1480) extensive alterations were implemented throughout and beyond the cloisters, while in Period IV (c 1480–1559) the emphasis seems to have been on repair-work although some larger-scale projects were undertaken, particularly within the East end of the church and within the Chapter house. It is thought that many of the modifications carried out in Periods III and IV resulted from damage wrought during the numerous conflicts that raged through the Border country after 1296.

6.1 PRE-AUGUSTINIAN ACTIVITY (PERIOD I)

THE MATERIAL EVIDENCE FOR A PRE-AUGUSTINIAN PRESENCE

Ecgred, Bishop of Lindisfarne, is known to have endowed two foundations at or near Jedburgh in c 830 (Arnold 1882, 52–3). There are few references to Jedburgh from the succeeding centuries, other than mention of a church in c 1080 (Arnold 1885, 198) and David I's confirmation of a monastery (OPS 1855, 367–9) which Cowan and Easson (1975, 18) refer to as a 'monasterium, large parish and dependent chapels'. Documentary sources have not equated the site of the Augustinian abbey with either of Ecgred's foundations; the artefactual evidence, however, is considerably more compelling.

The many pre-Augustinian artefacts retrieved from the abbey and its environs suggest that the early religious house was located there rather than at the alternative site, 5 miles up-river, proposed by some authorities (Cowan & Easson 1976, 92; Morton 1832, 2). Most of these objects, some of which were pre-Christian, were uncovered during previous investigations at the abbey. They comprise: a cup-and ring-marked stone, found at the abbey in 1903; a Roman altar, reused as a lintel over the entrance to the N stair in the church; part of the inscribed face of a Roman altar, reused in the presbytery of the church; three fragments (two from the abbey and one discovered in Ancrum) of a stone sarcophagus end, dated to c 700 and decorated with vine scrolls, birds and other animals; the spatulate head of a large cross, possibly late 8th or early 9th century; a terminal, of uncertain date, from a cross-head with a cable border; a fragment of a cross-shaft, perhaps 9th century; five stone fragments (two reused in the S wall of the refectory), all with coarse cable border and probably belonging to the same sculptured piece; a sandstone slab with interlaced pattern in relief; and a cross-shaft fragment with rope-moulding at one corner and leaf-scroll on one face, found when the manse was demolished in 1878 (Laidlaw 1905, 21–25; RCAHMS 1956, 200–208).

Large numbers of early coins have been found throughout Jedburgh, particularly at riverside locations. In 1827 about 90 'Saxon' silver coins were dug up at Bongate, 600m N of the abbey (NSAS 1845, 13). The same source also refers to 'many coins' of the reigns of Eadred, Eadwig and Aethelred (of the period 946–1016), and of Henry I, Henry III, Edward I and Edward III (1100–1377), which were discovered near Abbey Bridge. This second, rather mixed assemblage was probably deposited during landscaping and the regular tipping of refuse from the abbey.

The five pre-Augustinian artefacts recovered during the excavation consisted of: a Roman *dupondius*, from a disturbed drain in the East cloister alley (**4.5**, no 1 above); a coin of Aethelred II, from a late medieval context in the Chapter house (**4.5**, no 2 above); a probable 10th-century sculptured slab, reused in a late medieval wall (**4.7** above); a 9th- or 10th-century cross-shaft fragment, redeposited in the South cloister alley (**4.7** above); and an architectural fragment, perhaps dating to the late 9th or 10th century, found at the W end of the site.

The presence of a small number of Roman artefacts implies that there was a Roman camp a short distance from the abbey. The numerous 8th- to 11th-century stone fragments and coins found at or near the abbey are strong indications of a more permanent pre-Augustinian presence on the site, although this does not necessarily mean that that presence was unbroken over that period.

THE EXCAVATED FEATURES

Several factors should be taken into account when analysing the presumed pre-Augustinian features: none was fully defined; none could be dated; and their relationships with other important contexts were often difficult to establish. For example, the location and alignment of wall 915 corresponded to those expected for the S wall of the 18th-century 'John Preston's House' (Watson 1894, 95) (illus 12a); the stratigraphic evidence, however, pointed to this wall being 12th century or earlier. Furthermore, the N wall of John Preston's house was very different in style from wall 915 although the former's resemblance to an abutting wall (914) was quite pronounced. There was simply insufficient evidence to determine whether either or both of walls 914 and 915 were of pre-Augustinian, post-Reformation or even monastic origin.

A few patches of metalling (916) and a short stretch of walling (915) that might have been associated with it provided scant evidence from which to reconstruct the pre-12th-century landscape. Some skeletal remains, however, provide some indication of early habitation: the many residual bones, including those of females and juveniles, recovered from the Chapter house area suggest that a cemetery had been disturbed during the construction of the East range. Furthermore, investigations in the area of Murray's Green, to the E of the abbey, revealed crude stone cists at a considerable depth below presumed monastic stone coffins (Hilson 1872, 349). Hilson assumed the lower graves to be pre-Augustinian; indeed, they may even have been pre-Christian.

6.2 THE BUILDING OF THE ABBEY (PERIOD II)

THE INITIAL OCCUPATION (PRIMARY PERIOD II)

TERRACING AND COLONIZATION

The earliest phase of construction of the claustral complex after 1138 was reflected by two periods of timber building and terrace formation (illus 27), maximising the lower reaches of the slope as defined by the original course of the Jed Water. Evidence for both structures was fragmentary and later building had created merely isolated pockets of early Period II activity. Although the precise inter-relationship of each was obscured, enough remained to suggest possible connections.

Timber Structure 1 was of relatively sophisticated construction utilising a wide sill beam with offset, squared posts for its walls. The need to create a wider and lower terrace saw the abandonment of Timber Structure 1 and the truncation of its terrace in favour of a surface some 1.5m below. This lower terrace was ultimately to become part of Structure 8. The W extent of this terrace might be determined from the position of drain 490, the N end of which appeared to be turning northwards, following the edge of the flat surface which was to receive cobbling (304), ultimately associated with the 18th-century manse.

Similarly, the terrace immediately to the E of Timber Structure 2, which was absorbed into the open courtyard defined by Structure 10, dated from primary Period II. This surface and the W riverside terrace thus defined a raised, regular platform running E–W which supported a large, rectangular, wooden building.

To what extent these complex terraces were integral with the ultimate layout of the abbey ranges was difficult to determine, but it is arguable that they represented an independent programme of works dictated by the original N bank of the river. This programme created occupation/building platforms to answer the immediate needs of the incoming community rather than necessarily viewing it as part of the overall plan for the eventual stone abbey – a process which took well over a century.

The character of temporary structures which might have been built during the initial colonisation of monastic sites generally has been scantily documented and only a few examples have ever been identified through excavation. However, both the obvious attempts to terrace the site and the dateable artefacts found in association suggested that Timber Structures 1 and 2 dated from the 12th century and were not elements from an earlier, pre-Augustinian occupation phase.

The best documented accounts of the initial colonisation of abbey sites and the attempts to accommodate the basic requirements of a monastic foundation relate to Cistercian houses. The differences in the practices and preferences of that order compared with those of the Augustinians, did not necessarily preclude direct comparison once the site itself was selected.

While it was unwise to speculate too much on what was fragmentary evidence, it was reasonable to assume that temporary structures would have been necessary while the main building programme was under way – indeed, the evidence from the 1984 excavation suggested that over a century elapsed before the main elements of the W side of the complex were completed (Structure 8). The use of wood for such building was also to be expected as it was plentiful, cheap and relatively quick to build. However, whether such structures were built by the incoming colonists themselves or at the behest of King David, as founder, in anticipation of their arrival is not known. Furthermore, as both Timber Structures 1 and 2 were part of a common, west European tradition of timber building techniques, identifying the builder(s) from that standpoint was not possible. Certainly, members of the Cistercian order arriving from France expected the prior construction of 'an oratory, a refectory, a dormitory, a guest house and a gatekeeper's cell' (Lekai 1977, 448). In the case of the foundation at Meaux in south-east Yorkshire, two buildings were erected by the Earl of York, William 'Le Gros', in 1150; and at Kirkstead in Lincolnshire a contemporary account specifies 'that two years were spent raising the wooden buildings before the reception of the community' (Ferguson 1983, 79). The continuity found at Jedburgh between the early terraces and subsequent Period II building on the site was also a feature of the early buildings at Meaux which were absorbed into the main building programme at a later date. Count William (Le Gros)

> '. . . had a certain great house built with common mud and wattle where the hill is now established, in which the arriving lay brothers would dwell until better arrangements were made for them. He also built a certain chapel next to the aforementioned house, which is now the cellarer's chamber, where all the monks used the lower storey as a dormitory and the upper to perform the divine service. . .' (Chron Melsa, 82).

In general terms, therefore, while it was impossible on the surviving evidence to ascribe with any accuracy a specific function for either of the timber structures so far revealed at Jedburgh, they did represent a sequence of terrace construction and accommodation over an extended period. The reuse of Timber Structure 2 and its terrace, whereby they were adapted to the needs of the main stone phase in Period II, was paralleled by the later use of the early chapel at Meaux.

THE SEWAGE DITCH

There seems little doubt that the ditch (928) was used as a sewer – the bran and whipworm ova within the basal deposit of grey-green silt testify to that – although this was not necessarily its only function. It does not, however, appear to have been a defensive ditch for there was no evidence of any other defensive mechanism between the ditch's N terminal and the abbey church – a distance of 25m. Another cut of similar dimensions and alignment to those of the ditch was uncovered within the Chapter house although this cut did not extend beyond the limits of the building and has been interpreted as a robber trench for the E wall of the Period II building.

Presumably, the ditch had extended as far as the river before it was truncated, perhaps during the construction of the East range. Without a timber or clay lining, of which there was no evidence, much of the fluid waste would have drained away through the sandy subsoil, leaving solid matter to be removed manually.

The proximity of the ditch to the East range would have posed a serious threat to the stability of the building's foundations and hence it seems unlikely that the two features were co-existent. In addition, there was no evidence – either from excavation or from contemporary illustrations – that the ditch was associated with any of the post-Reformation structures in this area. Indeed, the artefacts retrieved from the ditch indicate that it was backfilled some time after 1161, in all probability in anticipation of the construction of the East range.

The weight of evidence, then, suggests that the ditch was a sewer dating to the early years of the Augustinian occupation. It was probably associated with a temporary, timber latrine although no physical evidence of such a structure was found during excavation. High concentrations of metallic lead in the underlying subsoil suggest that the water that flushed the sewer was carried along lead pipes, implying that at least some of the plumbing (for example, the drain at the S end of the East cloister alley (illus 15a)) had been installed during the early years of the abbey's construction. Less likely is that the metal was derived from a lead roof, for the only building to have been in such an advanced stage of construction at that time was probably the East end of the abbey church.

The source of the water has not been established. Although the pollen assemblage from the base of the ditch suggests that it came from a stream, such as the Skiprunning Burn, flowing from a nearby hill, the means by which it could have been transferred to the abbey is still open to speculation. To avoid pumping or otherwise manually carrying the water up the sides of the burn's steep-sided ravine, there would have had to be a long system of conduits commencing some distance away from the abbey. There may have been such a system although it has not been located. Alternatively or additionally, rainwater butts and wells could have supplied the abbey with its drinking water although the two wells that have been identified appear to be post-Reformation in date.

There was no definitive proof linking the remains of the torso with the nearby assemblage of artefacts (comb, buckle, seal/pendant and whetstone (illus 78; colour V; VI)) although the circumstantial evidence is persuasive. The objects belonged to a person of high social standing – perhaps a knight – who died in the mid- to late-12th century and who was not, it seems, given a Christian burial. It has been suggested that the corpse was that of Eadwulf Rus, who is alleged to have assassinated Bishop Walcher of Durham in 1080. Shortly afterwards Rus himself was killed and buried thereafter at Jedburgh, only for his body to be cast out by Walcher's successor, Bishop Turgot (RCAHMS 1956, 195). It is difficult to match this event with the ditch burial. If the corpse had been moved, it was done soon after death which, according to the artefactual evidence, was probably during the second or third quarter of the 12th century – too late for the body to be that of Rus. A similar assemblage, comprising a small iron chain, a small whetstone, a small square ivory comb and an ivory seal matrix of Godwin was found in association with skeletal elements at Wallingford, Berkshire, in 1879 (Hodges 1881, 183–4). Unfortunately, the full circumstances of the Wallingford collection are unknown and difficult to compare meaningfully with those from Jedburgh.

It is difficult to believe that the corpse lay exposed for long. It must be assumed, therefore, that either the body was thrown into the ditch and immediately covered or that the infill was disturbed for an unauthorised burial although the latter was not borne out by the evidence of excavation. Both possibilities point to murder – in this case of a person of high social standing. If the motive was theft, objects such as the comb must have been considered too distinctive to be taken.

THE MAIN BUILDING PHASE (illus 99)

THE ABBEY CHURCH

Previous investigations within the presbytery revealed masonry in a position similar to that of the wall foundations uncovered in 1990, 2.1m (7') W of the surviving E gable (RCAHMS 1956, 200). Although the accepted explanation of that masonry as representing the footings of the original E gable may be correct, the linear face on its W side renders its interpretation as the chord from which an apse projected seem less likely. It can only be assumed that the tusking projecting from the S presbytery wall, being more than 3m from the putative gable, was not the masonry to which the earlier investigators referred.

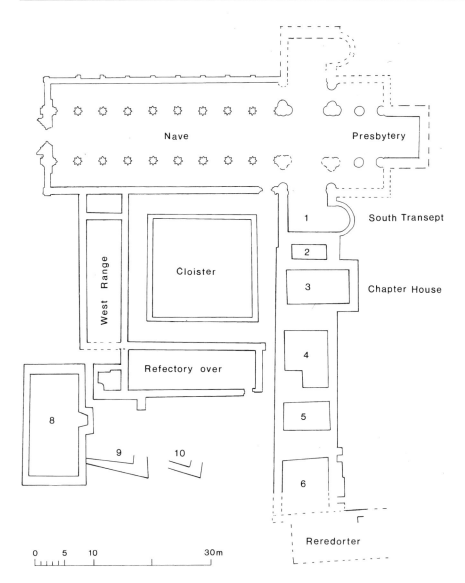

Illus 99
The layout of the abbey by the
mid-13th century.

There seems no obvious reason for siting the altar base off-centre. Its masonry had not been truncated and it can only be assumed that the altar itself was positioned towards the right side of its foundations.

No floor surface was uncovered. On the evidence of the wholesale disruption of floor levels throughout the church and within most of the claustral buildings, it can be assumed that floor tiles or flagstones were removed in the aftermath of the Reformation. The absence of a floor surface and the limited nature of the exercise did little to help date any of the excavated structures or the sarcophagus burial (Grave 42). The grave's resemblance to those of the group C burials within the Chapter house hints at contemporaneity although the Chapter house graves can only be said to pre-date the early 16th century.

THE EAST RANGE

It is generally accepted that the construction of the East range began adjacent to the abbey church in the 12th century and finished with the completion of the reredorter astride the re-routed Jed Water a century later (RCAHMS 1956, 205). This was difficult to verify because much of the relevant architectural evidence had been masked or destroyed during the programme of masonry consolidation that followed the 1936–37 excavation. However, the surviving stonework at the S end of the range, which had escaped the attentions of the earlier investigators, was certainly characteristic of the first half of the 13th century.

The South transept (Room 1)

Although excavation within the South transept was limited, the apse at the E end of the transept (illus 18) was shown to be authentic. Apsidal-ended transepts, common in many 12th-century churches, were frequently squared off in later centuries. For example, at Thetford and Castle Acre Priories the primary (12th-century) layouts included chapels within three apses at the E end of the choir and one at the E end of each transept whereas all but one in each of these monasteries were replaced during the following century. A similar development was also likely at Jedburgh, where there is evidence that both transepts originally had apsidal ends (**8** below).

Room 2

Room 2 occupied a position usually identified with that of the library, sacristy, vestry or slype (illus 18–20). At Jedburgh there was insufficient evidence to confirm how this room had been utilized although there were a few pointers to its likely role(s).

The room's position corresponds to that of the 'vault in the garden' shown in Winter's survey of 1760 (illus 67), the 'vault' perhaps being a reference to a vaulted passage or cellar or to an arched opening. Also in the vicinity of Room 2 was a single Romanesque-style arch, piercing what appears to be the ruined E wall of the East range, depicted in an early 19th-century engraving (illus 100). Taken together, these two illustrations suggest that there was a passage – or slype – through the East range, a suggestion supported by the squared sandstone footings in the room's NE and NW corners which may have been foundations for the jambs of a doorway.

It is conceivable that the masonry against the S wall of Room 2, was the foundation of bench seating, implying that the room was used as a parlour (RCAHMS 1956, 204). It is also possible, however, that this stonework was associated with the first phase of the Chapter house (see below). There was no evidence of major alterations to the fabric of Room 2 and it seems that, if this small chamber served both as a slype and as a parlour, it did so from the outset.

The Chapter house (Room 3)

It is not immediately obvious why the original Chapter house projected a mere 3m beyond the East range; in most monasteries it was either contained within the range or extended well beyond it. As the most important of the claustral buildings, however, the Chapter house was quite probably the first one to be built and at Jedburgh it may have stood in isolation until Room 2 was constructed. As a result, the dimensions of the original, free-standing building would not necessarily bear any relation to those of later, longer lasting structures. It has been suggested that the N wall of this putative free-standing structure is represented by the apparent wall face within the wall dividing Rooms 2 and 3 (illus 20), or that the outer face of the N wall of the Chapter house survived as the fragmentary remains visible (as 129) in Room 2.

On the evidence of architectural fragments retrieved from the overburden in the 1930s, it had been assumed that a late 12th-century Chapter house was remodelled, a century later, to include the earliest lierne vault in Scotland (RCAHMS 1956, 204). This interpretation is now considered to be erroneous, the fragments of vaulting bearing no relation to the date of deposition of the materials from which they were recovered. Indeed, even the near-complete excavation of the area in 1984 failed to yield sufficient evidence by which to accurately date the changes within the Chapter house or to provide accurate pictures of the building's superstructure prior to the Period IV remodelling.

Without doubt the primary building was small. Its internal area was only 52.5m^2 which is less than most other chapter houses of similar, or even lower, status – an indication, perhaps, of the building's temporary nature and the intention of its architect to extend it at the earliest opportunity.

There was no evidence of stone seating around the interior of the Chapter house. Indeed there were graves immediately adjacent to the N wall, making it likely that wooden benches were in use, at least in that part of the room.

Illus 100
An early 19th-century engraving, by J Greig from a painting by G Arnold, of the abbey viewed from the E.

Room 4

It was impossible to make an accurate interpretation of the architectural history of Room 4 without removing much of the masonry that had been consolidated and even rebuilt after the 1936–37 excavation. This was deemed impractical and hence no such programme was undertaken.

Room 4 occupied the position often assigned to the warming house – the only room, other than the kitchen, where the brethren were allowed the benefits of a fire. Although no medieval hearth was located (the one set into the N wall belonged to the overlying 18th-century house, Room 15), this may be because the evidence was obliterated in one of the attacks that plagued the abbey for centuries or during one of the more recent programmes of masonry consolidation.

The wall between Rooms 3 and 4 was up to 2.5m thick: substantial enough to help bear the weight of the overlying canons' dormitory or even to support its gable end. Alternatively, or indeed additionally, this may have been the site of the day stair, linking the dormitory with the cloister. There could have been a straight flight of steps, as at Dryburgh Abbey, or an arrangement similar to that at Haughmond Abbey, where access to the dormitory appeared to be directly from the Chapter house (Hope & Brakspear 1909, 296). The stair could also have been built upon the massive, L-shaped masonry foundations (120 and 215) and comprised steps, at least 2.0m wide, which descended to the S from the dormitory before turning to the E into the cloister – an arrangement similar to that at Chester Cathedral Priory. Another authority, however, suggests that the stairs were located between Rooms 2 and 3 (RCAHMS 1956, 204) although this seems less likely.

Room 5

The perils of building on a sloping river terrace were offset somewhat by the addition of buttresses against Rooms 4 and 5 and by thickening substantially the walls of the East range as it approached the river. While there were no real clues to help date the construction of Room 4, the tightly-jointed ashlar masonry and the piers supporting the roof of the two-bayed Room 5 and of the larger Room 6 were features typical of early 13th-century architecture.

Again, there was little to help interpret the function of Room 5 or to indicate whether it had undergone any significant alterations during its occupation. To interpret this small chamber as a day room (as its position might indicate), on the strength of the bench seating suggested by the linear masonry (276) and associated slot (242), would be to ignore its overall dimensions – a mere 8.0 by 4.7m. A more feasible suggestion is that Room 5 was the treasury.

Room 6

This basement chamber (illus 24) was a well-built structure with ashlar walls and a ceiling supported by quadripartite vaulting. The thickened walls were needed to carry the weight of the East range which must have towered to a considerable height at this point, allowing an additional floor level between the undercroft and the canons' dormitory.

The absence of windows, at least in the N bay, suggests that this was a storage cellar, its cool damp interior making it an ideal store for some types of food. Normally, most foodstuffs would have been kept in the West range (the domain of the cellarer) but at Jedburgh it was a rather insignificant building and its role appears to have been taken over by other buildings within (and perhaps beyond) the cloister. The doorway in the E wall of Room 6 would have allowed supplies to enter the abbey from the SE, rather than (or as well as) from the W. Access to the abbey's inner court was through a door in the W wall (since demolished) of the S bay and thence by steps between the East and South ranges or, less likely, by a stair in the NW corner of the cellar, another badly damaged part of the building.

Projecting further E from the E wall of Room 6 was a wall, which survived only as tusking, that perhaps barred the way to those who were allowed as far as the stores but who were not given access to the rest of the East range, the canons' burial ground or the infirmary.

The reredorter (Room 7)

Only a small portion of the reredorter (illus 24) was exposed although the resemblance between its masonry and that of Room 6 was unmistakable, even at foundation level. The building projected well beyond the line of the East range, as was customary in many monasteries (a good surviving example is Melrose Abbey), being aligned along the river course to facilitate the easy removal of waste.

THE WEST END OF THE ABBEY

The role of the Jed Water and a determination to take full advantage of the general topography of the natural eminence above a steep meander in the course of the river characterise the main building phase for the S and W of the site. Commencing in the first half of the 12th century while temporary buildings were still in use, the site was prepared by a series of stabilising measures in advance of the great weight of masonry which was to follow. The early, simple, scraped terraces were then extended to accommodate, on an appropriate scale, the required claustral buildings. This had to take account of the river and the original steep bend in its course which was exploited to facilitate removal of drainage waste and protected the new artificial building platforms.

A mid-13th-century date for the completion of Structure 8, with Structures 9 and 10 following in rapid succession, implied that the main focus for the building programme was the abbey church, cloister and East range while the S and W parts of the site were consolidated but not completed until over a century had elapsed since the first canons arrived from France. This was supported by the evidence of the architecture within the church itself (**8** below). Further evidence was the upgrading of certain simple drains (such as 2003 and 387) which survived from primary Period II buildings and terraces and which were only suitably improved when their associated waterfront buildings were well underway, if not virtually completed.

The precise function of Structure 8 – the biggest and most elaborate building from this phase on the W of the site – could not be readily deduced from the excavation because the best preserved section of the building had already been dug out. Structure 8 and ultimately Structure 13 saw many changes, including a period as a possible gun platform in 1548/9 (**6.4** below).

The structure was both large and domestic with at least two floors. A large fireplace and an elaborate drainage might have indicated kitchen activities at least at basement level with domestic accommodation above, as evidenced by the latrine chute. However, Structure 8 might have been either a guest accommodation or a private lodging for the abbot or one of the senior officials.

The pend and the waterfront were not fully exploited initially – the former being one way of utilising a steep gradient and a method of 'bridging' two important supporting cross walls (384 and 378). In its original form, the pend may have been no more than a convenient method for the disposal of rubbish while at the same time providing access to the river.

Of the examples of other sites where a distinctive angled waterfront was constructed, the most striking was the Premonstratensian abbey at Alnwick. This sprawling site followed a bend in the River Alne, creating a large fortified enclosure defined and defended to the S by the river. In particular, the double angled wall in the area of the kitchen which fronts onto the river was closely echoed by the angled frontage of Structures 9 and 10 at Jedburgh.

The use of a foundation raft of interlaced oak beams under at least part of the great S wall (378) and its extension (Period III wall 3006) was a consequence of the riverside location of Structure 8/13. Both the Period II timber work and that of Period III were part of a common tradition of wooden foundations, relying on horizontally laid beams. There were numerous examples of this technique from a wide range of contexts, applied mainly as a method of building across unstable, often waterlogged ground (see Stell 1984, 584–85). A similar use of interlaced beams was found beneath parts of Winchester Cathedral and beneath the tower of Holy Trinity Church, Hull which featured '. . . a timber raft of horizontal oak baulks crossing each other at right angles. . .' (Fox 1908, 260–1). The 16th-century King's College, Aberdeen was similarly built:

> 'The quholl foundatione of the colledge, being builded in marrish ground is under layde with great rafters of oake, which behoved to be great coast and travell' (Innes, 1842, 24).

6.3 REMODELLING AND REBUILDING IN THE 14TH AND 15TH CENTURIES (PERIOD III) (illus 101)

In terms of new building operations, this period was marked by efforts of the community to repair major structures damaged by warfare; and to take the opportunity to remodel the layout in order to reflect new trends in monastic discipline. The new works were both the result of practical expediency and the need for improvement within a less austere regime.

The community found itself inevitably drawn into a pattern of cross-Border warfare which persisted from the late 13th century until the mid-16th century. The chaos and panic created by the invasion of Scotland by Edward I in 1296 and his determination to maintain control of the Borders heralded an anxious period for the community. Abbot John Morel swore fealty to the English king at Berwick in August 1296. Edward had visited Jedburgh in May and June of that year and returned in October 1298 yet, despite the efforts of the Jedburgh canons to comply, the lead from the roof of the church was removed by English forces in 1305.

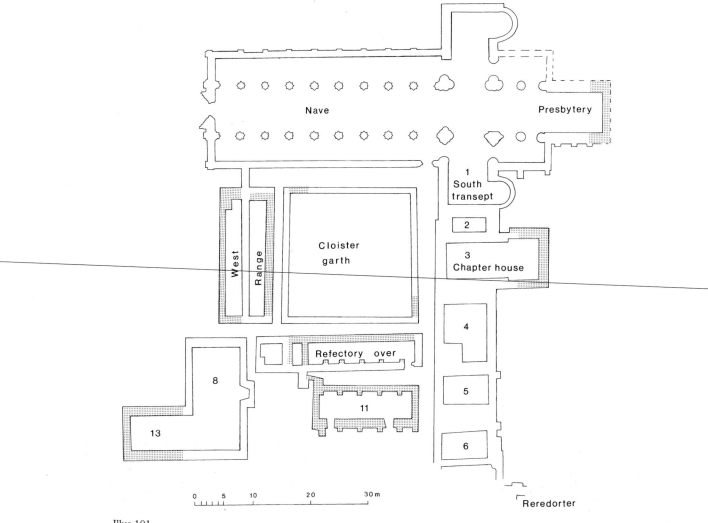

Illus 101
The layout of the abbey in the 14th and 15th centuries.

That the community supported the English cause is further suggested by the request of Edward II to Abbot William in 1307 to keep the peace (Bain 1881, 29). It is probable that the departure of some of the brethren between 1314 and 1324 to their lands in north Yorkshire was prompted by fear of retribution from the Scottish king Robert I. It was probably only when David II returned to Scotland in 1357 that relative stability returned to the area and a period of prosperity commenced which lasted more or less to the early years of the 15th century. The destruction of Jedburgh Castle by a local Scots force in 1409 after it had been held by the English since 1346 heralded a second, lengthy period of unrest. During that time the threat of war was never far away, culminating in the furious campaigns of the 16th century. The abbey was attacked twice by English forces in the 15th century – by Sir Robert Umfraville in 1416 and by the Earl of Warwick in 1464. The extent of the damage to the abbey is not known.

THE REMODELLED CLOISTER

The remodelling of the cloister coupled with the rebuilding of the Chapter house were most probably the results of damage to the site during the early 14th century. It was likely that work did not start until after 1326 when the exiled canons returned from Yorkshire.

The damage which prompted such major works, and which had significant structural implications for most of the Period II buildings on the cloister terrace, was thought to have been extensive. The documentary record is not specific: the main concern seemed to be about the robbing of lead from the church roof by Sir Richard Hasting in 1305. The evidence retrieved during the 1936 excavation (when the structures most affected were uncovered) seemed to show rebuilding over Period II walls which were somewhat erratically damaged. The most noticeable was the N wall of the secondary South cloister alley which overlay the N wall of the Period II refectory (compare the arrangement at Inchcolm Abbey: illus 102). In addition to the albeit limited stratigraphic evidence, there was no doubt that the Period III cloister belonged to an entirely separate building phase from that perceived in the 12th century. There is every indication that the Period II claustral ranges were completed by the mid-13th century as part of an integrated complex.

The need to re-establish the cloister and West range as well as the relative ease with which it was achieved could be explained by major structural damage to the site during the 14th century. The desire to extend and improve the facilities of the abbey linked the secondary West range with the extensions to Structure 8 and led to the creation of Structure 13.

'The rebuilding of a cloister, although sometimes conceived as a separate enterprise. . .was very often accompanied by the modernisation of the adjoining domestic ranges' (Platt 1984, 155).

Moreover, the new, wider, claustral circuit and Structure 13 generally improved the W side of the site and it might be possible to see these refinements as part of an implied upgrading of the western access to the abbey. The presence of the main entrance to the abbey complex via Abbey Close and documentary sources suggest that the upgrading of the abbey defences by the construction of Dabies Tower and the other towers to form a defensive line along Canongate coincided with the demise of the Castle in 1409. The limited evidence from excavation in the W of the site could be seen as a result of the increased wealth of the community which stimulated further efforts to protect that community.

Illus 102
Inchcolm Abbey: the refectory over the South cloister alley.

THE ADDITION OF STRUCTURE 13

'Separation of revenues and activities carried with it separation of lodging and staff, and by the end of the 12th century, the great abbots had quarters of their own, with a private chamber, hall, chapel and the rest' (Knowles 1956, 1, 273).

The Period II Structure 8 appeared to fit within this tradition, having been extended by the addition of Structure 13 (illus 56; 57) and by the upgrading of the garderobe arrangements. Because the level of the new basement of Structure 13 was appreciably lower than the undercroft in Structure 8, how the upper floor of the extension related to that of Structure 8 was not entirely clear. However, their upper floors were directly linked and shared access to the new garderobe chute. If the upper floor of the new building was at the same level as the upper floor of Structure 8, it would have given the new undercroft a ceiling height of some 5m. More likely there was some form of stepped access between the two – possibly steps up – from the upper floor of the Period III extension, through a doorway in the N wall of Structure 8 and into the upper chamber.

The location, role and complex chronology of Structure 13 were echoed to some extent by the abbot's lodging at Arbroath Abbey (illus 103) which progressed from a '. . .relatively modest first-floor suite of rooms. . . to form a handsome, semi-independent residence. . .' (Fawcett 1985, 23). There were many examples of the original, fairly minimal accommodation of the superiors of a monastic house being regularly refined and extended over the 14th and 15th centuries. This was seen as an attempt to keep pace with the increasing status of the heads of such houses in society at large. However, the extreme dilapidation of the remains of Structure 13, later referred to as 'the Abbot's Hall', renders more than the broadest comparisons impossible.

THE EAST RANGE

Excavation did not indicate that there had been substantial changes to Rooms 1, 2, 4 or 5 during these two centuries although the sparse archaeological record may reflect the destruction of the evidence. It is not even clear if the Chapter house was enlarged during this period or if such alterations were carried out at the same time as the construction of the rest of the East range. Caution, however, dictates that this event should be described here.

The extensive changes within Room 6 can be attributed with some justification to war damage, probably

Illus 103
Arbroath Abbey: the abbot's lodging.

during the Wars of Independence. Although reports broadcast by armies on campaign were usually little more than propaganda (McRoberts 1962, 427), Sir Richard Hastings' account of his assault on Jedburgh is usually given credence and his attack is believed to have caused considerable damage to the abbey. Morton (1832, 11) states that Hastings removed lead from the church roof and he describes the abbey as uninhabitable in 1300. Other authorities, probably correctly, reach the same conclusion for the year 1305 (Cowan & Easson 1976, 92). In all likelihood lead was also stripped from some of the claustral buildings, leaving them too in a ruinous state.

As a consequence, an extensive programme of repairs must have been of paramount importance. However, this scheme was apparently interrupted by the canons' flight to England around 1313 (Bain 1881, iii, 630; 894) and it must be wondered whether the abbey ever fully recovered from the trauma. As well as the re-organization of the S end of the East range, this programme of repair, upgrading and expansion probably included the remodelling of the refectory and the construction of new buildings such as Room 12 and a new range, represented by Room 11, on the abbey's southernmost terrace.

THE ENLARGED CHAPTER HOUSE

It has been suggested (**6.2** above) that the original Chapter house was a small, temporary, albeit stone, structure that was extended at a later date. This remodelling could have been contemporary with the construction of the adjacent Rooms 2 and 4 although the time span between the two building phases appears rather short. It is also possible that the Chapter house was enlarged in response to a growth in the monastic community – a familiar situation during the 13th century. More likely options, however, are that the Chapter house was expanded by an ambitious abbot, wishing to see his house grow in splendour; or that the canons were forced to rebuild parts of their abbey following one of the many raids inflicted on it over the centuries.

Whatever the cause, extending the building to the E was a relatively simple operation, involving the addition of one extra bay, probably only of one storey. Its width of only 5.3m would not have warranted an aisled arrangement: indeed, there was no evidence of pier bases either within the room's interior or within any of its walls.

Chapter houses were sometimes extended and simultaneously divided into two chambers. Between 1313 and 1321, the Chapter house at St Andrews Cathedral Priory, measuring 7.7 × 6.5m (roughly the same area as the Period II chamber at Jedburgh), was converted into a vestibule for a new Chapter house, measuring 14.0 × 6.5m (RCAHMS 1933, 236). The area of the new building was identical to that of the Period III Chapter house at Jedburgh although, if the latter had been partitioned, the new sub-divisions would simply have been too small to function effectively.

DESTRUCTION OF ROOM 6

The S end of the East range never recovered fully from the catastrophic damage to its upper storey(s). The insertion of a partition wall allowed the S half of the undercroft to be reused as the basement of a two (or more)-storeyed, free-standing building whereas the bays to the N of this wall remained derelict and were used subsequently as a midden. Artefacts retrieved from the midden point to its deposition beginning in the mid-14th century, thus placing the insertion of the partition wall at a similar, or earlier, date and the destruction of Room 6 earlier still. If the demolition was intentional, as seems likely, it was the probable result of the attack by Sir Richard Hastings early in the 14th century.

The range of finds within the midden points to it being a non-selective, general rubbish deposit. In apparent contradiction to this argument was the substantial proportion of mammal bones derived from high-meat joints although this may simply indicate that slaughtering and most butchery was done away from the claustral area. The abundance of bones suggests that the refuse did not come from the canons' kitchen or refectory where meat was supposedly absent, except on special occasions. However, many monasteries abandoned meatless diets in the later Middle Ages and the midden may well represent the waste derived from the canons' refectory during the 14th and 15th centuries. Other possible sources of this debris are the kitchens of the infirmary, guest houses, and lodgings of abbey officials, at least some of which would be within easy reach of Room 6. Room 11, for example, is thought to be the undercroft of a guest house or of an official's private chambers (perhaps those of the abbot or prior) and, by analogy with many other religious houses, the infirmary was probably located just beyond the East range and could perhaps be equated with Room 12.

From the proximity of the river, it might be reasonable to expect to find fishponds within the abbey precinct, yet no freshwater fish bones were found in the midden assemblage whereas the bones of marine species occurred in relative abundance. A likely reason was the non-availability of flat, riverside land, rather than a preference for seafood. Indeed, it has been argued (in a paper given by CK Currie to the Medieval Europe conference in 1992) that, during much of the medieval period, freshwater fish and fishponds were status objects, unlike sea fish which ranked very low. A similar situation was encountered during recent excavations at the late medieval Smailholm Tower, 16 km (10 miles) N of Jedburgh, where bones of freshwater fish were also absent (Barnetson 1988, 258).

The shortage of pig bones signifies either: a dislike for the animal's meat (unlikely outwith the Highlands); that it was reserved for special occasions; that it was limited to certain members of the community and guests; or, most likely, that an abundance of cattle and sheep, received as teinds or rents, discouraged the rearing of pigs. Similarly, the minimal effort put into catching wild species may have also stemmed from a cheap, readily available supply of beef and mutton/lamb.

ROOM 11 (SOUTH RANGE) (illus 53; 54)

The location of this range probably owed more to topography than to a strict adherence to a pre-ordained monastic layout. Level ground was at a premium and all suitable space – including this, the lowest terrace – was exploited to the full. Although this building has been dated to the 13th century (RCAHMS 1956, 206), the extensive use of the local, dark red sandstone suggests contemporaneity with the 14th-century remodelling of the refectory.

The building's function has not been positively identified although possible roles include: an infirmary; a guest house; or the lodging of an abbey official, perhaps the abbot or prior. By general analogy, the infirmary was likely to be outside the East range and may well have had some connection with Room 12 (see below). The infirmary would have housed the old and the sick brethren as well as those being bled; it would also have had its own chapel, kitchen, refectory and perhaps other rooms. The range that included Room 11 was limited to two storeys to allow adequate light into the adjacent refectory and was simply too small to be the infirmary. Furthermore, the garderobe chute in the SE corner of the building (the only one located) would have been woefully inadequate as the infirmary's only latrine.

At the priories of Ely Cathedral and Tynemouth the guest house and prior's lodging were both to the S of the refectory. One of these roles may have been assumed by Jedburgh's Room 11 which could be interpreted as a basement cellar below residential accommodation at first-floor level.

ROOM 12

This structure could not be closely dated nor its purpose easily identified from the limited evidence retrieved from excavation. However, both the stratigraphic sequence and a simple, visual comparison between its clay-bonded, rubble masonry and the superb ashlar of the East range confirmed that the doorway at the SW corner of Room 12, and hence the building integral with it, post-dated the construction of Room 6. This relative chronology and the similarity between the W wall of Room 12 and the secondary partition wall in Room 6 suggest that the former building dates from the phase of redevelopment that followed the demise of the S end of the East range. Most of the artefacts retrieved from levels associated with the construction of Room 12 pre-dated the destruction (and in some cases the construction) of the East range. This apparent anomaly can be explained by soil erosion and landscaping which redeposited these objects, some of them from ditch 928, perhaps after the ditch had been truncated.

It is not clear whether Room 12 replaced an earlier building or if it was an entirely new structure, built after the demise of the East range. From its location, it is more likely to have been an infirmary (or at least one of its ancillary buildings) rather than a guest house or the lodging of an abbey official. Indeed, it was the usual practice to site the infirmary beyond the East range, near to the monastic cemetery, and downstream of the reredorter, as was the case at nearby Kelso Abbey (Tabraham 1984, 401).

6.4 LATER REPAIRS AND ALTERATIONS
FROM THE LATE 15TH TO MID-16TH CENTURIES (PERIOD IV) (illus 104)

THE AREA OF THE EAST RANGE

THE CHAPTER HOUSE

It is easy to imagine that the Chapter house was enlarged by an ambitious abbot or because the community was expanding. It is difficult to believe that the subsequent contraction (illus 105) was provoked by anything other than structural damage, whether at the hand of man or by the ravages of time.

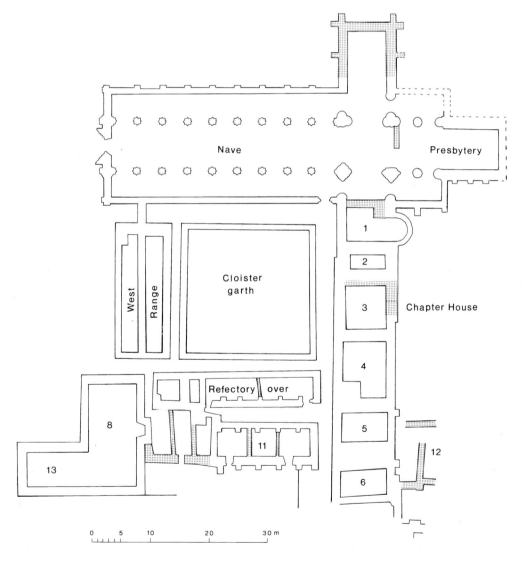

Illus 104
The layout of the abbey in the early 16th century.

A late 15th- or early 16th-century date for this radical change is suggested by the similarity between the octagonal pier in the centre of the chamber and those in the chapter houses at Cambuskenneth, Crossraguel and Glenluce abbeys (RCAHMS 1963, 128; MacGibbon & Ross 1896, III, 138; RCAHMS 1912, 106). The small number of interments (all coffin burials) that post-dated this change – three in the backfilled robber trench 888 and two adjacent to the N wall – support a relatively late date for this phase of reconstruction.

The Chapter house at Cambuskenneth is now demolished although its roof was evidently vaulted with transverse ribs. Glenluce is better preserved. There the rib-vaulted roof of the building (at 7.3m square, almost identical in size to that at Jedburgh) springs from a moulded central pier, 3.4m high, and from corbels in each angle and midway along the walls. Similarly, the ceiling of the four-bayed Chapter house at Crossraguel was rib-vaulted from a central, compound pier with corbels in the angles and vaulting shafts along all but the E wall, where a corbel had been substituted to allow for the abbot's seat below. At Glenluce (illus 106) an early 16th-century rebuild has been assumed from the evidence of tracery within two three-light windows in the E wall, whereas those in the E wall at Crossraguel may belong to the century before.

If the rebuilding of the Jedburgh Chapter house was contemporary with that at Crossraguel, then the architect of change was perhaps John Hall, abbot from 1478 until his death in 1484, or his successor, Thomas Cranston (1484–88). Hall initiated repairs to the East end of the church, perhaps damaged during a raid by the English in 1464 (although it may have also suffered from age), and he also began the reconstruction of the crossing tower (**8** below). The same attack may have also affected the Chapter house which, being such an important building to the monastic community, would have been a prime candidate for immediate restoration.

ROOM 4

According to one source, Room 4 was robbed of much of its masonry during the 18th century in order to build houses and to repair a nearby waulk mill (Watson 1894, 96). This may account for the paucity of information associated with the constructional phasing of the chamber. As a consequence, it was difficult to reconcile the layout of this room with that of the adjacent Period IV Chapter house.

OUTSIDE THE CHAPTER HOUSE (illus 47)

There is overwhelming evidence that the principal monastic cemetery was beyond the East range. Burials of probable monastic age were uncovered at Murray's Green, beyond Abbey Place, during the 19th century (Hilson 1872, 349) and large numbers of human skeletons were also unearthed when the same area was landscaped in recent years. Several graves had been disturbed by the insertion of a wall (960), after which 19 skulls and numerous other bones were re-interred against the wall's inside face. The presence of three stone coffins near to Rooms 1 and 2 are an indication that the cemetery extended up to the East range itself, the proximity of the graves to the Chapter house being a likely pointer to the incumbents' seniority.

Although the construction of the wall (960) post-dated that of the Period III Chapter house, excavation could

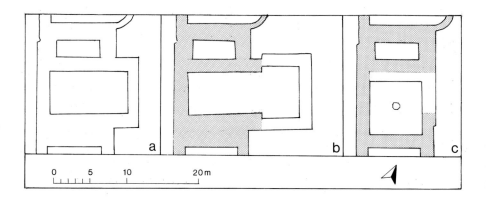

0   5   10   20m

Illus 105
The principal structural phases of the Chapter house:
a) Period II b); Period III; c) Period IV.

Illus 106
Glenluce Abbey: the interior of
the early 16th-century Chapter
house, its roof supported by a
central pier.

not determine whether it was built before or after the building's demolition. If the two structures coexisted, the wall must have been quite low in order to allow light to enter the window(s) in the E wall of the Chapter house, the gap between the two structures being only 2m. The angled wall, together with the N wall of the Period III Chapter house, may have lined a passage similar to those at Faversham Abbey (Philp 1968, 28) and at Crossraguel Abbey, the latter providing shelter between the church or Chapter house and the infirmary range (Pevsner 1962, 114). At Jedburgh this conjectural passage appears to lead from Room 2 (the slype) towards Room 12, tentatively interpreted as part of the infirmary range.

Investigations to the NE of the Chapter house were somewhat cursory and the role of the masonry feature there (966) remains unclear. It resembles an angled buttress although, if this was its function, the E–NE face of the adjacent wall 960 would have been external, rather than being on the inside of a passage. Other possible interpretations for the masonry 966 include the base of a door jamb associated with the inferred passage and a section of the same wall as is the tusking at the SE corner of the South choir chapel. The latter interpretation implies that at least some of the above alterations belonged to Abbot Hall's rebuilding programme of the late 15th century.

THE W AND S OF THE SITE

This period reflected the decline of a much reduced community in the face of relentless warfare and profound social change. In the W and S of the site, the evidence for building works during this period can be described under two headings: the partial and crude repairs of dilapidated Period II structures; and the possible slighting and conversion of elements of the conventual buildings to create a fortification after 1545.

Despite its size, Jedburgh Abbey was generally thought never to have had a very large community of canons and, despite the scanty documentation for the numbers in residence as compared with the other great Border abbeys at this time, the figures were modest indeed. Available documentation states the minimum numbers of canons after 1450 were as follows:

1464	8 canons	1547	7 canons
1516	10 canons and abbot	1553	5 or 6 canons
1528	10 canons and abbot	1542–53	1 canon
1542	7 or 8 canons		

Four canons of the abbey survived till 1560; three of whom were dead by 1583 (Dilworth 1983, 234–5). The extreme dilapidation of the conventual buildings was regarded as the main reason for the small size of the community although the abbey church cannot have been utterly ruinous even after the 1545 raid, services and ordinations being held there as late as 1550.

This small community was borne along by the general trend away from spiritual considerations in the face of increasingly secular interests and by extensive manipulation of monastic estates and revenues by local families. In the case of Jedburgh, the appointment of John and Andrew Home after 1513 was the imposition of a local laird's son as commendator – the suitability of either on religious grounds was questionable.

'In the 16th century, indeed, the Border abbeys were not regarded as spiritual power houses, but as sources of revenue and positions for royal servants or predatory individuals.' (Dilworth 1983, 247).

As the aims of the organisation were focused more on the secular than the spiritual, the impetus to maintain and repair church buildings receded:

'Neither the commendator nor the monks had any interest in maintaining buildings other than their domestic quarter, so that the Church decayed or, if damaged in military operations, was imperfectly repaired.' (Donaldson 1965, 135).

This policy was evinced by the crude masonry seen in the subdivisions of Structure 14 and in the buttresses (1215, 1216 etc) supporting the S wall of the church. The most striking characteristic of both areas of work was the extensive reuse of a variety of moulded stones. In walls 409 and 440 there were some fourteen fragments of round-section pillars varying in diameter from approximately 0.3–0.72m as well as numerous miscellaneous moulded fragments. The range of types and their general high quality implied that they originated in a complex ashlar building or buildings, possibly structure 9 from Period II. This use of residual stonework from demolished or redundant buildings nearby was also apparent in the crude building of buttresses bases 1215, 1216 and 1225: there was noticeable use of broken grave slabs – even more suggestive of hasty repair and unsentimental attitude.

6.5 THE DEVELOPMENT OF THE EAST RANGE

PERIOD II

The artefactual evidence has shown that ditch 928 was infilled some time after 1161, presumably in readiness for the foundations of the East range to be laid. Between then and the construction of the reredorter, several decades later, another temporary latrine – perhaps a timber building at the river's edge – must have been in use although none was identified by excavation.

The masonry at the N end of the range was too fragmentary to be dated with any accuracy whereas the style of the piers and vaulting ribs in Rooms 5 and 6 proclaim the work of early 13th- century craftsmen. Although the dating is far from precise, the evidence does suggest that the East range was begun adjacent to the church, perhaps in the third quarter of the 12th century, and finished at the river's edge about a half century later. Over this period architectural styles changed but, as at many medieval monuments, such changes were readily incorporated into the building programme.

Although it is difficult to visualize the overall appearance of the completed East range from the dearth of evidence that survived, much can be deduced by integrating certain aspects of the standard monastic plan with the results of excavation. The slype (Room 2), adjacent to the South transept, comprised a short passage with doors (probably within Romanesque arches) at each end, giving passage from the cloister to the monastic burial ground and probably also to the infirmary. It is not clear whether the Period II Chapter house (illus 105; 107), next to the slype, remained in operation during the 13th century or whether it had been replaced by the larger (Period III) building.

The day stair was probably reached from Room 4. Room 5 was probably accessed only from the cloister

Illus 107
The East range in 1987, showing the layout of the three phases of the Chapter house. The new visitor centre stands beyond the S end of the range.

whereas Room 6 appeared to have doors in its E and W walls. This southernmost chamber, evidently a simple storage cellar, was apparently windowless.

The reredorter was sited over the course of the Jed Water and extended some (unknown) distance to the E of the range, at right angles to it. The route from the canons' dormitory to the latrines was contingent on the number of storeys above Room 6: intermediate floors would have allowed for a simple passage (and a level roof); if the contours of the sloping ground were followed there would have had to be a flight of steps.

PERIOD III

Following the demise of the S end of the range, a free-standing building (perhaps a mill) was erected within, and possibly beyond, the S bays of Room 6. The N side of the room was abandoned and used thereafter as a midden.

PERIOD IV

During this period no further changes were apparent in Room 6 and, if Rooms 2, 4 or 5 had been altered, the evidence had been lost or masked before 1984. Hence, the only identifiable modifications to the East range were confined to the Chapter house and its environs, the change probably being linked to the restoration of the E end of the church by abbots John Hall and Thomas Cranston, between 1478 and 1488.

If the day stair had been adjacent to the Period II or III Chapter house it would not have survived the final remodelling programme, perhaps indicating that the stair was situated on the S side of Room 4 or that the dormitory had been abandoned by this stage. The latter hypothesis is further endorsed by the suggestion that the canons slept within the crossing and transepts during the 16th century (RCAHMS 1956, 202).

6.6 THE ABBEY FORTIFIED?

In addition to strictly monastic building programmes during this period, there was some evidence to suggest that the reduced abbey ranges saw limited re-use as a fortification, most notably in 1548 and 1549.

The extensive campaigns waged in southern Scotland by French, Scottish and English armies from the early 1520s to 1559 had profound impact on most of the Border towns and villages. Although never one of the well documented forts of either Franco-Scottish or English troops, Jedburgh, with its abbey and town defences, emerged as one of the secondary power bases and was occupied by both sides over the years.

The extant documentation concerning the construction of forts is concerned largely with works at the main centres. Perhaps because there was no reference to a fort at Jedburgh, the identification of the 16th-century campaigns with the 'Rampart' (which lay to the E and N of the church and cloister) was never made. There were problems in isolating distinctive earthworks from the mass of infilling and landscaping which the abbey site sustained after the Reformation. However, after the recent excavations, more evidence was found to justify a closer scrutiny of this intriguing possibility.

The abbeys of Jedburgh and Kelso were damaged in 1523 by the English during the rather half-hearted moves by a combined French and Scots army to invade England. It was with the birth of the future Mary Queen of Scots on 8 December 1542 that the impetus towards full-scale war across the Borders gathered momentum. King Henry VIII embarked on a policy of trying to coerce the Scots into the marriage of the infant Queen with his young son Edward. The 'Rough Wooing' was rigorously promoted by the Earl of Hertford and two armies during 1544 when they '. . .burned and looted from Leith to the Borders. . .' (Donaldson 1956, 70). On 27th May 1544, correspondence between Hertford and Henry described the abbey of Jedburgh as '. . .a house of some strength, and may be made a good fortress. . .' only if it was considered to be '. . .tenable without mayne armye. . .' (*ibid*, 393). In the event, '. . .the abbey likewise they burned, asmoche as they might for the stone worke. . .' on 12th June 1544 (Hamilton Papers II 393).

Hertford returned the following year to carry on the devastation and on 13th September 1545 the army moved from '. . .Kelso to Jedworth and then to Wark burning and wasting the country in their way'. On 18th September, after ten hours foray along the Water of Teviot and the destruction of fourteen or fifteen villages, Jedburgh abbey and town were burnt. (CSP 1898, 80).

The scale of the damage to the abbey fabric was not certain and it was generally assumed that Hertford exaggerated his successes for propaganda purposes. The English re-occupied Jedburgh after their victory at the Battle of Pinkie in 1547 when the town featured as one of a series of strong points maintained by both sides. Letters to Hertford (by now Protector Somerset) during January 1548 mentioned troops at Jedburgh under Sir Oswald Wolstrop but a French force under its commander, D'Esse, appeared to be the most likely candidate for refortifying the town and abbey. From the spring of 1548, a French garrison held the town from where they mounted regular attacks southward including, most notably, the destruction of Ferniehirst Castle. The gruesome fate of the English garrison there at the hands of Scots troops was a consequence of the tyrannical rule of the English commander: the French could do nothing to stop the slaughter. In response, an English army was ultimately despatched and the French, '. . .receiving intelligence of their design. . .' (*ibid*, 170), retreated into the countryside. They were much reduced by disease by this time, having no more than 1500 men and 500 horses (Jeffrey 1864 II, 170). This still represented a considerable French force under the command of a senior general, based in the town for some months. In addition, a letter to Somerset from Sir John Buttrell (at Broughty Fort, of 30th April 1548) mentioned that 'The abbot of Paisley brought hither two 'anseyns' of Frenchmen from Jedworth to scale the fort, and all his Fife adherents. . . .' (Bain 1881, 113).

The overwhelming characteristics of the fortifications erected by both sides in the campaigns of 1540s and 1550s were that they were built on the principles of 'Trace Italienne' and that they were primarily earthworks (Merriman 1982). These theories saw the introduction of new European designs of fortification, based essentially on a system of flanking fire from strategically located gun positions. Some forts during these campaigns were built entirely *de novo* (for example, Eyemouth, Haddington, Dunglass, Inchkeith and Lauder) but there were also attempts, particularly by the English, to adapt existing fortifications or, indeed, any convenient structure.

As has been already noted, Hertford considered using Jedburgh Abbey as a fort. He chose to fortify Hume and Roxburgh Castles although ecclesiastical sites were also being surveyed for this purpose throughout 1549; and a plan was drawn up for the conversion of Lindisfarne Priory by Giovanni di Rosetti. Although the work was never undertaken, it was evident that a monastic complex could have been easily converted into an effective artillery fort. Coupled with this policy was the regular practice of the local townspeople of both Kelso and Jedburgh to use the abbeys for defence. Certainly in 1523, Ker of Ferniehirst defended the abbey against Hertford '. . .in the midst of its burning ruins. . .' (Jeffrey 1864, 293).

The use of earthworks enabled the construction of the most sophisticated fortifications in a relatively short time and for relatively little cost. More modest ramparts could have been more easily thrown up, particularly when using the shell of an existing stone building. It was in this regard that elements of the later work at the abbey could have been associated with military defences rather than the more usual interpretation of stone robbing after the Reformation.

Although it was difficult to date the platform (449) in Structure 13, it was possible that the slighting of what may well have been an already badly damaged stone building after 1545 was not simply later municipal clearance.

As has been pointed out in the discussion of the coin evidence from the excavation (**4.5** above), there was a significant gap in the range of dates reflected by the coins found. This might be explained by the rapid abandonment of the site and the reoccupation of abbey buildings on a completely different basis.

This reoccupation, the presence of a major French occupying force in Jedburgh; the construction of the Rampart; and the obvious strategic and fortification potential of the abbey ranges suggested reuse along military lines. The need for security against the neighbouring English forts of Lauder, Hume and Roxburgh might demonstrate the necessity for a military base at Jedburgh.

The 'Rampart' was described in 1857 as being about 12 yards broad and 7 or 8 feet high, at one time forming '. . .the fashionable promenade of the burgh, but for the past few years has been nearly deserted. . .' (Jeffrey 1864, 109). These dimensions conformed well with the style and standard of earthworks erected during the campaigns of the 1540s elsewhere in Scotland. This implied that the East range formed part of the southern limits of a defensive line, with the Rampart cutting off the gap between the abbey church and the market place with its tower. This was a fair indication of the integration of upstanding abbey walls with a new earthwork to defend the abbey from attack from the E and from the Canongate bridge. It was also possible that the route, ultimately rationalised into the main river crossing at Abbey Bridge End, derived in part from a similar bank which augmented or 'vamured' the East range walls. The use of a redundant parapet as a promenade and the fact that it did not appear to have a monastic origin suggested that it was just such a bank which led to the development of the 17th-century street frontage now followed by the main route southwards out of the town.

The South range of the abbey served a similar function for the S defences; and access along the monastic riverside walk and pend under Structure 13 could have served the reused undercroft. The two platforms or paved areas (449, 502) could have represented two gun platforms set on a terrace within an old monastic building and the eroded bank (485) could have been the traces of an associated earthwork. This may have been the origin of the route of The Bow overlying reduced abbey masonry.

This arrangement provided a SW corner bastion or gun platform in a circuit defined by Dabies Tower to the NW, the Market Place Tower to the N, and the abbey church tower itself as the 'citadel'. Such a gun platform would have looked up the Jed valley and may even have provided flanking fire along the line of the South range. It was also worth considering that the deliberate backfilling of the lowest buildings in the South range may have dated from this period. This possibility was backed by some coin evidence which suggested a mid-16th century date for the abandonment of Structure 14 in advance of the development of The Bow. Certainly, these structures were not mentioned in the burgh charter of 1671 (Jeffrey 1864, 145) and were completely absent on any 18th-century map of the town.

6.7 POST-REFORMATION ACTIVITY (1559–1875) (PERIOD V) (illus 108)

OUTSIDE ROOMS 1 AND 2

The graveyard to the N of the abbey church served the parish from 1602 (and probably earlier) until the present century (Laidlaw 1905, 41), yet the preservation of many of the skeletons outside Rooms 1 and 2 indicate that the monastic cemetery also continued in use after the Reformation. This apparent anomaly should be considered in the light of evidence from the excavated graves, three specific points being worthy of note. Firstly, three of the post-monastic inhumations were of young children (one of them probably a newborn infant) who, if unbaptized at death, would have been debarred from burial in ground consecrated by the Reformed Kirk. Secondly, in contrast to the cemetery to the N of the church, there were no grave markers, either *in situ* or within disturbed contexts, in this area. Thirdly, grave-digging appeared to be somewhat haphazard, many of the burials (both monastic and later) being disturbed with two graves (29 and 30) deviating considerably from an E–W alignment. The last two points are indicative of a lack of organisation, suggesting that there was limited involvement by church officials. In turn, this implies that, after the Reformation, the monastic cemetery became the burial ground for paupers, unbaptized infants and others who, for whatever reason, could not be interred in the main graveyard.

ROOMS 15 AND 16

If the S and E walls of Room 15 overlay those of Room 4 (which could not be proved without removing 1930s masonry), then the building measured 10.6 × 4.3m internally and, if each wall was of similar thickness (0.8–1.0m) to the building's W wall, its overall size and position would be identical to those of the 18th-century house of Andrew Preston (illus 67–69). A similar date of construction was suggested by sherds of Staffordshire slipware retrieved from within the clay bonding of the W wall.

Illus 108
Buildings overlying the ruined East range in the early 19th century. From an original drawing by D Roberts.

Room 16 was identical in position and width (its full length was not revealed) to the 18th-century 'John Preston's House' (illus 67; 68; 70) and to the 'smithy' illustrated in the 1st edition (1857) Ordnance Survey map. Its N wall was built directly over the S wall of the Period III Chapter house whereas it was not clear whether the building's S wall overlay wall 915 or if the two were one and the same structure. Again, the adjacent stonework of 914 may have been a comparatively early feature or part of the 18th-century arrangement. Eventually, Preston's house appears to have become uninhabitable, for it was converted into a smithy during the following century, the putative anvil setting being placed over the demolished masonry of 914.

THE SE CORNER OF THE ABBEY

Two possible sources of the cereal chaff and seeds recovered from post-Reformation levels in this area are the nearby 'Mitchell's Stable' (illus 67) and the putative cornmill, of which Room 17 was the basement. This building, defined on its N side by a presumed 14th-century partition wall, could not be positively identified with any of the three mills operating in Jedburgh in 1610 (Jeffrey 1855, 129) for, although one was named 'abbey mill' so, too, was a later structure, situated about 100m down-river (illus 73).

The absence of structural remains on the site of the 'Town House' is probably due to the building's complete demolition prior to the creation of The Bow. The fragmentary remains overlying the infilled N bays of Room 6 were possibly part of 'Mitchell's Stable'. No trace of 'Mitchell's House' was found during the 1984 excavation although the stone steps exposed in 1936–37 and the well piercing the monastic masonry between Rooms 5 and 6 may have been associated with it.

6.8 IN CONCLUSION

Whether motivated by reforming zeal or by political and economic expediency, the decline and 'urbanisation' of the abbey ranges at Jedburgh fell into a pattern common in 16th-century Scotland. Typically, the abbey church was retained and adapted for use as the new Reformed parish church while what was left of the claustral ranges was variously demolished, robbed of stone or partially reoccupied. The impact on the town plans of post-medieval and modern Jedburgh of the abbey nucleus was very apparent. The natural constraints of the terraced site and the requirements of the Reformed Church minister appear to have prevented the wholesale absorption of the abbey ruins within street frontages – despite the increasing use of The Bow by a growing community towards the E and SE of the site. The development of the manse and its outbuildings along the W of the site and the numerous town houses and workshops to the E preserved the broad outlines of the conventual ranges.

Apart from these structural considerations, the effect of the abbey on the town was reflected, on one hand, by the development of an important 18th-century textile industry and, on the other, by the continued use of the monastic gardens as orchards cultivating (amongst other things) the celebrated 'Jeddart Pears'. Both developments, particularly the former, were significant factors in the economic revival of Jedburgh. They were the direct successors of 'abbey industries', although to what extent the sitings of the numerous 18th-century mills and their associated water supplies were based on those of their monastic predecessors, is not fully understood.

> 'The rule of the canons regular is the Rule of St Augustine, who drew his brethren to live together and tempered the rigour of his rule to their infirmity. Like a kind master, he did not drive his disciples with a rod of iron, but invited those who love the beauty of holiness to the door of salvation under a modern rule' (Clark 1897, 34).

Despite the inevitable emphasis on the structural aspects of the development and decline of Jedburgh Abbey, its full story is the result of the interaction between a constantly evolving, complex institution and a developing society. However, the abbey buildings themselves do constitute the most graphic reflection of the importance and the chequered history of the site – both in terms of the quality and complexity of its architecture and the profound impact it had on the subsequent development of the town of Jedburgh.

THE LAYOUT OF THE ABBEY
Dennis Gallagher

Whilst it seems reasonable to assume that some form of plan was produced before work on the construction of the abbey began in the 12th century, certain problems arise when trying to establish the architect's intentions concerning the overall layout of the monastery. Without documentary evidence it is difficult to be certain which points the architects considered significant. Fernie (1978) has demonstrated the dangers inherent in any speculation on the length of the original units used in a particular building; at Jedburgh investigations were also hampered by the fragmentary state of the surviving structures. Nevertheless, an examination of the principal dimensions of Jedburgh Abbey, as revealed by the recent excavations, strongly suggests that a geometric grid, based on a unit of 5' 6", and the limited application of a system of proportions were used to lay out the church and conventual buildings (illus 109).

7.1 THE EAST END OF THE CHURCH

The original plan of the E arm of the church appears to be based on 27' 6" squares with its sub-divisions into units of 5' 6". The crossing, measured from mid-pier to mid-pier, is 27' 6" (8.4m) square, the piers of the choir are 5' 6" (1.68m) wide and 11' (3.35m) high to their springing points, the width of the choir from mid-pier to mid-pier is 27' 7" (8.4m) and the footing of the W wall of the transept is 5" 4.5" (1.64m) wide. The loss of the N wall and the rebuilding of the S wall of the choir aisle make it difficult to estimate the original overall internal width of the presbytery and choir aisles, the present width between wall footings being 54' 10" (16.7m).

It is apparent that the E end was laid out using multiples of 5' 6" although it is not clear on which part of the structure the measurements were based. In the architect's mind, the church may have been conceived as a linear grid, similar to those illustrated by Villard de Honnecourt (Stalley 1987, 69). Simple linear grids would emphasise points at the mid-piers whereas measurements from wall faces would be of more practical use to builders. Nevertheless, there is some evidence to suggest that the inner face of the footings of the primary E wall of the presbytery was used as a base for measurement, the distance from it to the W faces of the footing of the NE and NW crossing piers being 55' (= 5' 6" × 10) (16.8m) and 82' 6" (= 5' 6" × 15) (25.2m), respectively. The area of the crossing, choir and choir aisles appears to be based on a 55' square, the W corners of which are centred on the responds at the junctions of the nave and the transepts. It seems reasonable to conclude that the builders adopted a flexible approach, basing their critical measurements on more than one point of the structure.

7.2 THE NAVE

From mid-pier to mid-pier, the nave is 27' 4" (8.33m) wide, a distance presumably intended as 5 units of 5' 6", and its overall width of 56' 5" (17.22m) is approximately 5' 6" multiplied by 10. The width of the South aisle, between the wall face and the centre of the S arcade, is 13' 10" (4.22m), roughly one quarter of the total internal width, or 2.5 units of 5.5' (13' 9"). The North aisle is 0.45m wider (15' 2") than the South aisle because, although the exterior wall faces of the nave aisles are aligned with those of the choir aisles, the N wall of the nave is narrower than those of the South aisle and choir.

The length of the nave from the footing of the respond at the E end of the S wall to the internal footing of the W wall is 126' 4" (= 5' 6" × 23) (38.5m). The bays of the nave arcade, from mid-pier to mid-pier, are 13' 9" (4.2m) wide, being 2.5 units of 5' 6", except for the three westernmost bays which are slightly wider.

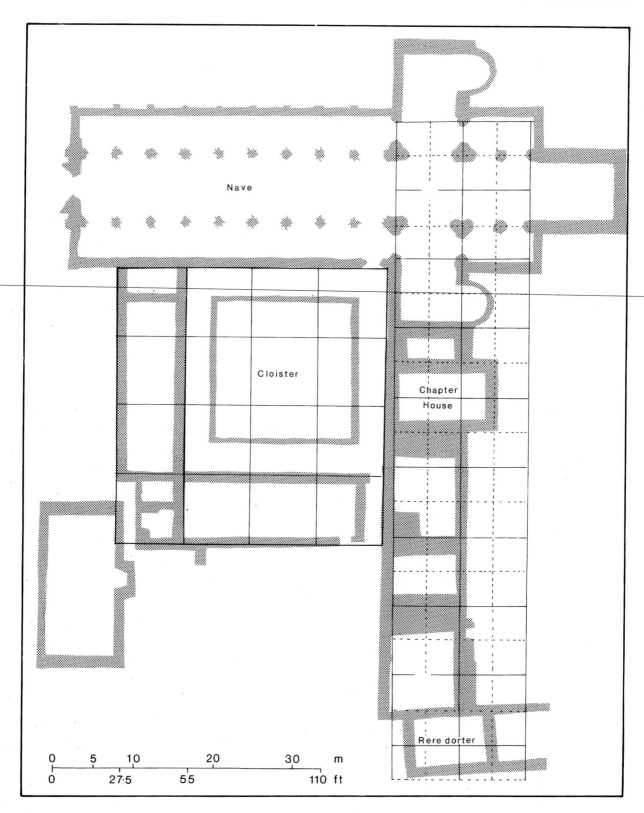

Illus 109
Gridded plan of the abbey.

It has been established that the proportion of 1: root 2 was in common use in major Anglo-Norman churches, especially when establishing the relative lengths of the nave and the total length of a church (Fernie 1976; Fernie 1979, 4; Singleton 1979) and such a relationship is evident at Jedburgh. The E arm of the church, measured from the interior footing of its E end to the line of the W edge of the base of the respond at the junction of the South aisle and transept, is 27.6 m. This figure multiplied by root 2 (1.414) is 39.03 m, only a slight deviation from the actual length of the nave which is 38.05 m.

7.3 THE CLAUSTRAL BUILDINGS

The East range appears to have been laid out as an extension to the 27' 6" square grid evident in the crossing. The distances from the S side of the crossing square to the N wall of the chapter house, to the S side of Room 4 and to the S limit of the East range, as defined by the SW corner of the reredorter are approximately 55', 110' and 220' respectively. It is not possible to take accurate measurements within the East range because the precise positions of the wall faces have been obscured or lost through stone robbing and the consolidation of foundations exposed during the present century. This apparent relationship between the E arm of the church and the East range suggests that the two structures were laid out at the same time although the buildings themselves were almost certainly not contemporary. However, the East range may have had priority over other claustral buildings as it not only contained the dormitory and chapter house but was also contiguous to a part of the church built early in the campaign and which helped define the cloister square. The exact size of the original chapter house is unknown. Subsequently, it was extended to the E beyond the limits of the range, the external walls of the projection forming a square with sides approximately 27' 6" (8.4m) in length.

The cloister, South range and West range were laid out within a 110' square, based on the external face of the S wall of the nave and hence not forming part of the same constructional programme as that associated with the East range. In all probability, the former structures were contemporary or near contemporary with the construction of the nave. The first phase cloister was 82' 8" (25.2m) square with the cloister garth measuring 55' 1" (16.8m) E–W and 54' 2" (16.5m) N–S, its area being one quarter of that of the combined cloister, South range and West range. Identical distances of 110' (33.5m) occur between the external face of the S wall of the nave and the external face of the S wall of the South range; and also from the exterior of the W wall of the West range to the exterior of the W wall of the East range. Measured between their external wall faces, the West and South ranges are both 27' 7" (8.4m) in overall width. The exact length of the West range is unknown although internally it appears to measure approximately 55' (16.8m). The internal measurements of the South range are obscured by later alterations although the building is approximately 82' 8" (25.2m) long.

Similar units appear to have been used for the construction of the Period II timber buildings. From the N wall of Timber Structure 1 to the N wall of Timber Structure 2 is approximately 4.25 m, the latter building also measuring 4.25m in width (N–S) which suggests that these two timber structures represent different phases of a single building. The total N–S measurement of approximately 8.5m across the two structures relates to a grid system of 27' 6" (8.4m) as discussed above. The N wall of Timber Structure 1 and the S wall of Timber Structure 2 are situated approximately 0.5m S of one of the E–W grid lines and the N terminal of ditch 928, a feature associated with the early Augustinian occupation, is the same distance from the church as is the N wall of Timber Building 1, a further indication of an overall plan for the layout of the monastic complex during its initial stage of development.

In summary, the abbey was laid out using a framework of squares, the choir and crossing and the cloister garth both consisting of 55' squares whilst the South range, West range and cloister were planned on a 110' square. The principal dimensions are 5' 6" (1.68m), 27' 6" (8.4m) and 55' (16.8m), all multiples of a basic unit of 5' 6" (1.68m). This unit, being one third of the standard perch of 16' 6" (Fernie 1985, 250), has a documented historical basis dating from the 7th century (Huggins 1981) and has been noted by Fernie (1976) in a study of Ely Cathedral. At Jedburgh, the widths of the nave and aisles and the lengths of the nave, the E arm of the church and the cloister were all measured in units of 5' 6" and bore simple arithmetic relationships to each other. The 5' 6" unit, being one third of a perch, may have appealed on the spiritual level as being an approximation to the average height of a man.

7.4 THE SIZE OF THE CLOISTER

In general, the size of a cloister was dictated by the number of residents within a monastery. Often, as at Jedburgh, the area of the cloister was increased subsequent to its original layout and, in many cases, its final dimensions were arbitrary, dictated only by the need to house a dormitory, Chapter house and other monastic buildings of adequate size in their traditional positions around the claustral precinct.

An examination of the surviving cloisters of Scottish Augustinian houses shows an arithmetic progression in size, based on a unit of 55'. The largest cloister is at St Andrews Cathedral Priory where dimensions of 164'(50m) × 162' (49.4m) (Cruden 1950, 12–13) are double those of Jedburgh (82' 8"). Several abbeys have cloisters and cloister garths similar in size to those at Jedburgh. For example, at Cambuskenneth, an Augustinian house observing the Order of Arrouaise, the cloister garth is approximately 55' square and the cloister measures approximately 80' (24.6m) N–S (RCAHMS 1963, 123). Recent survey work and excavation at Inchaffray suggest a cloister plan and length of nave very similar to those at Jedburgh (G Ewart pers comm). At the other end of the scale, the irregular cloister garth at Inchcolm measures approximately 44' x 42' (Fawcett *et al* nd, 32). Oronsay Priory has a cloister with sides varying from 39' 6" (12.1m) to 41' 6" (12.7m) long and a garth approximately 21' 6" (6.5m) square (RCAHMS 1984, 241).

It was usual for Augustinian houses to have either 13 or 26 canons although smaller numbers were also common. Unfortunately, information on the original numbers of canons in Scottish houses is not available. However, arranging monasteries into three categories according to cloister size (for example: St Andrews 164'; Jedburgh, Cambuskenneth and Inchaffray about 82'; and smaller houses such as Oronsay approximately 41'), suggests that an exact ratio of cloister size to the number of canons was common among Scottish Augustinians.

THE ARCHITECTURAL DEVELOPMENT OF THE ABBEY CHURCH

Richard Fawcett

The abbey church (illus 110) was the principal focus of the community of Augustinian Canons at Jedburgh between 1138 and 1560, and it is also the most complete structure to survive on the site. This chapter provides an outline account of its architectural development as an aid to fuller appreciation of the context against which the excavations took place.

8.1 THE CONSTRUCTION OF THE EASTERN LIMB AND TRANSEPTS

There seems to be no good architectural reason to doubt that construction of the eastern parts of the church of Jedburgh was begun soon after the abbey's foundation by David I and Bishop John of Glasgow in about 1138 (Cowan & Easson 1976, 92; Ross & Lorimer 1925; RCAHMS 1956, 194), and that masons trained in the Anglo-Norman tradition were brought up from England to carry out the work. It was the eastern parts which housed the most urgently needed areas of the presbytery for the high altar, at the far East end, and the choir, where the canons sang their daily round of services, a little further west. They were set out to an echelon plan, with semi-circular apsidal chapels to the transepts, as the outer element on each side of the formation, and with straight ends to the two-bay choir aisles next in the sequence.

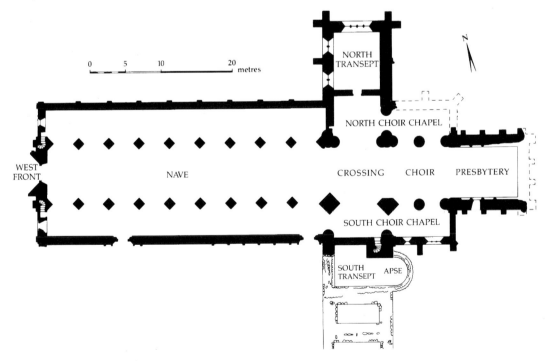

Illus 110
Plan of the abbey church.

The original form of the axial termination of the echelon, the presbytery's East end, however, is not known with certainty. The alternation between round and straight ends in the transept chapels and choir aisles might suggest that the presbytery would probably have had an apse as the culmination of the sequence. Certainly apses were the most common form of East end in major churches of the Anglo-Norman tradition by the first half of the 12th century, where there was no ambulatory or chapel beyond. On face value it might seem that a plan like that of Cerisy-la-Foret in Normandy, of a date around 1080 (Musset 1975, 156), is the most likely for Jedburgh. In apparent support of this, the architect Peter Macgregor Chalmers, claimed to have found 'somewhat limited' but 'sufficient' evidence for an apse in the course of inadequately recorded excavations in 1898 (Chalmers 1905, 185) although his coyness in giving details in itself leaves his findings open to doubt.

Against Chalmers' claims, excavations by the Office of Works in the 1930s located the foundations of a straight cross wall about 2m inside the later E gable, and this has been re-examined in the most recent campaign of excavations. On balance, although a case might be made that this straight line could have been some form of sleeper wall associated with the mouth of an apse, no evidence was found to support this view, and a rectangular E wall must thus be regarded as more likely. Straight East ends were certainly not unknown at this period. The presbytery of Archbishop Thomas of York's choir at Southwell in Nottinghamshire of between 1108 and 1114, for example, had a rectangular termination (Clapham 1934, 44, fig 13). It must be said, however, that since Bishop John spent much of his episcopal career fending off the predatory interests of the Archbishops of York in the Scottish church, it is perhaps unlikely that it was one of their churches which was the specific inspiration for Jedburgh.

Assuming that the presbytery was of rectangular plan, on the basis of these indications, we must next consider the evidence for its original internal elevations. This evidence is sparse, but is consistent with there having been two levels, corresponding with the arcade and gallery stages of the adjoining choir; both of these levels seem to have been at least partly pierced by windows. There are also clear indications of a mural passage at the upper level, and possibly also of a decorative wall arcade at the lower level. The evidence for the latter is a base beneath later masonry on both sides of the choir (illus 111), a short distance to the E of the E choir arcade responds which, from its scale and position, seems most likely to have belonged to the start of a decorative engaged arcade. At a higher level are two truncated sections of string course. One, above the choir arcade arch springing level, may have delineated the top of the wall arcading, while the other, at the base of gallery level, probably marked the sill level of the mural passage. Also at gallery level, on both sides of the presbytery, is a major respond shaft, which must have belonged to the start of the inner arcade of the mural passage, and provision for access to this passage may be seen at the E end of the choir galleries. Supplementing this evidence externally, on the N side there are traces of window jambs at both levels, immediately beyond the E wall of the aisle (illus 112). One of these would be within the wall passage at gallery level, while the other would be within the upper part of the wall arcade. On both sides there is additionally some evidence for the curved line of the lower window's arch springing.

After the highly tentative evidence for the presbytery, it is a relief to turn to the greater certainties of the two-bay aisled choir section of the E limb, which represents the most complete surviving part of the first campaign (illus 113). There are also substantial remains of the original transepts, which show that the design of the E limb was continued into the inner parts of the cross arms at the junctions with the choir and nave aisles. As supplementary evidence for the extent of work carried out in the first campaign, the form of the responds and two E arcade bases of the nave suggests that those bays had to be built – or rebuilt – later than the rest of that limb when the existing nave was built towards the end of the century. This could indicate that at least two bays of the nave had been built in the first operation and were only removed when the rest of the later nave was well advanced. These two bays would presumably have been required both to accommodate adequately the canons' choir and to abut the crossing area. On the N side, the stub of the first aisle wall may also still be observed, incorporated within the later stub.

The earliest surviving parts of the church are of particular interest because of the way in which they illustrate something of the range of architectural inspiration which was being sought by patrons at what must have been one of the most exciting and outward-looking periods in the history of the Scottish church (illus 114). At Jedburgh, as at others of the foundations in which David I played a part, there are good reasons for suspecting that it was the king himself, with his wide knowledge of the English church and its new buildings, who ◆ suggested the model on which the building was to be based.

Illus 111
A base of the wall arcading of the
early 12th-century presbytery is
on the right of this illustration.
Above it is the wall arcading of
the presbytery as rebuilt in the
later 12th century.

Illus 112
The external junction of choir and presbytery on
the N side at the upper level. Between the broken
E wall of the choir chapel and the first presbytery
buttress can be seen the vertical line of a window
jamb resting on a string course.

Illus 113
The external junction of choir and presbytery on
the N side at the lower level. Immediately to the
left of the broken E wall of the choir chapel is the
capital of a window arch.

The most striking feature of Jedburgh's first design is the way in which giant column-like piers with scalloped caps rise through both arcade and gallery stages. It may be mentioned, incidentally, that it seems to have cost the designing mason a considerable effort to contrive this arrangement satisfactorily, and resort had to be taken to a wide variety of forms of stilting to ensure that all of the orders of the arcade arches sprang from the required levels. The immediate inspiration for this design is now generally accepted as having been the E nave bays of the Benedictine nunnery church at Romsey in Hampshire. David's aunt, Christina, a sister of St Margaret, was a nun there, and his own sister, Matilda, had been placed in her care at Romsey before her marriage to Henry I in 1100 (Boase 1943, 152). There are thus good grounds for assuming that David would have had sufficient of a continuing acquaintanceship with the foundation to be able to point to it as a possible source of ideas. The date of Romsey's reconstruction is not known with certainty, although, following re-evaluation of the dating of architectural sculpture at Canterbury of a type that is related to examples at Romsey, it may now be thought unlikely to have been started much later than about 1100 (Zarnecki 1978, 39).

However, Jedburgh was clearly not designed simply as a derivative copy of Romsey, but must rather be seen as an integral part of the development of a strand of architectural thought of which Romsey was a part. So far as can now be judged, the earliest building to have had an elevation of this type was the choir of the Benedictine abbey church of Tewkesbury in Gloucestershire, an area where there was a particular interest in the use of arcade piers of giant proportions. Unfortunately, following the 14th-century remodelling of Tewkesbury it is now only the remains of cloured-off arches on the side of the truncated piers towards the aisles which give the clue to the original arrangement (Clapham 1952, 10). Nevertheless, having been started in about 1087, there are no known variants on the type which could be earlier, and the case for the primacy of Tewkesbury in this group appears to be supported by the rather uncertain way in which aspects of the

Illus 114
The original bays of the choir.

design were executed. As a consequence of its later remodelling both the precise details of, and the sources for, the design of Tewkesbury are the subject of a debate which has been summarised by Fernie (1985, 1). But in spite of this it seems possible that in some respects Jedburgh had more in common with Tewkesbury than with Romsey. Both Tewkesbury and Jedburgh have a rather tentative quality in the working out of the relationship between piers and arches, by comparison with which Romsey appears more assured.

Among the many questions posed by the first work at Jedburgh in its present state is what, if anything, was originally intended for the clerestorey? Romsey was certainly provided with a full clerestorey, even if it was only eventually built over those nave bays which are of this type of design after a considerable delay. But at Tewkesbury many scholars now believe that there was no clerestorey in the late 11th-century E limb although it does appear likely that there was a triforium passage immediately below either a stone vault or timber ceiling of semi-circular section (Thurlby 1985, 9). At Jedburgh the evidence is rather confusing. There is certainly clear evidence on the N side of the choir, at the junction with the transept (illus 115), of a phase of clerestorey construction pre-dating that which was eventually built, and on face value this might be taken to indicate the intention to have a clerestorey from the start. The evidence consists of an area of earlier masonry incorporating two stretches of chamfered string course and a fragment of corbel table. These string courses must be the relics of the mouldings at sill and arch springing level of a range of windows which would have been of considerably smaller size than those which were later built, while the corbel table belongs to a wall

Illus 115
The N side of the choir at gallery and clerestorey levels. The evidence for the early clerestorey, visible at the junction with the transept, consists of two string courses and a section of corbel table.

head rather lower than the one we now see. It is perhaps natural to assume that the clerestorey represented by this evidence must be contemporary with the choir, and that the original choir was thus of three storeys.

However, the string courses are of a different – and probably later – type than those used elsewhere in the choir, having no quirk (V-shaped indent) between the vertical and chamfered faces. Beyond this, comparison with related details in other parts of the church may also support the idea of a significantly later date for this clerestorey fragment. The first points of comparison are related stubs of clerestorey in the cross arms, particularly on the E side of the South transept. These have similar string courses at the same height as those of the choir clerestorey fragment, with which they must certainly be contemporary. But part of a window reveal and of a wall passage arcade respond also survive in the South transept clerestorey, and the details of those would appear to show that the clerestorey represented by these fragments is later than the first choir campaign. The window reveal has a narrow chamfered margin around the opening, with a rebate for a detached nook shaft, while internally the corresponding fragment of the wall passage arcade has a chalice cap. None of this is of a character likely to be before the later decades of the 12th century.

In support of a secondary dating for the transept clerestorey, a comparison for its chalice cap may be made with those used in conjunction with secondary pointed arches which were inserted into the rear plane of the gallery openings on the N side of the choir (illus 116). These added arches appear to belong to 'an attempt to

Illus 116
The N aisle wall of the nave where it joins the
North transept. The jagged line in the broken
stump of wall indicates the junction of the earlier
and later 12th-century work.

stabilise the structure, or even perhaps to strengthen it in order to receive a clerestorey which had not
originally been intended. It may also be mentioned that the imposts and abaci of these inserted arches are like
the strings of the choir clerestorey fragment in having no quirk between the vertical and chamfered faces. A
further, but perhaps rather less significant, comparison may be made with the surviving portion of a window
at the E end of the N nave aisle, which to some extent reflects the detail of the transept clerestorey in its rear
arch cap and external reveal, and which is certainly part of the first phase of the late 12th-century nave
campaign.

While all of this evidence cannot be regarded as entirely conclusive, there certainly appears to be at least a
strong possibility that the earliest surviving evidence for a clerestorey over the E arm thus post-dates the first
building campaign by some decades. If this was the case it would seem that Jedburgh, as first designed, was
rather closer to Tewkesbury than to Romsey in having been planned for a two-storeyed elevation. In this
respect it may be worth remarking that at Romsey the three-storeyed elevation had been established in the
choir, where the design was not of the Tewkesbury-Jedburgh giant order type; the use of a clerestorey over
the giant order bays in the nave there was thus conditioned by other factors.

Another respect in which Jedburgh may have been closer to Tewkesbury was the internal covering of the
choir. Nothing has survived of the original ceiling through the two clerestorey building operations, but a
pointer to what may be seen as one of the continuing aesthetic themes of the church may be seen in the
transepts. In both of the cross arms, as will be discussed below, a barrel vault was either projected or built at a
later stage of the abbey's history, and it may be not entirely unwarranted to speculate that such covering to
these lateral spaces could have been prompted by what already existed in the E arm. It must be said that the
structure of the choir suggests that it is unlikely that it ever had a stone vault. Nevertheless, taking account of

the fact that such a covering was eventually introduced or projected for the two transepts, and allowing for the possible initial influence of Tewkesbury, is it possible that Jedburgh's choir was originally finished at successive stages of its history in some related manner, perhaps in the form of a semi-circular timber wagon ceiling? Any such ceiling would continue the arc of the E crossing arch, the chevron-decorated springing of which still survives on the N side of the choir, rising from the string above the gallery. There can, however, be no possibility of certainty on this score. At this point reference must be made to an enigmatic, diagonally-set, corbel-like projection immediately adjacent to this springing. In its present worn condition no function can now be assigned to it with confidence, unless it was intended to carry an additional order of the tower arch.

Before leaving the first building campaign, brief mention must also be made of the internal disposition of the transepts. As has been said, at the aisle ends of choir and nave the transept elevations were essentially similar to those of the choir. Beyond this point, however, rebuilding has destroyed much of the evidence for the elevations. Nevertheless, on the S side we still have one respond of the arch which opened into the apsidal chapel there (illus 117), which has two orders of nook shafts carrying cushion caps towards the main body of the transept. In addition, in both transepts there is still evidence of two tiers of narrow windows with finely detailed rear-arches set between the arches into the choir aisle and gallery on one side, and the arch of the transept chapel on the other. At the upper level the provision of access around the transepts by mural corridors is indicated by narrow passages leading off the galleries above the choir aisles. On the S side, above the fragment of the transept chapel respond, is a portion of the inner wall of the mural passage, incorporating part of the respond of the mural passage opening at this point.

Illus 117
The surviving jamb and arch springing of the arch into the apsidal chapel of the South transept.

8.2 THE REMODELLING OF THE PRESBYTERY

Once the E parts of the church were completed, there is no evidence of further significant operations for some decades. Somewhat perversely, when work did start again, it seems to have been the E limb which received the first attention, in the form of a reconstruction of the presbytery to a slightly lengthened, plan (illus 118). Very little has survived from this operation, although inspection of the remaining evidence, together with the clues provided by earlier views (Watson 1894, f p 93), suggests that it was of a design related to the choir of the Benedictine priory church of Coldingham in Berwickshire. Like Coldingham, Jedburgh had decorative arcading to the lower walls, and upper walls with an alternating rhythm of low and tall arches. This upper arcade ran in front of a wall passage, with windows on the outer face corresponding to the taller arches. Although a *terminus post quem* for Coldingham is usually taken to be an attack by King John of England in 1215/16 (MacGibbon & Ross 1896, I, 443), there seems to be little reason on stylistic grounds to doubt that in fact it dates from the later decades of the 12th century. The waterleaf and crocket capitals of the Jedburgh presbytery also point to a similar date. A small group of churches of similar design in northern England, such as Nun Monkton in Yorkshire and St Bees in Cumberland provide further support for a date around the 1180s (Pevsner 1959, 383; Pevsner 1967, 183).

Looking at this group of churches with elevations related to that of the rebuilt Jedburgh presbytery, the question again arises as to whether a clerestorey was intended for its E limb. Certainly no clerestorey above the main rank of windows was intended for Coldingham, St Bees or Nun Monkton, the relevant parts of which were not flanked by the aisles which might have made an upper tier of windows seem essential. Similarly, the presbytery of Jedburgh was aisle-less, and therefore arguably without need of a rank of windows above those corresponding to the choir galleries. Indeed, the choice of such a design for the presbytery, with what appears to have been the natural wall-head level rising to the same height as the top of the choir gallery, might be thought to strengthen the case which has already been made for the choir not originally having had a clerestorey. Nevertheless, it has to be said that the grandest of all variants on this design type, the nave of the collegiate church of Ripon in Yorkshire, did have an upper rank of windows. However, Ripon, which was

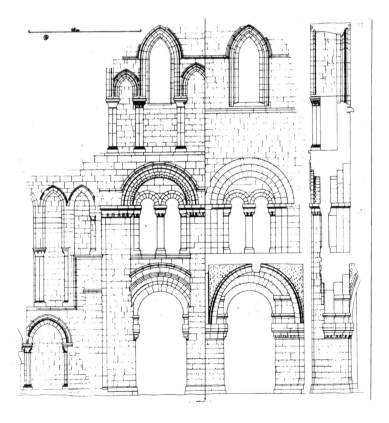

Illus 118
Measured elevations of the choir and presbytery.

started by Archbishop Roger of York shortly before his death in 1181, was altogether more ambitious than the other members of the group, and should not be regarded as offering the closest parallels for the Jedburgh presbytery. A proposed reconstruction of the original nave at Ripon is illustrated in Hearn (1972, 39).

However, if a clerestorey had not yet been planned for the E limb at the time the presbytery was rebuilt, it must have been very soon after it was completed that one was started. The stub of an earlier clerestorey on the N side of the choir, the evidence for which has already been discussed, seems likely to have been started in the last decades of the 12th century.

8.3 THE ADDITION OF THE NAVE

In fact the last decades of the 12th century saw simultaneously renewed activity at Jedburgh on a heroic scale, although the most important aspect of this activity was not in the E limb but in the nave. By comparison with the E limb, the nave is strikingly complete (illus 119), resulting from the use of the lower storeys of its western parts as a parish church between 1668 and 1875. It also appears markedly homogeneous. Nevertheless, examination of the details of the work indicates that it was probably completed in a number of closely consecutive phases. It has already been suggested above that the E bays of the nave may initially have been built as a continuation of the operations in the E limb in the early 12th-century campaign and only replaced after the rest of the nave had been started. At a higher level a change in the design of the gallery stage may be noted: whereas the four E bays have basically quatrefoil piers with additional smaller shafts on the N–S axis (except for the second bay on the N, which was not sub-divided), the five W bays have only pairs of major shafts separated by smaller shafts.

However, as a dreadful warning against over-neat conclusions based on such evidence, it should be noted that changes in the *tas-de-charge* of the aisle vaults complicate the picture. Those above the piers of the two E bays of the S aisle vaults incorporate heavier and thus seemingly earlier transverse ribs than those of the other bays, although the corresponding *tas-de-charge* in the outer aisle wall are of essentially the same type as in the other bays. Clearly, in a part of the building in which the constituent phases were separated by no great gap of time, it would be dangerous to place too great a burden of proof on excessively slight changes of detail.

The lower storey of the West front was probably among the earliest parts of the new nave to be started. The chief focus of this front is the cavernous processional entrance, surmounted by a triplet of gables above a horizontal string. Although it is not coursed in with the flanking masonry, it seems unlikely to represent a later addition. It has five principal orders, once carried on disengaged shafts and with caps of mainly Corinthianesque forms; these shafts alternate with continuous mouldings. The engaged inner order has classically-inspired foliage to the arch, and in the jambs there is similar foliage alternating with heads in quatrefoils; at impost level this order has pairs of delightful wyvern-like creatures. The proliferation of various types of chevron decoration to both arch and jambs introduces a note of late Romanesque elaboration which is remarkably absent from the rest of the nave, other than in the two processional doorways from the cloister into the S aisle, one of which is a complete restoration. Garton (1987, 69) suggests that the W doorway is secondary to the West front; however, although the idea is an attractive one, the present author feels that this is not supported by the structural evidence.

Internally the masonry of the lower part of the West front (colour illus VIII) is differentiated from that of the upper parts by the alarming downward slope towards the S of its bedding. This had to be corrected above the string course which runs at the level of the gallery sill. Further evidence for a break in the West front building operation is observable inside the two stair turrets which rise at the ends of the arcade walls. Above a level corresponding with the arch springing of the galleries, there is a change from steps of composite construction, formed on the extrados of a helical barrel vault, to steps of monolithic key-hole shape incorporating an integral newel.

Nevertheless, despite these changes, the basic design of the front is likely to have been determined at the start of the work, and the immediate inspiration for the upper part, rising through both gallery and clerestorey

Illus 119
The abbey church from the NW.

levels, may have been the nearby Tironensian abbey of Kelso, where the West front appears likely to have been started a few years before that of Jedburgh. At both, the main feature of the upper part of the design is a single lofty window, flanked by decorative arcading – a pair of intersecting arches at Kelso (RCAHMS 1956, 240) and a triplet of simple arches at Jedburgh. The links with Kelso are supported by similarities in the moulded detail, which may even suggest that some of the Jedburgh nave masons had come from there.

Some precedents for such a facade design may be found in the areas of France within which many of the ideas which eventually took root in Scotland first originated. Among examples which show something of a related approach to design is the Burgundian Cistercian church of Pontigny, of about 1155 (Dimier 1982, pl 111) although it is very likely that there were northern English intermediaries which provided the immediate stimulus for the choice of such a design. The influence of ideas which had originated in Burgundy and reached Scotland through northern England, where the activities of the Cistercian order provided fertile ground for the reception of ideas from eastern and northern France, is also apparent in a number of other aspects of the nave design (colour illus IX).

The piers themselves are of the clustered shaft type which, after a brief vogue in France in the 11th century, had been taken up by the Cistercians in their earliest surviving house at Fontenay in Burgundy – the area in which the order was born. The small-scale examples in the Chapter house there date to about 1155. Such piers were then quickly copied on a larger scale in northern England, reached Scotland soon after 1160 at St Andrews Cathedral, and had a considerable vogue on both sides of the Border in the later decades of the 12th century. (For a discussion on clustered shaft piers see Bilson (1909, 185), Ferguson (1975, 155) and Wilson (1986, 86)).

Other details of the Jedburgh arcade also show close links with both the north of England and St Andrews.

These include the earlier of the two nave arcade base types, in which the lower roll ends in a vertical face. By comparison, the bases at the E end of the nave are of the later type which has a full lower roll below a water-holding hollow with a filleted rim. Further links with both England and St Andrews are to be seen in the arcade arches, in which the angles of each order are relieved by a form of roll, while the soffits show variants on a triplet of rolls. Beyond this, telling comparisons may be made between at least one of the elaborated waterleaf caps at Jedburgh and examples at the Cistercian abbey of Byland, the luxuriantly fleshy carving of which shows a very similar approach.

In the general design of its internal elevation (illus 120), Jedburgh belongs within an Anglo-Scottish group, of which the Tironensian abbey of Arbroath in Angus and the Augustinian priory of Hexham in Northumberland (Hodges 1888) are the best surviving examples. All have arcades carried on keeled octofoil clustered shaft piers, and all have a relatively tall gallery stage, with two pointed arches contained by a semi-circular arch in each bay. Although there are differences at clerestorey level, all have a continuous open arcade in each bay, in front of the mural passage at that level. A number of the sculptural and architectural details of Arbroath and Hexham suggest they could be marginally later than Jedburgh. Among these pointers may be included the general use of waterleaf and crocket foliage at Jedburgh as opposed to the use of stiff leaf in comparable situations at the others, and the use of earlier base types in the main body of the Jedburgh arcade. In addition, the relatively larger size of the gallery stage at Jedburgh appears typologically earlier than those of Arbroath and Hexham.

While the difference in date between Jedburgh on the one hand and Arbroath and Hexham on the other is likely to have been slight, it does seem there may be a case for arguing that it was Jedburgh which set the pattern for the others; but, if so, what was the immediate inspiration for Jedburgh itself? Since so many buildings have been lost there can be no certain answer, but one very likely source of ideas is the choir of Scotland's most important cathedral, at St Andrews, to which reference has already been made on a number of counts. St Andrews was, like Jedburgh, the home of a community of Augustinian canons, and had been started in or soon after 1160, but it is important to remember that work there was still in progress throughout the whole time that Jedburgh's nave was being built (Cant 1976, 11; Cambridge 1977, 277). Beyond this, despite St Andrews' much greater size, assuming that the relative proportions of the three stages of the elevation there were the same in the choir as in the aisle-less presbytery, they must have been very similar to those of Jedburgh. St Andrews therefore seems to offer a convincing prototype for Jedburgh's nave in a number of respects.

8.4 THE CLERESTOREYS OF THE NAVE AND CHOIR

That there was a pause before the construction of the nave clerestorey is suggested by the change in the stair turret construction already mentioned; but the use of waterleaf or chalice capitals throughout this level probably suggests that the pause was not a long one. Nevertheless, the design of the clerestorey as built does seem to embody changes from the original design. Externally a large respond and arch springing at the W end on both sides, along with the large pilasters which define the bays at the jamb level of the arches, may suggest that originally the upper part of the clerestorey was to have been thicker; although the motive behind this may have been no more than the provision of an adequate wall walk to either side of the main roof.

It was presumably the resumption of work on the nave clerestorey which led to the decision to rebuild the choir clerestorey – but not that of the South transept – to a greater height, so that its wall head would be on a level with that of the nave. Whatever the external benefits of this heightening in the overall balance of the building, internally the consequent disproportionate relationship with the arcade and gallery below is one of the less pleasing features of the E limb. The new choir clerestorey may well have been started before the squatter one which was apparently started only a few years earlier had been taken very far. Indeed it may even have been started before the nave clerestorey itself was complete if the use of square abaci in the choir as opposed to polygonal abaci in the nave may be taken as as significant.

Here again, however, as with the vault ribs of the nave aisles, it may be that too much should not be

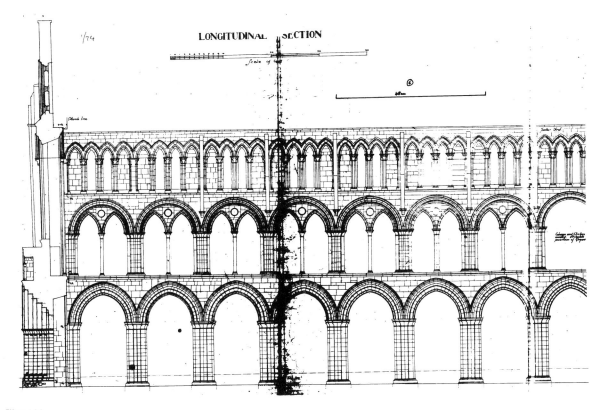

Illus 120
Measured elevation of the nave.

concluded from such slight changes. In fact the architectural evidence suggests that construction was underway in all parts of the abbey church throughout the decades at the turn of the 12th and 13th centuries, and that different teams of masons with varying architectural vocabularies were at work. The net result for the canons must have been that they were hard pressed to recite their offices anywhere within the church in anything approaching peace.

The form of the stiff leaf foliage to be found associated with some of the finishing touches of the both the nave and of the choir clerestorey indicates that the operation may not have been finally wound down until several years of the 13th century had passed. The parts which have this type of foliage include the S clerestorey of the choir and, somewhat unexpectedly, the fourth bay from the E of the N nave gallery. This latter also has the later form of rounded abacus and therefore seems only to have been completed at a very late stage of the operations; possibly this bay was possibly left open to allow access for materials.

It is perhaps not surprising that, once the building was complete, the canons appear to have chosen to leave the structure well alone until Border warfare, and maybe also some degree of structural instability, forced them to take action in the 15th and 16th centuries. One slight change to the choir clerestorey which may be noted here is the lowering of the sills of its N windows at some stage although it is not known quite when this was done.

8.5 THE RECONSTRUCTION OF THE NORTH TRANSEPT

Despite accounts of attacks in the course of the wars of independence, including references to the removal of lead roofing in about 1305 (Bain 1888, no 1727), there is little evidence of repairs to the church around that time. The first major operation to have left its mark on the fabric after the completion of the church in the early 13th century is the reconstruction of the North transept. This took place in the central decades of the 15th century. It is known that the abbey suffered attacks in 1410 and 1416, and it may have been those which were the cause of rebuilding although the more extended plan given to the transept suggests that the need for additional altar space was also a factor. An additional motive for rebuilding may be indicated by the tomb recess under the N window, suggesting that at least one altar in the transept was destined to serve a chantry foundation.

The new transept (illus 110) was laid out to a rectangular plan, re-using much of the 12th-century masonry in the reconstructed walls, with a blank E wall to accommodate the retables of the altars placed against it. The stubs of the demolished apse appear to have been adapted for use as buttresses. Direct light for the altars came from a pair of two-light windows in the W wall, and there was a magnificent four-light window with curvilinear tracery in the N wall. Above this window is a shield with arms which are now badly worn, but which have been identified with Bishop William Turnbull of Glasgow (1447–54). Although doubt has been cast upon this identification, the near identicality of the window with one at Melrose would seem to support such a date, since at Melrose the comparable window is associated with the arms of Andrew Hunter, who was abbot between 1444 and 1471 (Fawcett 1984, 176). Additionally, Turnbull's concern for Jedburgh is indicated by the presence of his arms on the S choir chapel although any work he did there was soon to be subsumed within more extensive operations. It may be noted here that one of his successors in the see of Glasgow also seems to have had an interest in the transept, since the arms of Archbishop Robert Blackadder (1483–1508) are placed on the rebuilt tomb chest within the recess below the N window.

On the evidence of the roof creases, and of returned mouldings from the flanking choir, it appears that the reconstruction of the transept involved the destruction of an existing clerestorey, and that the transept as rebuilt was thus lower than its predecessor. However, there is some reason for thinking that this represented a change of plan, and that the re-furbished transept was originally intended to rise to a similar overall height as its predecessor. On the E side of the transept, immediately adjacent to the tower, is what seems to be the springing of a barrel vault, while within the transept are the the vertical joints of what appear to have been the rear-arches of a row of windows below the springing of such a vault. In addition, towards the N end of the E wall there are the lower external reveals of one such window. If this vault had ever been completed, it would have given the transept a characteristically Scottish Late Gothic appearance, in marked contrast with the rest of the building. But, on balance, it appears unlikely that it was ever carried higher than we now see.

8.6 OPERATIONS IN THE AREA OF THE CROSSING AND SOUTH TRANSEPT

The next operations on the abbey church are liberally indicated as their own contribution by Abbots John Hall and Thomas Cranston who successively held office between 1478 and 1488. The immediate cause of the work was probably an English attack of 1464 although this may have exacerbated long-standing structural weaknesses which have left much evidence in this area, particularly in the N crossing piers. Hall's work included the reconstruction of the pier at the SE corner of the crossing. An arch springing near the level of the choir gallery floor (illus 121) shows that he also intended either to brace the S crossing arch by a transverse strainer arch at that level, or perhaps even to extend the gallery across the transept. However, by the time that Cranston rebuilt the SW pier, together with three of the high crossing arches, this idea had been abandoned. Hall also remodelled the S choir chapel to which Bishop Turnbull had earlier made some now unidentifiable contribution, and in the process he reconstructed the vault, re-using some of the earlier ribs.

As part of the same strengthening operations, several of the openings into the aisles and galleries of choir and transepts were either remodelled or simply blocked, and there was extensive reconstruction of the Romanesque work at the SW corner of the choir. It was probably also as an element of this campaign that a stone barrel vault was constructed over the South transept, following the arc of the crossing arch. In building

Illus 121
The rebuilt SE crossing pier,
showing the cap and springing
of the arch intended to cross the
transept at gallery level.

this vault there seem to have been doubts about the capacity of the transept walls to support it, since it was constructed above gallery rather than clerestorey level, and as a consequence the clerestorey over this part of the building was blocked internally. The culmination of this phase of the work was the extensive reconstruction of the central tower, the stone vault at the top of which – like that in the South transept – suggests a real concern for fire-proof construction. This work was perhaps left incomplete on the death of Cranston, since the arms of Archbishop Blackadder (1483–1508) on the parapet indicate that it was under his patronage that it was finished.

One other 15th-century alteration which may be mentioned at this point is the reconstruction of the W gable in the nave, although there is no way of knowing its precise place in the sequence of operations. As the main focus of the new work a handsome twelve-light rose window was installed, which is very similar to one which was inserted in the W gable of the refectory at Dryburgh Abbey, and which may well have been the work of the same mason (Fawcett 1984, 179).

8.7 THE FINAL MEDIEVAL BUILDING OPERATIONS

The results of the contribution of Abbots Hall and Cranston, whilst not sitting entirely sympathetically with the earlier work, do at least point to the continuing aspirations of a community which was still concerned to provide a worthy and even beautiful setting for its worship. By contrast, the final works for which the fabric offers evidence are indicative of no more than damage control operations by a community which was both spiritually and financially exhausted, and which was not to have the opportunity to recover as a corporate institution.

The need for the work was almost certainly created by devastating English attacks in 1523, 1544 and 1545. There is no way of being sure of the precise sequence of the various reconstruction works undertaken, but it seems most likely to have been after the burning of the abbey in 1523 by the Earl of Surrey that the roofs were replaced at a lower pitch. The evidence for this is to be seen in the creases against the tower and the W walls of the transepts, and in the chases cut into the back walls of the galleries above arch springing height. This must have represented a massive effort for the impoverished abbey although the aesthetic consequences can hardly have been entirely happy. The partial or total blocking of the gallery openings which must have been involved in the lowering of the aisle roofs would have been particularly unfortunate.

Work on all of this can have been only newly completed when the attacks of 1544 and 1545 were delivered. There is even less certainty of what works followed these, but it is inherently likely that the truncation of the South transept on the line of the flanking aisle walls and with a stair at the E end of the cross wall, was a part of the operation. The wall below the E crossing arch may also be of this period. If these were indeed the efforts of damage control which followed the English attacks it is likely that they were instigated as a stop-gap exercise pending the collection of funds to undertake a more thorough-going reconstruction. However, the Reformation intervened to prevent further repairs by the Augustinian canons, and it was this small area within the truncated transept and crossing which was first taken over as their parish church by the local population.

REFERENCES

Allan, JP 1984 *Medieval and Post-Medieval Finds from Exeter 1971–1980*. Exeter: Exeter City Council.

Allen, JR & Anderson, J 1903 *The Early Christian Monuments of Scotland*. III. Edinburgh: Soc Antiq Scot.

Anderson, J 1899 *Calender of the Laing Charters*. Edinburgh: Univ Press.

d'Archimbaud, GD 1980 *Les Fouilles de Rougiers*. Paris: Centre National de la Recherche Scientifique.

Arnold, T (ed) 1882 *Symeon of Durham (Rolls Series)*. i, *Historia Dunhelmensis Ecclesiae*. London: Surtees Society.

Arnold, T (ed) 1885 *Symeon of Durham, (Rolls Series)*. ii, *Historia Regum*. London: Surtees Society.

Bailey, RN 1980 *Viking Age Sculpture in Northern England*. London: Collins.

Bain, J (ed) 1881 *Miscellaneous Public Documents II. Calender of Documents relating to Scotland preserved in Her Majesty's Public Record Office, London*. Edinburgh.

Barnard, FP 1917 *The Casting-Counter and the Counting Board*. Oxford: Clarendon Press.

Barnard, FP 1924 'The Types of Coinage of Certain Early Nuremberg Reckoning-Pennies used in England', *Num Chron*, 5th ser, 4 (1924), 261–309.

Barnetson, L 1988 'Faunal Remains' *in* Good & Tabraham 1988, 231–66.

Barrow GWS 1971 *Regesta Regum Scottorum II: The Acts of William I*. Edinburgh: Univ Press.

Bateson, JD 1982 'The Coin Finds' *in* Wordsworth & Gordon 1982, 111–14.

Beresford, G 1987 *Goltho. The Development of an early medieval manor c.850–1150*. London: HBMCE.

Bilson, J 1909 'The architecture of the Cistercians. . .' *Archaeol J* 2 ser, 66 (1909), 185–280.

Boase, TSR 1953 *English Art 1100–1216*. Oxford: Clarendon Press.

Brooks CM 1980 'Medieval pottery from the kiln site at Coulston, E Lothian', *Proc Soc Antiq Scot*, 110 (1978–80), 364–403.

Brothwell, DR 1981 *Digging Up Bones*. Oxford: Brit Mus.

Burnett, G (ed) 1880a *The Exchequer Rolls of Scotland, III: 1379–1406*. Edinburgh: HM General Register House.

Burnett, G (ed) 1880 b *The Exchequer Rolls of Scotland, IV: 1406–1436*. Edinburgh: HM General Register House.

Burns, E 1887 *The Coinage of Scotland*. Edinburgh: Adam and Charles Black.

Butler, L & Given-Wilson, C 1979 *Medieval Monasteries of Great Britain*. London: Michael Joseph.

Caldwell, DH & Dean, VE 1981 'The post-medieval pottery industry at Throsk', *Scott Pottery Hist Rev*, 6 (1981), 21–27.

Callander, JG 1924 'Fourteenth-Century Brooches and Other Ornaments in the National Museum of Antiquities of Scotland', *Proc Soc Antiq Scot*, 58 (1923–24), 160–84.

Cambridge, E 1977 'The early building history of St Andrews Cathedral. . .', *Antiq J*, 107 (1977), 277–88.

Cant, R 1976 'The Building of St Andrews Cathedral' *in* MacRoberts, D (ed) *The Medieval Church of St Andrews*, 11–32. Glasgow: Burns.

Chalmers, PM 1905 'A thirteenth century tomb in Glasgow Cathedral', *Proc Roy Philosoph Soc*, (1904–05), 184–88.

Chron Melsa (ed Bond, EA) 1866 *Chronica Monasterii de Melsa*, I (Rolls ser). London.

Clapham, AW 1934 *English Romanesque Architecture after the Conquest*. Oxford: Clarendon Press.

Clapham, AW 1952 'The form of the early choir of Tewkesbury and its significance', *Archaeol J*, 108, supplement.

Clark, JW 1897 *The Observances in use at the Augustinian Priory of St Giles and St Andrew at Barnwell*. Cambridge: MacMillan & Bowes.

Clark, J 1986 *Medieval Horseshoes*. Medieval Finds Res Group. (= *Medieval Finds Res Group datasheet*, 4.)

Cowan, IB 1975 'Early Ecclesiastical Foundations', *in* McNeil, P & Nicholson, R (eds), *An Historical Atlas of Scotland c 400–c 1600*. St Andrews: Univ.

Cowan, I & Easson, D 1976 *Medieval Religious Houses, Scotland*. London: Longman.

Cox, E 1984 'Petrological examination of the ceramic material from pits BY and AQ', *in* Tabraham, CJ 1984, 386–95.

Cramp, R 1974 'Early Northumbrian sculpture at Hexham', *in* Kirby, DP (ed), *St Wilfred at Hexham*, 115–40. Newcastle: Oriel Press.

Cramp, R 1983 'The Anglian Sculpture from Jedburgh' *in* O'Connor, A & Clarke, DV (eds) *From the Stone Age to the 'Forty-Five*, 269–84. Edinburgh: John Donald.

Cramp, R 1984 *Corpus of Anglo-Saxon Stone Sculpture in England, I, County Durham and Northumberland*. Oxford: Univ Press.

Crossley, FH 1936 *The English Abbey*. London: Batsford.

Crowdey, A 1986 'The Pottery' *in* Dixon, P 'Excavations in the Fishing Town of Eyemouth', *Borders Burghs Archaeol Project Monogr*, ser 1, 38–55. Edinburgh.

Cruden, S 1950 *St Andrews Cathedral*. Edinburgh: HMSO.

Cruden, S 1964 'Holyrood Abbey', *Arch J*, (1964), 181–3.

Crummy, N 1988 *The post-Roman small finds from excavations in Colchester 1971–85*. Colchester: Archaeol Trust. (= *Colchester Archaeol Rep*, 5.)

CSP 1898 *Calender of State Papers relating to Scotland, 1. The Scottish Series of the reigns of Henry VIII, Edward VI, Mary, Elizabeth 1509–1589*, 8, no 80. London.

Cunnington, C & Cunnington, P 1973 *Handbook of English Medieval Costume*. London: Faber.

Dalton, R & Hamer, SH 1916 *The provincial token coinage of the 18th Century*, part XII. London: Robert Stockwell.

Davey, PJ 1982 'Clay pipe fragments', *in* Hunter, JR 'Medieval Berwick-upon-Tweed', *Archaeol Aeliana*, 5 ser, 10 (1982), 67–124.

Davey, PJ 1987 *The archaeology of the clay tobacco pipe*. BAR: Oxford. (= *BAR Brit ser*, 178).

Day, LF 1909 *Windows: a book about stained and painted glass*. 3 ed. London: Batsford.

Dickinson, JC 1950 *The origins of the Austin Canons and their introduction into England*. London: Church Hist Soc.

Dickinson, JC 1968 'The buildings of the English Austin Canons after the Dissolution of the Monasteries', *J Brit Archaeol Assoc*, 3rd ser, 31 (1968), 60–75.

Dilworth, M 1983 'The Border Abbeys in the Sixteenth Century' *Scott Church Hist Soc*, (1983), 21, 233–47.

Dimier, A 1982 *L'art Cistercian, France*. La Pierre-qui-Vire: Zodiaque.

Donaldson, G 1965 *Scotland: James V to James VII*. Edinburgh: Oliver & Boyd. (= *The Edinburgh History of Scotland*, 3).

Duncan, AAM 1975 *Scotland: The making of the Kingdom*. Edinburgh: Oliver & Boyd. (= *The Edinburgh History of Scotland*, 1).

Fawcett, R 1984 'Scottish Medieval Window Tracery', in Breeze, D (ed), *Studies in Scottish Antiquity*, 148–86. Edinburgh: John Donald.

Fawcett, R 1985 *Scottish Medieval Churches*. Edinburgh: HMSO.

Fawcett, R, McRoberts, D & Stewart, F nd *Inchcolm Abbey and Island*. Edinburgh: HMSO.

Ferguson, P 1975 'The south transept of Byland Abbey', *J Brit Archaeol Assoc*, 3 ser, 38.

Ferguson, P 1983 'First Architecture of the Cistercians in England', *J Brit Archaeol Assoc*, 136 (1983), 74–86.

Fernie, E 1976 'Observations on the Norman Plan of Ely Cathedral', *Medieval Art and Architecture at Ely Cathedral*, 1-7. (= Brit Arch Assoc Conference Trans).

Fernie, E 1978 'Historical metrology and architectural history', *Art Hist*, 1, 4 (1978), 383–99.

Fernie, E 1985a 'Anglo-Saxon Lengths: The Northern System, the Perch and the Foot', *Arch J*, 142 (1985), 246–54.

Fernie, E 1985b 'A note on the historiography of Tewkesbury Abbey', *Medieval Art*, (1985), 1–5.

Ford, B & Walsh, A 1987 'Horseshoe nails' *in* Holdsworth, P 1987, 137.

Fox, F 1908 'Foundations: the use of divers and the grouting machine', *J RIBA*, 3 ser, 15 (1907–8), 249–72.

Gage, J 1982 'Gothic Glass: two aspects of a Dionysian Aesthetic', *Art History*, 5, 1 (1982), 36–58.

Gallagher, DB 1987a 'Edinburgh pipemakers in the seventeenth century, the documentary evidence', in Davey, PJ 1987, 3–13.

Gallagher, DB 1987b 'Tobacco pipemaking in Glasgow, 1667–1967', *in* Davey, PJ 1987, 35–109.

Gallagher, DB 1987c 'Kelso', *in* Davey, PJ 1987, 279–91.

Gallagher, DB 1987d 'Thomas White, tobacco pipe manufacturer of Canongate, Edinburgh', *in* Davey, PJ 1987, 26–28.

Gallagher, DB 1988 'Clay tobacco-pipes', *in* Good & Tabraham 1988, 231–66.

Garton T 1987 'The transitional Sculpture of Jedburgh Abbey', *in* Stratford, N (ed) 1987, 69–82.

Genoves, S 1969 'Sex Determination in Earlier Man', *in* Brothwell, D & Higgs, E (eds) *Science in Archaeology*, 429–39. London: Thames & Hudson.

Gilyard-Beer, R 1970 *Fountains Abbey, Yorkshire*. London: HMSO.

Glasgow Registrum 1843 *Registrum Episcopatus Glasguensis*. Edinburgh: Bannatyne & Maitland Clubs.

Good, GL & Tabraham, CJ 1988 'Excavations at Smailholm Tower, Roxburghshire', *Proc Soc Antiq Scot*, 118 (1988) 231–66.

Goodall, AR 1983 'The Finds: non-ferrous metal objects', *in* Mays, P & Butler, L *Sandal Castle Excavations 1964–1973*. Wakefield: Hist Soc.

Graves, CP 1985 *Scottish Medieval Stained and Painted Glass*. Unpub dissertation. Glasgow: Dept Archaeol Univ Glasgow.

Graves, CP forthcoming 'Window glass', *in* Sides, R *Excavations at St Wilfred's Parish Church, Hickleton, South Yorkshire*.

Grieg, S 1933 *Middlealderske Byfund Fra Bergen Oc Oslo*. Oslo: AW Broggers: Boktrykkeri.

Haggarty, GR 1980 'The pottery', *in* Ewart, GJ 'Excavations at Stirling Castle, 1977–78', *Post-Medieval Archaeol*, 14 (1980), 23–51.

Haggarty, GR 1984 'Observations on the Ceramic Material from Phase 1 Pits BY and AQ', *in* Tabraham, CJ 1984, 395–8.

Hamilton Papers 1892 *The Hamilton Papers II 1543–1590*. Bain, J (ed), 1890–92. Edinburgh: Scott Rec Office.

Hannay, RK 1932 *Collections of Acts and Proceedings. The Register of the Privy Council of Scotland*, 3rd ser, 9. Edinburgh: Scott Rec Office.

Hanson, W & Maxwell, G 1983 *Rome's North West Frontier: the Antonine Wall*. Edinburgh: Univ Press.

Harman, M 1985 'Objects of Bone and Ivory', *in* Ayers, B 'Excavations within the North East of Norwich Castle, 1979' *East Anglia Archaeol*, 28 (1985), 44–7.

Hearn, MF 1972 'On the Original Nave of Ripon Cathedral', *J Brit Archaeol Assoc*, 3 ser, 35 (1972), 39–45.

Henshall, A 1956 'The Long Cist Cemetery at Lasswade, Midlothian', *Proc Soc Antiq Scot*, 89 (1955–56), 252–83.

Higgins, FC 1892 *Copper Coins of Europe Till 1892*. London: Swann Sonnerschein & Co.

Higgitt, J 1987 'The Jedburgh comb', *in* Stratford, N (ed) 1987, 119–27.

Hilson, J 1872 'Notes on the Cist opened at Lanton Mains, Roxburghshire, in October, 1870', *Hist Berwick Nat Club*, 6, (1869–72), 349–50.

Hinton, DA 1982 'Stone, with a note on the gemstone', *in* 'Excavations at Castle Acre Castle, Norfolk, 1972–77: Country House and Castle of the Earls of Surrey', *Archaeol J*, 139 (1982), 255–64.

Hirst, SM, Walsh, DA & Wright, SM 1983 *Bordesley Abbey II: Second report on excavations at Bordesley Abbey, Redditch, Hereford-Worcestershire*. Oxford: BAR. (= *BAR Brit Ser*, II).

Hodges, C 1888 *The Abbey of St Andrew, Hexham*. Hexham: Abbey Press.

Hodges, JK 1881 *The History of Wallingford*. London.

Holdsworth, P 1987 *Excavations in the Medieval Burgh of Perth 1979–1981*. Edinburgh: Soc Antiq Scot. (= *Soc Antiq Scot Monogr Ser*, 5).

Holmes, NMMcQ 1989 'Coins and Jetton', *in* Stones, J A (ed), *Three Scottish Carmelite Friaries: excavation at Aberdeen, Linlithgow and Perth 1980–86*. Edinburgh: Soc Antiq Scot. (= *Soc Antiq Scot Monogr Ser*, 6).

Hope, WHStJ & Brakspear, H 1909 'Haughmond Abbey, Shropshire', *Archaeol J*, 2nd ser, 16 (1909), 281–310.

Huggins, P 1981 'Yeavering measurements: an alternative view', *Medieval Archaeol*, 25 (1981), 150–3.

Hunter, DM 1967 'Kinneil Church', *Trans Glasgow Archaeol Soc*, new ser 15 (1967), 189–99.

Innes, C (ed) 1842 *Abredoniae utriusque descriptio. . .* Aberdeen: Spalding Club. (= *Spalding Club*, 5.)

Janaway, R 1990 'The Conservation and Analysis of Textiles from Christ Church, Spittalfields, London', *Archaeol Textiles*, 36–40. (= *Occas Pap Proc United Kingdom Inst Conservation*, 10).

Jeffrey, A 1864 *The History and Antiquities of Roxburghshire and adjacent districts*, 4 vols (1855–64). Edinburgh: TC Jack.

Jennings, S 1981 'Eighteen Centuries of Pottery from Norwich', *E Anglian Archaeol*, 13.

Kelly, PV 1926 'A bridge of monastic date and other finds at Furness Abbey', *Trans Cumberland Westmorland Antiq Archaeol Soc new ser*, 26 (1926), 262–69.

Kelso 1805 *Kelso Mail*, Jan 3rd and 7th 1805.

Kelso 1857 *Kelso Mail*, July 9th 1857.

Knowles, D 1959 *The Religious Orders in England, III*. Cambridge: Univ Press.

Knowles, JA 1936 *Essays in the History of the York School of Glass-Painting*. London: Soc Promoting Christian Knowledge.

Krogman, WM 1962 *The Human Skeleton in Forensic Medicine*. Springfield, Illinois: Charles C Thomas.

Laidlaw, W 1905 'Sculptured and Inscribed Stones in Jedburgh and Vicinity', *Proc Soc Antiq Scot*, (1904–05), 21–54.

Lawrie, AC (ed) 1905 *Early Scottish Charters prior to 1153*. Glasgow: James MacLehose & Sons.

Lekai, LK 1977 (trans Lachner, B K) *The Cistercians: ideals and reality*. Ohio: Kent State Univ Press.

Lewis, JH 1984 'Jedburgh Abbey', Medieval Britain and Ireland in 1983', *Medieval Archaeol*, 28, (1984) 259.

Lewis, JH forthcoming *Excavations at the Episcopal Palace of Spynie, Moray*.

MacDonald, G 1920 'The Mint of Crosraguel Abbey', *Proc Soc Antiq Scot*, 54 (1919–20), 20–44.

MacGibbon, D & Ross, T 1896 *The Ecclesiatical Architecture of Scotland*, I. Edinburgh: David Douglas.

MacGregor, A 1985 *Bone, antler, ivory and horn. The technology of skeletal materials since the Roman period*. London: Croom Helm.

MacGregor, AG & Eckford, RJA 1952 'The Upper Old Red and Lower Carboniferous Sediments of Teviotdale and Tweedside, and the Stones of the Abbeys of the Scottish Borderland', *Trans Edinburgh Geol Soc*, 14, ii (1952), 230–52.

MacAskill, NL 1982 'Pottery', *in* Wordsworth, J 'Excavation of the settlement at 13–21 Castle Street, Inverness, 1979', *Proc Soc Antiq Scot*, 112 (1982), 322–91.

MacRoberts, D 1962 'Material destruction caused by the Scottish Reformation', *in* MacRoberts D (ed), *Essays on the Scottish Reformation, 1513–1625*, 415–62. Glasgow: Burns.

Margeson, S 1985 'The artifacts/small finds', *in* Evans, DH & Carter, A (eds), *Excavations in Norwich II: Excavations on 31–51 Pottergate*, 52–67. Norwich: Norwich Survey.

Medieval Art 1985 *Medieval Art and Architecture at Gloucester and Tewkesbury*. Oxford: Oxbow Books. (= *Brit Archaeol Assoc Conf Trans 1981*.)

Merriman, MH 1980 'The Fortifications in Scotland, 1547–50', *in* Colvin, HM *The History of the King's Works*, 694–726. London: HMSO.

Metcalf, DM 1977 'The Evidence of Scottish Coin Hoards for Monetary History, 1100–1600', *in* Metcalf, DM *Coinage in Medieval Scotland (1100–1600)*, 1–59. Oxford: BAR. (= *Brit Archaeol Rep*, 45.)

Micklethwaite, JT 1892 'On the indoor games of school boys in the Middle Ages', *Archaeol J*, 49 (1892), 319–28.

Moorhouse, S & Wrathmell, S 1987 *Kirkstall Abbey roll. The 1950–64 excavations: a reassessment*. West Yorkshire Archaeol Service.

Morton, J 1832 *The Monastic Annals of Teviotdale*. Edinburgh: W Easton.

Mossop, HR 1970 *The Lincoln Mint c 890–1279*. Newcastle–upon–Tyne: Corbitt & Hunter.

Myres, JNL 1933 'Butley Priory, Suffolk', *Archaeol J*, 90 (1933), 177–282.

Muir, JW 1956 *The Soils of the country around Jedburgh and Morebattle*. Edinburgh. (= *Mem Soil Surv Gr Brit*, sheet 17).

Musset, L 1975 *Normandie Romane*, 1. La-Pierre-qui-Vire: Zodiaque.

Nathan, H 1962 'Osteophytes of the Vertebral Column', *J Bone Jt Surg*, 44A (2) (1962), 243–68.

North, JJ 1980 *English Hammered Coinage*. I. 2 edn. London: Spink & Son.

NSA 1845 *New Statistical Account of Scotland, III*. Edinburgh: W Blackwood & Son.

Oakley, GE 1979 'The Copper Alloy Objects – lace tags', *in* Williams, J (ed) *St Peter's Street, Northampton Excavations 1973–1976*, 248–64. Northampton: Northampton Development Corporation.

O'Connor, DE 1989 'The Medieval Stained Glass of Beverly Minster', *in* Wilson, C (ed) *Medieval Art and Architecture in the East Riding of Yorkshire*, 62–90. (= *Brit Archaeol Assoc Conference Transactions*, 1983.)

O'Connor, DE & Haselock, J 1977 'The Stained and Painted Glass', *in* Aylmer, GE & Cant, R (eds) *A History of York Minster*, 313–94. Oxford: Clarendon Press.

OPS 1855 *Origines Parochiales Scotiae*, Bannatyne Club Publication, 1851–55. Edinburgh.

Oswald, A 1963 'Excavation of a 13th-century wooden building at Weoley Castle, Birmingham, 1960–61', *Medieval Archaeol*, 6–7 (1962–63), 109–34.

Parsons, D 1982 'The Romanesque Vices at Canterbury', *in* Coldstream, N & Draper, P *Medieval Art and Architecture at Canterbury before 1220*, 39–45. (= *Brit Archaeol Assoc Conference Trans*).

Pevsner, N 1959 *The Buildings of England: Yorkshire, the West Riding*. Harmondsworth: Penguin.

Pevsner, N 1962 *The Buildings of England: North-West and South Norfolk*. Harmondsworth: Penguin.

Pevsner, N 1967 *The Buildings of England: Cumberland and Westmoreland*. Harmondsworth: Penguin.

Philp, B 1968 *Excavations at Faversham, 1965: the royal abbey, Roman villa and Belgic farmstead*. Crawley: Kent Archaeol Res Group Counc.

Pirie, EJE 1986 *Post-Roman Coins from York Excavations 1971–81*. London. (= *York Archaeol Trust*, fasc 18/1.)

Platt, C 1984 *The Abbeys and Priories of Medieval England*. London: Secker and Warburg.

Platt, C & Coleman-Smith, R 1975 *Excavations in Medieval Southampton 1953–1969*. Leicester: Univ Press.

Rahtz, P 1979 *The Saxon and Medieval Palaces at Cheddar, Excavations 1960–62*. Oxford: BAR. (= *BAR Brit Ser*, 65.)

Rahtz, P & Hirst, S 1976 *Bordesley Abbey, Redditch, Hereford-Worcester: First report on excavations, 1969–1973*. Oxford: BAR. (= *BAR Brit Ser*, 23).

Ramsay, NL 1987 'Medieval Artists and their techniques', in Alexander, J & Binski, P (eds) *Age of Chivalry art in Plantagenet England 1200–1400*, 382–83. London: Weidenfield and Nicholson.

RCAHMS 1912 Royal Commission on the Ancient and Historical Monuments of Scotland, *Inventory of Monuments and Constructions in Galloway*. Edinburgh: HMSO.

RCAHMS 1933 Royal Commission on the Ancient and Historical Monuments of Scotland, *Inventory of Monuments and Constructions in the Counties of Fife, Kinross and Clackmannan*. Edinburgh: HMSO.

RCAHMS 1951 Royal Commission on the Ancient and Historical Monuments of Scotland, *Inventory of the Ancient and Historical Monuments of Edinburgh*. Edinburgh: HMSO.

RCAHMS 1956 Royal Commission on the Ancient and Historical Monuments of Scotland, *Inventory of the Ancient and Historical Monuments of Roxburghshire*, 2. Edinburgh: HMSO.

RCAHMS 1963 Royal Commission on the Ancient and Historical Monuments of Scotland, *Inventory of the Ancient and Historical Monuments of Stirlingshire*. Edinburgh: HMSO.

RCAHMS 1982 Royal Commission on the Ancient and Historical Monuments of Scotland, *Argyll 4: an Inventory of the Ancient Monuments*. Edinburgh: HMSO.

RCAHMS 1984 Royal Commission on the Ancient and Historical Monuments of Scotland, *Argyll 5: Islay, Jura, colonsay and Oransay, an Inventory of the Ancient Monuments*. Edinburgh: HMSO.

Rigold, SE 1981 'Numismatica', *in* Woodfield, C 1981, 118–25.

Richardson, JS & Tabraham, CJ 1987 *Dryburgh Abbey*. (Historic Buildings and Monuments guide book). Edinburgh: HMSO.

Ritchie, A 1977 'Excavation of Pictish and Viking Age farmsteads at Buckquoy, Orkney', *Proc Soc Antiq Scot*, 106 (1976–77), 174–227.

Robertson, N 1966 'The Game of Merelles in Scotland', *Proc Soc Antiq Scot*, 98 (1964–66), 321–23.

Robinson, DM 1980 *The Geography of Augustinian Settlement in England and Wales*. Oxford: BAR. (= *BAR Brit Ser*, 80.)

Ross, T & Lorimer, R (eds) 1925 *National art survey of Scotland*, 3. Edinburgh: Nat Gall Scot & Roy Incorporation Architect Scot.

Sharratt, P & Sharratt, F 1985 *Ecosse Romane, France*. Paris: Zodiaque.

Sherlock, D 1976 'Discoveries at Horsham St Faith Priory, 1970–3', *Norfolk Archaeol*, 36 (1974–77), 202–23.

Shirreff, AG 1953 'The Sparsholt nine men's morris', *Berkshire Archaeol J*, 53 (1952–3), 110–15.

Simpson, AT & Stevenson, S 1981 *Historic Jedburgh, the archaeological implications*. Edinburgh: Scott Burgh Survey.

Singleton, B 1981 'Proportions in the Design of the Early Gothic Cathedral at Wells', *in* Medieval Art 1985, 10–17.

SO 1959 Scottish Office: SC21970/01 (1950–59).

SRO 1833 Scottish Record Office: MW/1/1259 (1823–33).

SRO 1938 Scottish Record Office: MW/1/1088 (1919–38).

SRO 1942 Scottish Record Office: MW/1/1090 (1942).

Stalley, R 1987 *The Cistercian Monasteries of Ireland*. London: Yale Univ Press.

Stell, G 1984 'Stone buildings with timber foundations: some unanswered questions', *Proc Soc Antiq Scot*, 114 (1984), 584–85.

Stewart, IH 1967 *The Scottish Coinage*. London: Spink & Son.

Stones, JA (ed) 1989 *Three Carmelite Friaries: excavation at Aberdeen, Linlithgow and Perth 1980–86*. Edinburgh: Soc Antiq Scot. (= *Soc Antiq Scot Monogr Ser*, 6.)

Stratford N (ed) 1987 *Romanesque and Gothic: Essays for George Zarnecki*. Woodbridge: Boydell.

Tabraham, CJ 1984 'Excavations at Kelso Abbey', *Proc Soc Antiq Scot*, 114 (1984), 365–404.

Tatton-Brown, T 1975 'Excavations at the Custom House site, City of London, 1973. Part II', *Trans London and Middx Archaeol Soc*, 26 (1975), 154–67.

Thomas, C 1987 'Leather', *in* Holdsworth, P 1987, 174–90.

Thoms, LM 1982 'Trial Excavation at St Ann's lane, Perth', *Proc Soc Antiq Scot*, 112 (1982), 437–54.

Thurlby, M 1985 'The Elevations of the Romanesque Abbey churches of St Mary at Tewkesbury and St Peter at Gloucester', *in* Medieval Art 1985, 36–51.

Tweddle, D 1986 *Finds from Parliament Street and Other Sites in the City Centre*, York: Archaeol Trust.

Urry, W 1967 *Canterbury under the Angevin Kings*. London: Univ London Hist Stud.

Watson, G 1909 *The History of Jedburgh Grammar School*. Jedburgh: Reprinted from the Jedburgh Gazette.

Watson J 1894 *Jedburgh Abbey: Historical and Descriptive*. Edinburgh: David Douglas.

Westlake, NHJ 1881 *A History of Design in Painted Glass*. London: James Parker & Co.

Wilson, C 1986 'The Cistercians as missionaries of Gothic in Northern England', *in* Norton, C & Park, D (eds) *Cistercian Art and Architecture in the British Isles*, 86–116. Cambridge: Univ Press.

Woodfield, C 1981 'Finds from the Free Grammar School at the Whitefriars, Coventry, *c* 1545–*c* 1557/8', *Post Medieval Archaeol*, 115 (1981), 81–159.

Wordsworth, J & Gordon, AR 1982 'Lesmahagow Priory: Excavations 1978', *Glasgow Archaeol J*, 9 (1982), 76–114.

Zarnecki, G 1978 'The Romanesque capitals in the south transept of Worcester Cathedral', *in Medieval Art and Architecture at Worcester Cathedral*, 38–42. Leeds. (= *Brit Archaeol Assoc Conf Trans*.)

INDEX

Italicised references at the end of an entry denote illustration numbers